AN INVITATION TO POETRY

AN INVITATION TO POETRY

JAY PARINI

Middlebury College

PRENTICE-HALL, INC., ENGLEWOOD CLIFFS, NEW JERSEY 07632

Library of Congress Cataloging-in-Publication Data

PARINI, JAY.
An invitation to poetry.

Includes index.
1. English poetry. 2. English poetry—History and
criticism. 3. American poetry. American poetry—
History and criticism. 5. Poetry. I. Title.
PR1175.P3572 1987   808.1   86-18662
ISBN 0-13-505546-6 (pbk.)

Editorial/production supervision and
   interior design: *Hilda Tauber*
Cover design: *Bruce D. Kenselaar.*
Cover photo by *Eliot Porter*
Manufacturing buyer: *Ray Keating*

The acknowledgments on pages 319-322
constitute an extension of the copyright page.

© 1987 by Prentice-Hall, Inc.
A Division of Simon & Schuster
Englewood Cliffs, New Jersey 07632

Printed in the United States of America

10 9 8 7 6 5 4 3 2 1

ISBN 0-13-505546-6   01

PRENTICE-HALL INTERNATIONAL (UK) LIMITED, *London*
PRENTICE-HALL OF AUSTRALIA PTY. LIMITED, *Sydney*
PRENTICE-HALL CANADA INC., *Toronto*
PRENTICE-HALL HISPANOAMERICANA, S. A., *Mexico*
PRENTICE-HALL OF INDIA PRIVATE LIMITED, *New Delhi*
PRENTICE-HALL OF JAPAN, INC., *Tokyo*
PRENTICE-HALL OF SOUTHEAST ASIA PTE. LTD., *Singapore*
EDITORA PRENTICE-HALL DO BRASIL, LTDA., *Rio de Janeiro*

To ROBERT PACK—poet, critic, and friend

Contents

A Word to the Teacher

What is different about *An Invitation to Poetry?* Let me say first what is *not* different. In the tradition of Brooks and Warren, this textbook stresses well-known techniques of close reading. Assuming that most students are unfamiliar with the established canon of English and American poetry, I have reprinted many of the classic poems from Chaucer to Yeats. Likewise, the approach to poetry found in these pages is classical, with an emphasis on the study of verse as a formal discipline evolving through time. I have pointedly avoided trendiness. However much I admire Bob Dylan and Jackson Browne, I prefer not to pretend that their lyrics deserve the kind of attention one might lavish on, say, Milton's "On His Blindness." This does not mean I prize "difficulty" in poetry. If anything, I have sought out poems that students will find accessible, even entertaining. There is good reason why Robert Frost is the most quoted poet in this book. I believe, with A. E. Housman, that a poem should make one's scalp tingle. Throughout, I emphasize the sensual as well as the intellectual pleasures poetry affords.

You will also find here an awareness of what has happened to the act of reading *since* the New Critics, who, in their insistence on the primacy of the poem, sometimes imagined it to be autonomous. A poem is not a self-enclosed world, as more recent critics have taught us. Language, as with other sign systems, both informs and feeds on the culture around it. Language is rooted in history. *An Invitation to Poetry* is among the first introductory textbooks that urge students to read "through" the poem, to take into account its context, the psychological and social factors that help to determine meaning. Of course, it is futile to ask students to read *through* a poem before they have learned to focus *on* the text itself. In Chapter 2, I present the case for close reading while exploring in detail Frost's famous poem "The Road Not Taken." I pursue the wider implications of close reading in Chapter 14 (see, especially, the section about reading, From the Outside In) and in the study questions throughout the book. My last chapter, "Poets in Dialogue," opens the question of influence—a thorny issue for beginning readers, but an interesting one. I provide several examples of the ways poets make use of other poems, implicitly arguing against naive assumptions about originality. Students are often surprised to learn the extent to which poets make use of earlier texts while still managing, as Pound once said, to "make it new."

To the familiar poems in this textbook I have added a substantial number of contemporary poems, most of which have never been anthologized before. A new generation of poets has appeared on the scene since Lowell and Roethke. I offer a generous sampling of work by poets such as Seamus Heaney, Anne Stevenson, Philip Levine, Louise Gluck, and others. This generation has rediscovered the tradition, and has refreshed and extended it. I hope your students will come to see that poetry is very much alive, as urgent today as it was in the time of Chaucer.

Finally, a word about the anthology section. Instead of arranging poems by chronology, I have grouped them by theme, mixing classic with contemporary poems on similar subjects such as "Aspects of Love" or "War, and Rumors of War." This section is ideal, I think, for browsing, and it should stimulate classroom discussion and topics for papers. Reading through these poems, students should come to realize that poetry is a continuing dialogue on issues of enduring human concern. With any luck, they will learn to *like* poems as well, to seek them out for help in living their lives and for the kind of knowledge that poetry offers.

A Word to the Student

An Invitation to Poetry is what the title suggests—an invitation for you to explore and understand poetry in the context of your everyday life. Poetry may seem a long way from your present concerns, something you have been forced into studying before, in high school, and now must study even more seriously for a college degree. Our hope is that by the end of this course, you will have discovered that poetry has a lot to say to you about your own life and about the way you live—that, far from seeming a chore, reading poetry will become a regular, meaningful part of your life.

Remember that poetry and song are closely related. You probably listen to music quite often in the course of a busy week. Rock music is full of poetry. Think about the effect of those song lyrics on your daily life. Don't phrases from Jackson Browne, Bob Dylan, and the Bee Gees, the Talking Heads, whomever, come into your head from time to time? Song has always played an important part in the lives of human beings, and so has poetry, though the educational system has locked up poems in imposing books and relegated them to the classroom and the library.

The purpose of this book is to bring poetry into the open, to give it its proper place in the culture beside song. The book is designed to teach you, step by step, ways of reading and *hearing* poems. We also hope that by learning how to read closely, to read the words on the page *well,* you will learn how to "read" the world, to interpret events and what might be called "sign systems" (such as TV commercials or political speeches) that exist everywhere around you. We want to help you develop a critical eye. That, after all, is the main purpose of a college education.

This book divides into two main parts, a textbook section and an anthology. The textbook is arranged so that the parts build on each other. You should not skip ahead. The chapters are designed to be readable and enjoyable. There are many study questions and exercises in each chapter that should prove interesting and helpful in understanding the main points. The anthology has been arranged according to key themes in poetry, such as "Life and Death" or "War, and Rumors of War." These categories are purposefully broad to encompass a wide range of English poems (and a few translations). Not incidentally, the poems in this book have all been chosen to represent different eras of English poetry as well as different approaches to the art of poetry.

Perhaps the most unique aspect of this book is its inclusion of many new, younger poets, such as Richard Kenney, Seamus Heaney, Rosanna Warren, Pamela White Hadas, Richard Tillinghast, and others. Many of the poems in *An Invitation to Poetry* have never before appeared in a textbook. We hope that these poems, written in this decade, will speak especially to you, in a language not distanced from you by time.

We should also mention the bias of this book. The emphasis is strongly on what might be called the "classical" aspects of poetry, as well as the formal aspects. Poets write in a tradition; they make poems that reflect the work of earlier poets. In a sense, poets write *to each other*, and readers are privileged to listen in on this fascinating conversation. One special chapter, "Poets in Dialogue," tries to explain some of the ways in which poets "talk" to each other. Notice that we are avoiding the word *influence*, which has been often misunderstood and certainly overused.

Read this book and enjoy it. The poems belong to all of us. But your response to individual poems is, of course, a very private thing. The best we can hope to do, as teachers, is to help you interpret your own complicated, powerful responses to the poems themselves. Good luck. And good reading.

AN INVITATION TO POETRY

WHAT IS POETRY?

I am always interested in hearing what a poet has to say about the nature of poetry, though I do not take it too seriously.

—W. H. AUDEN

No one, including the poets themselves, has ever been quite sure how to define poetry. As W. H. Auden has said (see the epigraph), it is always interesting to see what poets have to say about their art, but they can't be taken too seriously. Perhaps nobody should be trusted on this topic, including writers of textbooks on poetry. Poetry is not a science, and so interpretation and value judgments must play a crucial part in all discussions. The only thing we can be sure of is that poetry is not prose; it consists of lines that do not usually run to the end of the page. Anything else we might care to say about poetry is subjective, though we must not assume that subjective judgments are necessarily inaccurate.

To a student, poetry may well seem superfluous, just another subject to be studied in school. It's true that few people read poems after high school or college. But the fact is that hardly any culture has ever existed, from the ancient Greeks on, in which people did not make up poems. The greatness of a culture is often measured by the quality of its art, and poetry is among the highest forms art can take. It represents the most refined way human beings have ever found for expressing themselves in language; indeed, it satisfies an almost primitive need for conjuring experience in vivid, memorable language.

In ancient cultures, poets were holy men or prophets, in some instances more powerful and feared than kings or tribal leaders. Poetry was thought to possess a magical quality, and poems were passed from generation to generation like secret chants. Something of the legendary power and mystery of poetry still attaches itself to poets and poetry, though in America today poets are revered only by a minority who still read and study poems out of a sense of need; much of the aura once attached to poets has been transferred to rock musicians and song writers. In fact, many people nowadays experience the pleasures of poetry mostly through music, much as they did in the days of ancient Greece, when poems were sung to the accompaniment of the lyre.

For the most part, poetry frightens or bores the general public, often for good reasons. Modern poetry is too often obscure, and—like all disciplines—poetry is most accessible to people who already know a good deal about its **conventions**, the rules, special features, and traditions that have made their way into the present from earlier times. Baseball, for instance, seems either boring or confusing to many foreigners, although nearly every American can easily understand, appreciate, and enjoy the game. Those who understand the conventions of baseball are able to compare the batting styles of Babe Ruth, Mickey Mantle, George Brett, and Reggie Jackson. Every new player works within the rules and features of the game, but the good ones add something of their own to the sport, too. The same is true of poets. The good ones understand the conventions of poetry, yet they extend the art by their innovations, by the addition of their own private speaking voice, which invariably owes a lot to other voices and earlier times.

A working knowledge of the conventions of poetry is indispensable to the reader who wants to get as much out of poetry as the art has to offer. Just as you could not judge one player over another if you didn't know what to look for in a good player, you cannot appreciate quality in poetry without knowing what to look for in a poem. So part of our purpose in this book is to outline and explain the elements of poetry, such as rhythm and rhyme, imagery, the use of figurative language, and the use of forms. Your understanding these elements will make it possible for you to evaluate poems, to judge their relative worth among other, similar poems. Without this knowledge, the act of judgment becomes almost whimsical.

To read a poem well, to enjoy it, and to judge its worth fairly is no mean feat. Poetry is demanding, and those who would learn to read it well must pay close attention to the words on the page, their full meaning and context. This is called **close reading**, and it is stressed throughout this book. The enormous subtlety that good poems exhibit is an aspect of their quality, and our purpose here is to encourage the kind of attentive reading that respects this subtlety.

People who don't enjoy poems on a gut level will never really understand poetry. Another part of our purpose here, then, is to get you to react to the poems themselves, to shiver and smile when the words—and the way the poet arranges the words—strike you as especially true or beautiful or moving. Alastair Reid, a Scottish poet, has written a poem about those special moments when a phrase, a sight, a bar of music, or a line of poetry exactly mirrors your mood or penetrates to the heart of your reality.

ALASTAIR REID (1926–   )

Oddments, Inklings, Omens, Moments

Oddments, as when
you see through skin,
when flowers appear
to be eavesdropping,
or music somewhere   5
declares your mood;
when sleep fulfils
a feel of dying
or fear makes ghosts
of clothes on a chair.   10

Inklings, as when
some room rhymes
with a lost time,
or a book reads
like a well-known dream;   15
when a smell recalls
portraits, funerals,
when a wish happens
or a mirror sees
through distances.   20

Omens, as when
a shadow from nowhere
falls on a wall,
when a bird seems
to mimic your name,   25
when a cat eyes you
as though it knew
or, heavy with augury,
a crow caws
cras cras from a tree.   30

Moments, as when
the air's awareness
makes guesses true,
when a hand's touch
speaks past speech   *35*
or when, in poise,
two sympathies
lighten each other,
and love occurs
like song, like weather.   *40*

Reid is talking about those wonderfully eerie moments when the mind clarifies, when reality seems lucid and shining. Poetry is one of the chief means writers have always had for catching such experiences in the net of language.

To go back to basics: How is poetry different from prose, apart from the way the lines look on the page? Both depend on language for their effects, and both use it in similar ways to create images, gather certain rhythms, and employ figures of speech like metaphors and similes. The differences are not nearly so great as many think, and there is sometimes a fine line between poetry and **poetic prose**. The simple answer is that poetry is language that bows to the conventions of poetry; it is written in lines of varied length that ask to be read as a poem, with close attention to its rhythms, the sounds the words make, and their patterns on the page. In general, poems are short, they proceed by way of images, and they compress their meanings as much as possible. Prose is usually more discursive, making abstract statements and connecting ideas in a detailed and logical fashion. Poems, like dreams, often have a logic of their own; they usually avoid talking "about" things. They *are* things in themselves—verbal objects. A poem, unlike a story or a novel, can be hung on a wall. But these distinctions between poetry and prose are necessarily crude. The final truth is that you, the reader, either recognize a poem as poetry or you don't.

EXERCISE

In the following poems, poets talk about what their art means to them, how they use poetry to explain the conditions of their lives. Often, they meditate on the differences between life and art. Sometimes they talk about the inadequacies of poetry, too—its limited power, for instance, in the face of real grief or joy. In all cases, the poets whose poems follow show an abiding fascination with the power and function of poetry in their lives. Characterize their different views on the nature of poetry as found in each poem. Which seems most attractive to you? Why?

DYLAN THOMAS   (1914–1953)

In My Craft or Sullen Art

In my craft or sullen art
Exercised in the still night
When only the moon rages
And the lovers lie abed
With all their griefs in their arms,   5
I labor by singing light
Not for ambition or bread
Or the strut and trade of charms
On the ivory stages
But for the common wages   10
Of their most secret heart.
Not for the proud man apart
From the raging moon I write
On these spindrift pages
Not for the towering dead   15
With their nightingales and psalms
But for the lovers, their arms
Round the griefs of the ages,
Who pay no praise or wages
Nor heed my craft or art.   20

ARCHIBALD MACLEISH   (1892–1984)

Ars Poetica

A poem should be palpable and mute
As a globed fruit,

Dumb
As old medallions to the thumb,

Silent as the sleeve-worn stone   5
Of casement ledges where the moss has grown—

A poem should be wordless
As the flight of birds.

                *   *   *

A poem should be motionless in time
As the moon climbs,   10

Leaving, as the moon releases
Twig by twig the night-entangled trees,

Leaving, as the moon behind the winter leaves,
Memory by memory the mind—

A poem should be motionless in time   *15*
As the moon climbs.

             *   *   *

A poem should be equal to:
Not true.

For all the history of grief
An empty doorway and a maple leaf.   *20*

For love
The leaning grasses and two lights above the sea—

A poem should not mean
But be.

WILLIAM SHAKESPEARE   (1564–1616)

Sonnet 55
Not Marble, Nor the Gilded Monuments

Not marble, nor the gilded monuments
Of princes, shall outlive this powerful rhyme;
But you shall shine more bright in these conténts
Than unswept stone, besmeared with sluttish time.
When wasteful war shall statues overturn,   *5*
And broils root out the work of masonry,
Nor Mars° his sword nor war's quick fire shall burn   *Roman god of war*
The living record of your memory.
'Gainst death and all-oblivious enmity
Shall you pace forth; your praise shall still find room   *10*
Even in the eyes of all posterity
That wear this world out to the ending doom.°   *Judgment Day*
So, till the judgment that yourself arise,
You live in this, and dwell in lovers' eyes.

NIKKI GIOVANNI   (1943–   )

Kidnap Poem

ever been kidnapped
by a poet
if i were a poet

i'd kidnap you
put you in my phrases and meter   *5*
you to jones beach
or maybe coney island
or maybe just to my house
lyric you in lilacs
dash you in the rain   *10*
blend into the beach
to complement my see
play the lyre for you
ode you with my love song
anything to win you   *15*
wrap you in the red Black green
show you off to mama
yeah if i were a poet i'd kid
nap you

SEAMUS HEANEY   (1939–   )

Personal Helicon

For Michael Longley

As a child, they could not keep me from wells
And old pumps with buckets and windlasses.
I loved the dark drop, the trapped sky, the smells
Of waterweed, fungus and dank moss.

One, in a brickyard, with a rotted board top.   *5*
I savoured the rich crash when a bucket
Plummeted down at the end of a rope.
So deep you saw no reflection in it.

A shallow one under a dry stone ditch
Fructified like any aquarium.   *10*
When you dagged out long roots from the soft mulch
A white face hovered over the bottom.

Others had echoes, gave back your own call
With a clean new music in it. And one
Was scaresome for there, out of ferns and tall   *15*
Foxgloves, a rat slapped across my reflection.

Now, to pry into roots, to finger slime,
To stare, big-eyed Narcissus, into some spring
Is beneath all adult dignity. I rhyme
To see myself, to set the darkness echoing.   *20*

MARIANNE MOORE   (1887–1972)

Poetry

I, too, dislike it; there are things that are important beyond all
    this fiddle.
  Reading it, however, with a perfect contempt for it, one discovers
    in it after all, a place for the genuine.
    Hands that can grasp, eyes   5
  that can dilate, hair that can rise
    if it must, these things are important not because a

high-sounding interpretation can be put upon them but because they are
  useful. When they become so derivative as to become unintelligible.
  The same thing may be said for all of us, that we do not admire what   10
  we cannot understand: the bat
    holding on upside down or in quest of something to

eat, elephants pushing, a wild horse taking a roll, a tireless wolf under
  a tree, the immovable critic, twitching his skin like a horse that
    feels a flea, the base-   15
  ball fan, the statistician—
    nor is it valid
    to discriminate against 'business documents and

school-books'; all these phenomena are important. One must
    make a distinction   20
  however; when dragged into prominence by half poets, the result
    is not poetry,
nor till the poets among us can be
    'literalists of
    the imagination'—above   25
    insolence and triviality and can present

for inspection, 'imaginary garden with real toads in them',
    shall we have
  it. In the meantime, if you demand on the one hand, the raw
    material of poetry in   30
  all its rawness and
  that which is on the other hand
    genuine, then you are interested in poetry.

CLOSE READING

The truest poetry is the most feigning.

—WILLIAM SHAKESPEARE

The importance of reading a poem closely can hardly be overempha-sized. Poets choose each word with great care, and they want the reader to acknowledge this care by reading with wide open eyes and ears. Poems must first be read for their **literal meaning**, the basic level at which we ask such questions as, "What's happening in this poem?" "Where does it take place?" "Who is speaking?" These questions refer to the factual or situational aspect of the poem—the level at which the poem tells a story or sets a scene. Once you have grasped the literal meaning of a poem, you can proceed to its **figurative meaning**—the implicit, often hidden, reality that the poem is trying to suggest. It would be naive to assume that the literal and figurative meanings of a poem exist inde-pendently of one another, like shelves on a wall; in reality, these two kinds of meaning usually play off, complement, and reinforce one another.

It is best to begin by asking the obvious questions, because there is no set way to proceed for literal understanding. In many poems, finding out *who is speaking* or *what the subject is,* is not easy. The locale, too—where the poem takes place—may be in question. It may even be insig-nificant, though you should understand that this is the case. Without a grip on the situation of the speaker, you will never be able to read a poem closely. Let's examine the following well-known modern poem:

ROBERT FROST   (1874–1963)

The Road Not Taken

Two roads diverged in a yellow wood,
And sorry I could not travel both
And be one traveler, long I stood
And looked down one as far as I could
To where it bent in the undergrowth;   *5*

Then took the other, as just as fair,
And having perhaps the better claim,
Because it was grassy and wanted wear;
Though as for that the passing there
Had worn them really about the same,   *10*

And both that morning equally lay
In leaves no step had trodden black.
Oh, I kept the first for another day!
Yet knowing how way leads on to way.
I doubted if I should ever come back.   *15*

I shall be telling this with a sigh
Somewhere ages and ages hence:
Two roads diverged in a wood, and I—
I took the one less traveled by,
And that has made all the difference.   *20*

Robert Frost could be cunning and deceptive. He enjoyed teasing people, especially his readers. Even those experienced in close reading often misread this poem, which looks much easier on the surface than it really is. A typical **paraphrase** or prose summary of "The Road Not Taken" runs like this:

> Robert Frost writes about the importance of taking the road "less traveled by"—the individual path, as opposed to the commonly traveled path. He is advocating nonconformity, suggesting that those who go their own way in life will look back on their decision, when they are old, with satisfaction. They will understand that taking the less traveled road has made all the difference, and that their life has been much better because they were willing to take a risk.

Is this the sort of paraphrase of the poem you would make?

A closer look at "The Road Not Taken" reveals that the speaker in the poem—who should never be confused with the poet, because we cannot assume that Frost is speaking as himself—is not at all confident about taking the less traveled road. The narrator begins, in the first

stanza—that cluster of lines, like paragraphs, which divides many poems into sections—by saying that there were two roads diverging in a yellow wood. The speaker in the poem pauses. He is at a crossroad. This, then, is the literal level: A man appears in the woods at a crossroad, probably in autumn, because the leaves are yellow. In the obvious figurative reading of the poem, we might suggest that the man in question has reached an important juncture in his life. Let's say that he is trying to decide whether or not to go to *X* or *Y* College. The speaker looks down one road carefully, wondering if it is really the right one to take, the right college to choose.

In the second stanza, he says that he took the other one, which is *just as fair*. In other words, neither road is really "fairer" than the other. Notice how the narrator seems uncertain about this point of "fairness." The road he actually took seemed grassy and in need of wear, he says; but he quickly takes that back: "Though as for that the passing there / Had worn them really about the same." Look closely: *really about the same*. So really, the two roads were equally worn. Neither had a better claim to being less traveled by.

That this is Frost's conclusion about the two roads in the poem seems confirmed by the first line in the next stanza:

> And both that morning equally lay
> In leaves no step had trodden black.

There was simply no difference between the roads. So the traveler keeps the road not taken "for another day." Yet, knowing "how way leads on to way," he wisely doubts that he will ever have the chance to take that other road; a situation not unlike choosing College *X* over College *Y*. You may think you can always transfer to *Y* if *X* doesn't work out, but the truth is that you can't go back to the same point in your life and stand there as you once were. You can only have your "real" first term at one college, and if you transfer, the experience will be a new one, not the one you *would* have had if you had gone there in the first place. You can never keep one choice "for another day," as Frost's narrator would like to think he can.

In the final stanza, the speaker acknowledges that one day he will be telling his story with "a sigh." What is that sigh? How are we to interpret it? Perhaps it is a subtle signal to the reader that the speaker knows that, one day, when he claims to have taken the "road less traveled by," that he will be kidding himself and know it. The previous three stanzas repeat—again and again—that both roads that morning were equal. This makes the final line, "And that has made all the difference," deeply **ironic**. In other words, we are not to take what is said at face value. Indeed, the choice made by the speaker in the poem may well have made all the difference for the worse instead of the better. The poet will never know, just as we can never know if our choice of *X* over *Y* College will make any difference for good or ill in the long run. Furthermore, Frost is acknowledging that we mortals are likely to want to deceive ourselves in the end, to say "I made the difficult choice—am I not wonderful?" But we ought really to know that it is a little fiction we have made up to make ourselves feel good about our choice.

As you can see, "The Road Not Taken" is much more ambiguous—even devious—than it first seems. A close reading takes us beyond the naive reading that an initial look at the poem produces. This is not to say that a naive reading is totally wrong: Frost seems almost willfully to mislead the reader toward the end of the poem; he may well have been trying to fool himself about the two roads! But the poem has the more complex meaning built into its structure, and our job as readers is to listen closely to every word. Great poetry demands our fullest attention. (The broader implications of close reading are discussed in Chapter 14.)

POEMS FOR FURTHER READING

Read the following poems and answer the questions on each.

GEORGE GASCOIGNE   (1542–1577)

A Farewell

'And if I did, what then?
   Are you aggrieved therefore?
The sea hath fish for every man,
   And what would you have more?'

Thus did my mistress once   5
   Amaze my mind with doubt;
And popped a question for the nonce,
   To beat my brains about.

Whereto I thus replied:
   'Each fisherman can wish,   10
That all the seas at every tide
   Were his alone to fish.

'And so did I, in vain,
   But since it may not be,
Let such fish there as find the gain,   15
   And leave the loss for me.

'And with such luck and loss
  I will content myself,
Till tides of turning time may toss
  Such fishers on the shelf.   20

'And when they stick on sands,
  That every man may see,
Then will I laugh and clap my hands,
  As they do now at me.'

QUESTIONS

1. Let's examine the way the poem begins. What is the situation of the speaker? Who is talking to whom?
2. The speaker, in the third stanza, tells a little story about fishermen and fish. What's the point of this story? How does it relate to the rest of the poem? How are lovers like fish or fishermen?
3. How would you characterize the speaker's attitude to the situation described in the poem? Look carefully at the last stanza.

THOMAS HARDY   (1840–1928)

Channel Firing

April 1914

That night your great guns, unawares,
Shook all our coffins as we lay,
And broke the chancel window-squares,
We thought it was the Judgment-day

And sat upright. While drearisome   5
Arouse the howl of wakened hounds:
The mouse let fall the alter-crumb,
The worms drew back into the mounds,

The glebe° cow drooled. Till God called, "No;   *pasture*
It's gunnery practice out at sea   10
Just as before you went below;
The world is as it used to be:

"All nations striving strong to make
Red war yet redder. Mad as hatters
They do no more for Christés sake   15
Than you who are helpless in such matters.

"That this is not the judgment-hour
For some of them's a blessed thing,
For if it were they'd have to scour
Hell's floor for so much threatening. . . .   *20*

"Ha, ha. It will be warmer when
I blow the trumpet (if indeed
I ever do; for you are men,
And rest eternal sorely need)."

So down we lay again. "I wonder,   *25*
Will the world ever saner be,"
Said one, "than when He sent us under
In our indifferent century!"

And many a skeleton shook his head.
"Instead of preaching forty year,"   *30*
My neighbor Parson Thirdly said,
"I wish I had stuck to pipes and beer."

Again the guns disturbed the hour,
Roaring their readiness to avenge,
As far inland as Stourton Tower,°   *35*
And Camelot, and starlit Stonehenge.°

³⁵*Stourton Tower:* tower built in the eighteenth century to commemorate a victory.

³⁶*Camelot:* the legendary site of King Arthur's court; *Stonehenge:* an ancient site dating back to 1200 B.C.

QUESTIONS

1. Who is talking, and what is the situation? What lines or phrases make this clear?
2. God speaks in the third stanza. What is Hardy's God like? Be specific, using quotations to justify your response.
3. What is Parson Thirdly's attitude toward what is going on?
4. What effect does the list of places—some mythical (Camelot), some real (Stonehenge)—have at the end? Can you isolate the poet's attitude toward the situation? Where?

THEODORE ROETHKE   (1908–1963)

Orchids

They lean over the path,
Adder-mouthed,
Swaying close to the face,

Coming out, soft and deceptive
Limp and damp, delicate as a young bird's tongue;   5
Their fluttery fledgling lips
Move slowly,
Drawing in the warm air.

And at night,
The faint moon falling through whitewashed glass,   10
The heat going down
So their musky smell comes even stronger,
Drifting down from their mossy cradles:
So many devouring infants!
Soft luminescent fingers,   15
Lips neither dead nor alive,
Loose ghostly mouths
Breathing.

QUESTIONS

1. Make a list of the different things to which orchids are compared, beginning with the adder (a snake) in the second line.

2. What conclusions can you draw from this list about the poet's sense of what orchids represent?

3. Compare the two stanzas. Is there any obvious transition from the first to the second?

4. Read the poem out loud. What effects does the poet achieve simply by changing the lengths of each line?

5. Write your own poem about a flower or plant, making sure that the flower or plant takes on a strange life of its own, as do Roethke's orchids.

3

THE POET'S VOICE:
TONE AND CONTEXT

When we encounter a natural style we are always surprised and delighted, for we had thought to see an author and found a man.

—BLAISE PASCAL

Everyone has a distinct voice, one as different from every other voice in the world as his or her own fingerprint. Recognizing this uniqueness defines our humanity. When you know people very well, for instance, you learn to recognize the unique ways that each uses language. Most people have certain favorite words or expressions; their **diction**—or choice of words—bears the mark of their individuality. Their words, too, reflect their distinctness. The way you might string certain words together, your **syntax**, will differ, however slightly, from everyone else's way of saying the same thing. A professional linguist could analyze the idiosyncrasies of anyone's language and come up with a rational explanation for its special qualities; normally, though, we don't need a linguist to persuade us that differences exist.

Scholars of ancient Greek and Latin can now program a computer to recognize the diction and syntax of a particular ancient author. Thousands of unidentified fragments of ancient texts have been discovered by archaeologists, who have turned to these scholars for help in the work of identification. Until computers could do this kind of analysis, detailed linguistic studies such as these took years. Today, it can be done quickly and well, and our knowledge of the ancient world has grown enormously as a result.

If you have any favorite authors, you will probably recognize their voices quite easily. You can easily recognize a page by a novelist such as Hemingway, for instance, whose broad idiosyncrasies of diction and syntax seem quite exaggerated. They include his fondness for short words, abrupt sentences, and repetitions, as well as his habit of linking brief declarative sentences with the conjunction *and*. Most good writers, whether they write fiction, essays, or poetry, have a discernable **style,** which might be defined as the sum of any writer's idiosyncrasies.

Poetry is the ultimate refinement of style. Poets learn how to listen closely to fine shadings of language, and to pare away everything that does not fit the inner contours, the idiosyncrasies, of their own voice. Doing this is like listening to and imitating one's own heartbeat; it requires discipline and concentration, as well as talent, and it partly explains why the number of truly great poets in any age can be counted on one hand. A good close reader must cultivate the ability to recognize the idiosyncrasies and refinements of language that account for a poet's individual style.

The most crucial aspect of any given passage is **tone**, or the poet's stance toward the subject at hand. A good reader will try to determine how poets feel about the subjects of their poems, whether they are cynical or indifferent, bemused or earnest, sarcastic or sentimental. This overall tone may be thought of as a poet's **attitude** in the poem. Summing up a poet's tone or attitude in one word is not always easy. You have to explore attitude through tone, sizing up the different, often contradictory, aspects of a poet's feeling about the subject. Without a solid understanding of the author's attitude toward the subject of a poem, it is easy to misread that poem badly.

Words always constitute the right place to begin any study of a poem. In our reading of Frost's "The Road Not Taken" in the previous chapter, we had to look at what the speaker in the poem actually said, to try to discover who was talking and what was going on. If you know *who is talking* you have come a long way toward discovering the tone of any given passage, especially if you also know *who is being addressed*. These questions form the basis of any analysis of tone.

Some critics find it useful to distinguish between a poem's **subject** and its **theme**. A poem's subject is usually quite straightforward. Look at the following poem:

WILLIAM WORDSWORTH   (1770–1850)

My Heart Leaps Up

My heart leaps up when I behold
  A rainbow in the sky;
So was it when my life began;

So is it now I am a man;
So be it when I shall grow old,   5
    Or let me die!
The Child is father of the Man;
And I could wish my days to be
Bound each to each by natural piety.

The subject of the poem is the poet's continuing delight in rainbows. Its theme is the importance of responding to nature in a simple, childlike manner at every age, because children have a natural piety in the presence of nature, an instinctual admiration for natural phenomena. One excellent line, "The Child is father of the Man," sums up Wordsworth's theme succinctly. But, in truth, one should beware of isolating a poet's theme without regard for his or her overall tone or attitude. No poets would ever want their poems reduced to prosy single sentences. It is always best to talk more in terms of attitude than theme, because readers can more usefully characterize an attitude.

QUESTIONS

1. Look again at "My Heart Leaps Up." How would you describe Wordsworth's attitude toward the subject of that poem? How does this relate to its theme (as characterized in the preceding paragraph)?
2. Choose one of the poems in the Anthology section of this book and discuss the development of the poet's tone as the poem moves from line to line or stanza to stanza. Then try to summarize the poet's attitude in the poem toward the subject of that poem.

Assessing a poet's attitude toward the subject and theme of a poem can be difficult, since it's common for poets to adopt a **mask**, a guise, which is often called a **persona** (from the Latin word for mask). In other words, the poet speaks as somebody else, perhaps someone quite different from himself or herself. This tradition goes back to ancient Greece, where poetry was most often spoken on stage in highly formalized theatrical productions. Only a limited number of masks were available, representing the familiar gods and heroes of Greek legend and mythology; poets had to apply to the Keeper of the Masks for permission to use certain personae or masks. It was unheard of for a poet to write in his or her own voice. Today, poets still resort to masks, even when they write as themselves. The "I" of a lyric poem is rarely meant to be the poet's own voice. In poetry as in daily life, self-dramatization often depends on a certain amount of fictionalizing. So it is important that, as a close reader of poems, you identify the relationship between the poet and the speaker of the poem.

This judgment can be easy or difficult. When Alastair Reid begins a poem, "I am a lady three feet small," we can be fairly sure that Mr. Reid is not speaking in his own voice. But when John Milton writes a poem on the subject of his own blindness, we can feel equally confident that the "I" in the poem is at least closely identified in Milton's mind with himself. Let's look at Milton's famous poem:

JOHN MILTON   (1608–1674)

On His Blindness

When I consider how my light is spent
  Ere half my days, in this dark world and wide,
  And that one talent which is death to hide
  Lodged with me useless, though my soul more bent
To serve therewith my Maker, and present   5
  My true account, lest he returning chide;
  "Doth God exact day-labor, light denied?"
  I fondly ask; but Patience to prevent
That murmur, soon replies, "God doth not need
  Either man's work or his own gifts; who best   *10*
  Bear his mild yoke, they serve him best. His state
Is kingly. Thousands at his bidding speed
  And post o'er land and ocean without rest:
  They also serve who only stand and wait."

It certainly helps to know that John Milton went blind in middle age. Without this knowledge, it would be possible to misunderstand the poem, even though the title lays out this clue quite clearly. (Milton did not put this title on the poem himself. His editors did, and the title has stuck.) Even without the title, reading the first two lines makes it possible to figure out that the poet was blind. In any case, the context of the poem—the fact of Milton's blindness—is central to a full comprehension of the tone of "On His Blindness."

EXERCISE

Go through Milton's poem, line by line, and discuss his changing tone. Begin by looking at specific words in context. Where does the tone change? How do the various tones, at last, accumulate an overall tone or attitude? What *is* Milton's ultimate response to his own blindness?

Sometimes a poet will take on a mask to dramatize, perhaps to exaggerate or ridicule, aspects of his own personality, as T. S. Eliot does in "The Love Song of J. Alfred Prufrock." (This poem is enormously musical and should be read aloud.)

T. S. ELIOT   (1888–1965)

The Love Song of J. Alfred Prufrock

S'io credesse che mia risposta fosse
A persona che mai tornasse al mondo,
Questa fiamma staria senza piu scosse.
Ma perciocche giammai di questo fondo
Non torno vivo alcun, s'i'odo il vero,
Senza tema d'infamia ti rispondo.*

Let us go then, you and I,
When the evening is spread out against the sky
Like a patient etherized upon a table;
Let us go, through certain half-deserted streets,
The muttering retreats   5
Of restless nights in one-night cheap hotels
And sawdust restaurants with oyster-shells:
Streets that follow like a tedious argument
Of insidious intent
To lead you to an overwhelming question . . .   10
Oh, do not ask, "What is it?"
Let us go and make our visit.
In the room the women come and go
Talking of Michelangelo.

The yellow fog that rubs its back upon the window-panes   15
The yellow smoke that rubs its muzzle on the window-panes
Licked its tongue into the corners of the evening,
Lingered upon the pools that stand in drains,
Let fall upon its back the soot that falls from chimneys,
Slipped by the terrace, made a sudden leap,   20
And seeing that it was a soft October night,
Curled once about the house, and fell asleep.

And indeed there will be time
For the yellow smoke that slides along the street,
Rubbing its back upon the window-panes;   25
There will be time, there will be time
To prepare a face to meet the faces that you meet;
There will be time to murder and create,

---

*These words come from Dante's *Inferno* (XXVII.61–66). In the scene from which this quotation is taken, Dante and Virgil, his guide through Hell, encounter Guido da Montefeltro, who, like everyone in this ring of Hell, is wrapped in a flame. This is the Chasm of Hell where false counselors are put. The lines from Dante say: "If I believed my reply were given to anyone who might go back to the world, this flame would stand motionless. But since nobody has ever gone back alive from this abyss, if what I hear is true, I answer you without fear of infamy."

And time for all the works and days° of hands
That lift and drop a question on your plate;   30
Time for you and time for me,
And time yet for a hundred indecisions,
And for a hundred visions and revisions,
Before the taking of a toast and tea.

In the room the women come and go   35
Talking of Michelangelo.

And indeed there will be time
To wonder, "Do I dare?" and, "Do I dare?"
Time to turn back and descend the stair,
With a bald spot in the middle of my hair—   40
[They will say: "How his hair is growing thin!"]
My morning coat, my collar mounting firmly to the chin,
My necktie rich and modest, but asserted by a simple pin—
[They will say: "But how his arms and legs are thin!"]
Do I dare   45
Disturb the universe?
In a minute there is time
For decisions and revisions which a minute will reverse.

For I have known them all already, known them all:
Have known the evenings, mornings, afternoons,   50
I have measured out my life with coffee spoons;
I know the voices dying with a dying fall
Beneath the music from a farther room.
   So how should I presume?

And I have known the eyes already, known them all—   55
The eyes that fix you in a formulated phrase,
And when I am formulated, sprawling on a pin,
When I am pinned and wriggling on the wall,
Then how should I begin
To spit out all the butt-ends of my days and ways?   60
   And how should I presume? And I have known the arms already,
        known them all—
Arms that are braceleted and white and bare
[But in the lamplight, downed with light brown hair!]
Is it perfume from a dress   65
That makes me so digress?
Arms that lie along a table, or wrap about a shawl.
   And should I then presume?
   And how should I begin

*   *   *

---

[29]*Works and Days* is the title of a famous Greek poem by Hesiod, written in the eighth
century B.C.

Shall I say, I have gone at dusk through narrow streets   70
And watched the smoke that rises from the pipes
Of lonely men in shirt-sleeves, leaning out of windows? . . .
    I should have been a pair of ragged claws
Scuttling across the floors of silent seas.

*   *   *

And the afternoon, the evening, sleeps so peacefully!   75
Smoothed by long fingers,
Asleep . . . tired . . . or it malingers,
Stretched on the floor, here beside you and me.
Should I, after tea and cakes and ices,
Have the strength to force the moment to its crisis?   80
But though I have wept and fasted, wept and prayed,
Though I have seen my head (grown slightly bald) brought in
        upon a platter,°
I am no prophet—and here's no great matter;
I have seen the moment of my greatness flicker,   85
And I have seen the eternal Footman hold my coat, and snicker,
And in short, I was afraid.

    And would it have been worth it, after all,
After the cups, the marmalade, the tea,
Among the porcelain, among some talk of you and me,   90
Would it have been worth while,
To have bitten off the matter with a smile,
To have squeezed the universe into a ball
To roll it toward some overwhelming question,
To say: "I am Lazarus, come from the dead,°   95
Come back to tell you all, I shall tell you all"—
If one, settling a pillow by her head,
    Should say: "That is not what I meant at all.
    That is not it, at all."

    And would it have been worth it, after all,   100
Would it have been worth while,
After the sunsets and the dooryards and the sprinkled streets,
After the novels, after the teacups, after the skirts that trail along
        the floor—
And this, and so much more?—   105
It is impossible to say just what I mean!
But as if a magic lantern° threw the nerves in patterns on a screen:

---

[82]John the Baptist was beheaded by King Herod (see Matthew 14:1–12).
[95]Lazarus was raised from the dead by Jesus (see John 1:1 to 2:2).
[107]*lantern:* an antique type of projector.

Would it have been worth while
If one, settling a pillow or throwing off a shawl,
And turning toward the window, should say: *110*
    'That is not it at all,
    That is not what I meant, at all.'

*   *   *

No! I am not Prince Hamlet, nor was meant to be;
Am an attendant lord, one that will do
To swell a progress, start a scene or two,   *115*
Advise the prince; no doubt, an easy tool,
Deferential, glad to be of use,
Politic, cautious, and meticulous;
Full of high sentence, but a bit obtuse;°
At times, indeed, almost ridiculous—   *120*
Almost, at times, the Fool.

I grow old . . . I grow old . . .
I shall wear the bottoms of my trousers rolled.°

Shall I part my hair behind? Do I dare to eat a peach?
I shall wear white flannel trousers, and walk upon the beach.   *125*
I have heard the mermaids singing, each to each.

I do not think that they will sing to me.

I have seen them riding seaward on the waves
Combing the white hair of the waves blown back
When the wind blows the water white and black.   *130*

We have lingered in the chambers of the sea
By sea-girls wreathed with seaweed red and brown
Till human voices wake us, and we drown.

We find in this poem a complex mingling of tones. The title itself associates the romantic notion of a "love song" with the name of "J. Alfred Prufrock," thus moving from the sublime to the ridiculous. Notice Eliot's tone in the title alone, his attitude toward the name. He is clearly cynical, because the name is ridiculously pompous, which alerts the reader that Mr. Prufrock has certain problems of self-conception that the poet is aware of. (It's amusing to note that Eliot, as a young man recently graduated from college, used to sign his name, "T. Stearns Eliot.") It also

---

[119]In Shakespeare's play *Hamlet,* Polonius is a ridiculous adviser, full of fancy speeches or "high sentence."
[123]A fashionable thing for young men to do.

alerts readers that Eliot wants to maintain a strong separation between himself and the speaker in his poem.

EXERCISE

Characterize the difference in tone that would be implied in the following alternative titles to Eliot's poem:

"The Love Song of J. A. Prufrock, M.A."
"The Love Song of John Prufrock."
"Jack Prufrock's Love Song"

From the beginning of Eliot's poem, the reader discovers a strange mix of images, as when evening is compared to "a patient etherized upon a table." Throughout the poem, the speaker, J. Alfred Prufrock, presents an image of himself that is both funny and sad, a bit like Charlie Chaplin, though the element of sadness seems to dominate. Read the poem again carefully, then answer the following questions.

QUESTIONS

1. When Prufrock says, "Let us go then, you and I," to whom does he refer? (This is tricky, so be inventive. Read the poem again before answering.)
2. What specific words or phrases alert the reader to Prufrock's attitude toward the city in the first stanza?
3. Note the refrain: "In the room the women come and go/Talking of Michelangelo." What is Prufrock's attitude toward these women? Admiring? Cynical? How can you tell?
4. Prufrock seems obsessed with time. He wonders, especially, if there will be time to wonder, "Do I dare?" What does daring have to do with Prufrock's portrait of himself? What do you think he wonders if he might dare?
5. When Prufrock says he should have been "a pair of ragged claws/Scuttling across the floors of silent seas," how does he regard himself? How is that different from the image of him near the end, where he walks along the beach with his white trousers rolled above the ankles?
6. How many different ways of looking at himself does Prufrock enumerate? List them.
7. How would you differentiate between subject and theme in this poem? How would you describe the overall tone or attitude (as distinct from theme)?

POEMS FOR FURTHER READING

Read the following poems carefully and answer the questions on each.

CHIDIOCK TICHBORN   (d. 1586)

Elegy

My prime of youth is but a frost of cares,
My feast of joy is but a dish of pain,
My crop of corn is but a field of tares,
And all my good is but vain hope of gain:
The day is past, and yet I saw no sun,   5
And now I live, and now my life is done.

My tale was heard, and yet it was not told,
My fruit is fall'n, and yet my leaves are green,
My youth is spent; and yet I am not old,
I saw the world, and yet I was not seen: 10
My thread is cut, and yet it is not spun,
And now I live, and now my life is done.

I sought my death, and found it in my womb,
I looked for life, and saw it was a shade,
I trod the earth, and knew it was my tomb,   15
And now I die, and now I was but made:
My glass is full, and now my glass is run,
And now I live, and now my life is done.

QUESTIONS

1. "Elegy" was written in the Tower of London shortly before Tichborn was
   executed for his part in a Catholic plot to overthrow the Protestant British
   queen, Elizabeth I. How does the addition of this biographical knowledge
   affect your sense of the poem's overall tone?
2. Paradoxes (statements that seem, at least on their surface, self-contradictory)
   play a central role in the way this poet forms his lines. Explain the paradoxical
   (self-contradictory) nature of the tone found in these lines.

A. E. HOUSMAN   (1859–1936)

Into My Heart an Air That Kills

Into my heart an air that kills
From yon far country blows:
What are those blue remembered hills,
What spires, what farms are those?

That is the land of lost content,   5
I see it shining plain,
The happy highways where I went
And cannot come again.

QUESTIONS

1. What is the "land of lost content" and why can't the poet go back there?
2. How would you describe the setting of this poem? (Find particular words or phrases that call up a specific geographical region or kind of region.)
3. Does the tone shift from the first to the second stanza? In what way?
4. How would you characterize the tone of the last line? Does this accurately describe the overall tone or attitude of the poet in the poem as a whole?

THEODORE ROETHKE   (1908–1963)

My Papa's Waltz

The whiskey on your breath
Could make a small boy dizzy;
But I hung on like death:
Such waltzing was not easy.

We romped until the pans   5
Slid from the kitchen shelf;
My mother's countenance
Could not unfrown itself.

The hand that held my wrist
Was battered on one knuckle;   10
At every step you missed
My right ear scraped a buckle.

You beat time on my head
With a palm caked hard by dirt,
Then waltzed me off to bed   15
Still clinging to your shirt.

QUESTIONS

1. What tone does Roethke adopt in the title? Consider carefully the word "waltz."
2. When the poet says, "Such waltzing was not easy," what is he trying to imply? Discuss this in terms of tone.
3. How is the mother portrayed in relation to the father?
4. What emotions does the poet attribute to the boy in the poem?
5. What is the poet's overall tone or attitude? Cite specific lines to verify this.

IMAGE AND IDEA

Image and after-imagery are about all there is to poetry.

—ROBERT FROST

Imagery is central to all poetry. As John Dryden (1631–1700) once said, "Imaging is, in itself, the very height and life of Poetry." But what defines an image? An image is a picture in words, some would argue. That is true, but it represents only a rough stab at a definition. Let's begin, as usual, with a specific example. The Greek poet, Sappho (seventh century B.C.) wrote the following little poem that depends for its splendid effects almost entirely on one image:

> In gold sandals
> dawn like a thief
> fell upon me.
> —*translated by Willis Barnstone*

This startling poem presents one crisp image, that of dawn as a thief who creeps up on the sleeping speaker, taking her unaware. We have all seen these "gold sandals" on the horizon. The poem wakens in our minds a lovely and mysterious picture that also frightens us, because most of us have imagined how terrifying it would be for a thief to "fall on us" and waken us suddenly.

Chinese and Japanese poets have long recognized the importance of sharp imagery. Read the following brief Oriental poems and notice the quality of images invoked:

Liu Ch'ang Ch'ing (8th century)

SNOW ON LOTUS MOUNTAIN

Sunset, Blue peaks vanish in dusk.
Under the Winter stars
My lonely cabin is covered with snow.
I can hear the dogs barking
At the rustic gate.
Through snow and wind
Someone is coming home.

—translated by Kenneth Rexroth

Hsieh Ling Yuen (385–433)

BY T'ING YANG WATERFALL

A strange, beautiful girl
Bathes her feet in the flowing water.
The white moon, in the midst of the clouds,
Is far away, beyond the reach of man.

—translated by Kenneth Rexroth

Chiang K'uei (1155?–1235?)

WRITTEN AT LAKESIDE RESIDENCE

The wind over the lake is mild, the moon fair;
I lie down and watch the clouds' shadow on the glass.
A light boat suddenly passes by the window,
Disturbing one or two green reeds.

—translated by Chiang Yee

A poetic image must not tell us *about* something; it must present the thing itself. It is one thing to say, "I saw a beautiful sunset this morning." It is another to show someone a sharp photograph of that sunset. A poem, in theory, should present a vivid picture that *embodies* an idea or a feeling, as in the preceding Chinese poems. "Snow on Lotus Mountain," for instance, etches an impression in the reader's mind. The sunset, the blue mountain peaks that seem to vanish in the dusk, and the lonely cabin deep in snow convey feelings of isolation and coldness. That "someone is coming home" through the wintry weather adds a human touch to the landscape; the reader begins to appreciate humanity's aloneness under the stars, whether or not he or she lives in a lonely winter cabin. Saying little, the poet Liu Ch'ang Ch'ing has called to mind a picture worth a thousand words.

EXERCISE

Examine in detail the other two Chinese poems printed above. Describe the emotion or idea that each poem embodies in its images.

In its original definition, the word *idea* was associated with mental pictures. Many linguists argue that all language begins with concrete pictures, and that it is only over time that words become abstract. Ralph Waldo Emerson (1803–1882), the American poet and philosopher, once said: "The etymologist finds the deadest word to have been once a brilliant picture," pointing out that abstract words like *right* and *wrong* originally meant *straight* and *crooked*. The "right" path to a destination was the "straight" path, as the crow flies. The "wrong" path was simply the crooked one. If you study the history of words, as etymologists do, you will find that most abstract words were once connected to images. The word *abstraction* itself is a good example. In Latin, it means "pulling away from." The Latin verb *tractare* is buried in the word. It is the same as our English word, *tractor,* a machine that pulls something along. Abstraction represents a pulling of language away from its concrete embodiment in an image.

The word *idea* now seems permanently connected to abstract or philosophical thought, though poets have long considered it one of their tasks to restore ideas to their sensuous or pictorial context, to "embody" ideas or make them physical again; after all, as T. S. Eliot once observed, a thought *is* a feeling. Modern poets, in particular, have tended to think of poetry itself as **concrete** language, thus separating it from philosophical discourse, which is **abstract**. Indeed, the terms *concrete* and *abstract* have, somewhat naively, become opposites, with preference going to the former.

It is naive to oppose abstract and concrete so absolutely because an image is *not* simply "a picture in words." Samuel Taylor Coleridge (1772–1843) put his finger on the problem:

> Images, however beautiful . . . do not of themselves characterize the poet. They become proofs of original genius only as far as they are modified by a predominant passion; or by associated thoughts or images awakened by that passion.

Another poet, Ezra Pound (1885–1972), understood the necessity to extend the meaning of the poetic image beyond its merely pictorial quality. He defined the image itself as "an intellectual and emotional complex in an instant of time"—that is, the image itself involves more than just visual description. Readers' thoughts and feelings ought to be touched as well as their mental retinas. Pound's definition rightly points to the juxtaposition of image and idea that occurs in the best poems.

Let's examine a couple of recent poems that use images in the complex sense of Ezra Pound's definition.

LOUISE GLUCK (1944–   )

Happiness

A man and woman lie on a white bed.
It is morning. I think
Soon they will waken.
On the bedside table is a base
of lilies; sunlight   5
pools in their throats.
I watch him turn to her
as though to speak her name
but silently, deep in her mouth—
At the window ledge,   10
once, twice,
a bird calls.
And then she stirs; her body
fills with his breath.

I open my eyes; you are watching me.   15
Almost over this room
the sun is gliding.
Look at your face, you say,
holding your own close to me
to make a mirror.   20
How calm you are. And the burning wheel
passes gently over us.

"Happiness" *does,* of course, present a number of bold visual images. We can actually see the man and woman lying on the white sheets—an image of purity and serenity, which is reinforced by the images of the lilies in their vase, the sunlight pooling in the couple's throats. Beyond this visual imagery, there is sound: "once, twice, / a bird calls." Taste and smell are involved in the image of her body filling with his breath at the close of the first stanza. The poem ends with the strange image of a burning wheel, the sun, as it passes over. The wheel is a complex image, often associated with desire, which comes over people in a cyclical fashion. Hinduism uses the wheel of life, the *mandala,* as its central image; it considers the wheel as something to which souls are bound through various reincarnations. Gluck may have had this in mind when she described the sun as a wheel, though the wheel might also be the sky itself, which appears (from our inferior human vantage point) to revolve over the earth. Yet much more is involved than these visual and sensual images. Gluck is trying to convey an impression of happiness and the cyclical nature of happiness, and she is trying—as Coleridge insisted a good poet must—to modify the image by a passion. One finds, certainly, strong feelings of affection, even love, in this poem. That the man is watching the woman when she opens her eyes suggests fondness or, at least, real attentiveness. That she has already taken his breath into herself is a sign of their closeness, if not affection. The general aura of gentleness, ease, and warmth adds to the overall impression. The poem's imagery, then, is complex, and it involves much more than merely pictorial descriptions.

Drama, too, can play a great role in the effectiveness of a poet's imagery. The following poem by Theodore Roethke provides an excellent example of that drama:

THEODORE ROETHKE   (1908–1963)

Child on Top of a Greenhouse

The wind billowing out the seat of my britches,
My feet crackling splinters of glass and dried putty,
The half-grown chrysanthemums staring up like accusers,
Up through the streaked glass, flashing with sunlight,
A few white clouds all rushing eastward,   5
A line of elms plunging and tossing like horses,
And everyone, everyone pointing up and shouting!

Roethke limits the drama to one perilous moment, with the child poised on top of the greenhouse. Notice how the language enacts the drama: Verbs like *billowing, crackling, staring, plunging,* and *tossing* add to the excitement by their participial form, which implies action. The very fact that the entire poem consists of a sentence fragment—a sentence without a main subject or verb—enhances the expectancy of the reader, who is left, like the sentence, dangling, incomplete. The sun, the clouds, and the trees all seem to participate in the potentially violent scene; meanwhile the brevity of the poem, all that is left unsaid, adds to its intensity and focus. The deep image at the center of this poem creates what Pound called for, an emotional and intellectual complex in time.

POEMS FOR FURTHER READING

Read the following poems carefully and answer the questions on each.

EMILY DICKINSON   (1830–1886)

He Fumbles at Your Soul

He fumbles at your Soul
As Players at the Keys
Before they drop full Music on—
He stuns you by degrees—
Prepares your brittle Nature   5
For the Ethereal Blow
By fainter Hammers—further heard—
Then nearer—Then so slow
Your Breath has time to straighten—
Your Brain—to bubble Cool—   10
Deals—One—imperial—Thunderbolt—
That scalps your naked Soul—

When Winds take Forests in their Paws—
The Universe—is still—

QUESTIONS

1. Who is the "He" that Dickinson mentions at the beginning of the poem?
2. What is implied by the word "fumbles" and how does it relate to the rest of the poem?
3. The poem builds to a terrifying climax. What do you make of the final image, "When Winds take Forests in their Paws"?
4. What is Dickinson's attitude toward death in this poem?

ROBERT HERRICK   (1591–1694)

Upon Julia's Clothes

Whenas in silks my Julia goes,
Then, then, methinks, how sweetly flows
That liquefaction of her clothes!

Next, when I cast mine eyes and see
That brave vibration each way free,   5
—O how that glittering taketh me!

QUESTIONS

1. How does the word "liquefaction" in the first stanza develop the image of Julia walking in her clothes?
2. What important change occurs in the second stanza?

PERCY BYSSHE SHELLEY   (1792–1822)

Ozymandias°

I met a traveler from an antique land
Who said: Two vast and trunkless legs of stone
Stand in the desert . . . Near them, on the sand,
Half sunk, a shattered visage lies, whose frown,
And wrinkled lip, and sneer of cold command,   5
Tell that its sculptor well those passions read
Which yet survive, stamped on these lifeless things,
The hand that mocked them, and the heart that fed:
And on the pedestal these words appear:
"My name is Ozymandias, king of kings: 10
Look on my works, ye Mighty, and despair!"
Nothing beside remains. Round the decay
Of that colossal wreck, boundless and bare
The lone and level sands stretch far away.

°Ozymandias is the Greek name for Ramses II, Egyptian King of the thirteenth century
B.C., who is said to have erected a huge statue of himself.

QUESTIONS

1. What impression does the word "antique" in the first line make on you?
2. How does the image of the statue contrast with the setting?
3. Is the image itself ironic? Why?
4. The poem presents a central image, then what Robert Frost calls an "after-image" or follow-up image, the "lone and level sands." What effect does that produce?

WILLIAM CARLOS WILLIAMS   (1883–1963)

The Red Wheelbarrow

so much depends
upon
a red wheel
barrow
glazed with rain   5
water
beside the white
chickens.

QUESTIONS

1. This poem has, for many reasons, remained among the most popular that Williams ever wrote, yet there is very little here apart from one commonplace image. What is so good about this poem?

2. What do you think might be the "so much" that "depends" on a red wheelbarrow? (Think about your own response to—or need for—objects in the world.)

3. Compare this poem to "In March" by Anne Stevenson, which you will find in the Anthology II section of this book.

4. Write your own little poem beginning "So much depends upon. . . ." See if you can produce a clear image upon which much might depend.

HILDA DOOLITTLE (H. D.)   (1886–1961)

Evening

The light passes
from ridge to ridge,
from flower to flower—
the hypaticas, wide-spread
under the light   5
grow faint—
the petals reach inward,
the blue tips bend
toward the bluer heart
and the flowers are lost.   10

The cornel-buds are still white,
but shadows dart
from the cornel-roots—
black creeps from root to root,
each leaf   15
cuts another leaf on the grass,
shadow seeks shadow,
then both leaf
and leaf-shadow are lost.

QUESTIONS

1. The first stanza of "Evening" creates an image of motion that ends when that motion stops and "the flowers are lost." How does Doolittle manage to convey an impression of motion? How would you describe this motion if you were asked to make a diagram of it?

2. Is the second stanza menacing? Why or why not?

3. Is there a sense of despair at the end of this poem? If not, what is your final impression?

ALFRED CORN (1943–)

Grass

At this range, it's really monumental—
Tall spears and tilted spears, most
Blunted by the last mowing.
A few cloverleafs (leaves?)   5
And infant plantains fight
For their little plot of ground.
Wing-nuts or boomerangs, the maple seeds
Try to and really can't take root.
There's always more going on   10
Than anyone has the wit to notice:
Look at those black ants, huge,
In their glistening exoskeletons.
Algebraically efficient,
They're dismembering a dragonfly—   15
Goggle-eyed at being dead
And having its blue-plated chassis,
Its isinglass delicately
Leaded wings put in pieces.
When you get right down to it,   20
The earth's a jungle.
The tough grass grows over and around it all,
A billion green blades, each one
Sharply creased down the spine.
Now that I've gotten up to go,   25
It's nothing but a green background
With a body-shaped dent left behind.
As the grass stretches and rises,
That will go, too.

QUESTIONS

1. This is a poem about perspective, about not trusting the image, because it
   has many sides and only the sum of those sides is the "real" thing. What are
   some of the problems the poet has with "taking in" the image of grass?

2. "When you get right down to it," says the poet, "The earth's a jungle." How
   many different ways can you look at this remark?

3. How has Corn modified the image of grass by adding feelings or thoughts?
   Has he?

FROM METAPHOR
TO SYMBOL

The greatest thing by far is to have a command of metaphor. This alone cannot be imparted by another. It is the mark of genius.

—ARISTOTLE

An image alone does not make a poem. The image has to refer to a complex field of thought and feeling beyond itself; it has to suggest or call up a parallel idea, to become what we call a **metaphor**. A metaphor is a comparison that suggests that one thing is similar to another. (If the word *like* is actually used, we call this comparison a **simile**, as in the statement "His heart is like a stone.") The word *metaphor* itself derives from two Greek words which mean "to carry over," and *meaning* is what the poet "carries over." As Aristotle pointed out over 2000 years ago, metaphors are fundamentally illogical, because they imply that one thing is another. For instance, if a woman says, "My husband is a real workhorse," she has said something basically crazy. Her husband isn't really what she says he is—at least, we can hope not! She means that he is *like* a workhorse—hardworking and reliable or having whatever other characteristics we might reasonably associate with a workhorse. A transference of meaning takes place.

In a lecture called "Education by Poetry," Robert Frost explains the nature of metaphorical thinking:

> Poetry begins in trivial metaphors, pretty metaphors, "grace" metaphors, and goes on to the profoundest thinking that we have. Poetry provides that one permissible way of saying one thing and meaning another. People

say, "Why don't you say what you mean?" We never do that, do we, being all of us too much poets. We like to talk in parables and in hints and in indirections—whether from diffidence or some other instinct. I have wanted in late years to go further and further in making metaphor the whole of thinking.

Like all poets, Frost understood the centrality of metaphor, of comparison, to human thought. We can't even begin to think about something without comparing it to something else: Such comparison is the first step in all forms of analysis. We can only judge the value of one thing by setting it against something else.

Metaphor lies at the heart of poetry. (The preceding statement itself makes use of a metaphor. Can you tell how?) Let's examine a famous poem that employs an obvious metaphor.

ROBERT BURNS (1759–1796)

A Red, Red Rose

O, my luve is like a red, red rose,
    That's newly sprung in June.
O, my luve is like the melodie,
    That's sweetly played in tune.

As fair art thou, my bonnie lass,   *5*
    So deep in luve am I,
And I will luve thee still, my dear,
    Till a' the seas gang dry.°

Till a' the seas gang dry, my dear,
    And the rocks melt wi' the sun!   *10*
And I will luve thee still, my dear,
    While the sands o' life shall run.

And fare thee weel, my only luve,
    And fare thee weel awhile!
And I will come again, my luve,   *15*
    Though it were ten thousand mile!

[8]till all the seas go dry.

This poem fairly explodes with traditional metaphors, as Burns compares his love to a rose newly sprung in June and to a melody played in tune. He leaves it to us, because it is quite obvious, to decide his love compares to the rose and the melody. (Roses are beautiful flowers, but they can also be thorny! Presumably Burns's love was the former and not the latter.) Note that these metaphors are actually similes, since the poet calls attention to the comparisons by using *like* or *as* in the formulations.

Notice, too, the extremely conventional aspect of Burns's metaphors. In love poems written by men, women have traditionally been referred to as flowers of one kind or another. Today, however, such metaphors seem rather sexist, because flowers are inherently pretty to look at but quite "useless" otherwise. They are objects to be admired but not taken seriously.

EXERCISE

Could Burns's poem have been written by a woman about a man? If not, how would it have to be changed? (This is a good exercise in thinking about male and female stereotypes, which inevitably underevaluate real people.)

Burns employs metaphor on the simplest level. He makes comparisons, then drops them. In the best poems, comparisons are developed in a more thorough way, as we see in "The Silken Tent" by Robert Frost.

ROBERT FROST   (1874–1963)

The Silken Tent

She is as in a field a silken tent
At midday when a sunny summer breeze
Has dried the dew and all its ropes relent,
So that in guys° it gently sways at ease,   *ropes*
And its supporting central cedar pole,   5
That is its pinnacle to heavenward
And signifies the sureness of the soul,
Seems to owe naught to any single cord,
But strictly held by none, is loosely bound
By countless silken ties of love and thought   10
To everything on earth the compass round,
And only by one's going slightly taut
In the capriciousness of summer air
Is of the slightest bondage made aware.

Throughout the poem, Frost analyzes his lover or wife in terms of the silken tent of the title. An extended metaphor or simile, such as this one, is often called a **conceit** or a **metaphysical conceit**. (Poets who belonged to the "Metaphysical School" of poets, who wrote in the early seventeenth century, adored conceits and often employed them on an elaborate scale.) A fair number of the best poems in English make use of this technique, because it gives a poem a great deal of unity.

QUESTIONS

1. How often, and where, does Frost refer explicitly to the woman in question?
2. Why does Frost refer to noon in the poem?
3. The supporting tent pole is also a crucial part of this elaborate comparison. What does the pole stand for?
4. Discuss the phrase "countless silken ties of love and thought" in the context of the entire metaphor as it develops.
5. What does Frost hope to suggest by the final image of the silken ties that go taut when the wind slightly blows the tent? Focus on the word "capriciousness," which you might want to look up.
6. How does Frost's attitude toward his lover differ from that of Robert Burns in "The Red, Red Rose"? Look carefully at the two metaphors for women and compare the difference in the ways Burns and Frost think of their ideal lovers. What are the differences? How do you respond to these conceptions?

A natural progression occurs from idea to image, from image to metaphor, from metaphor to symbol. A **symbol** is simply the extension of a metaphor to include things beyond its immediate field or scope. When you throw a stone into a pond, for instance, its first plunk is the bull's eye of metaphor. The progressive, concentric rings that flow outward in decreasing levels of force but ever-widening scope represent the symbolic waves that flow out from the metaphorical image. A **conventional symbol** is a common symbol whose associations are familiar. A flag is a symbol of one's country, for instance. It suggests patriotism and cultural solidarity and many other commonly felt ideas. If you came across a skull and cross-bones image in a story or a poem, it would carry obvious connotations of death and destruction. It would be called a conventional symbol.

Because we began our discussion of metaphor with Robert Burns's famous rose, let's look at the rose, in another way, as a symbol, in a poem by William Blake.

WILLIAM BLAKE (1757–1827)

The Sick Rose

O Rose, thou art sick!
The invisible worm
That flies in the night,
In the howling storm

Has found out thy bed   5
Of crimson joy,
And his dark secret love
Does thy life destroy.

We have come a long way here from Burns's rose, which has newly
sprung in June. Blake's rose is sick. As always, it is important to judge
a poem on its literal level first. Let's assume that the poem is first about
a plant, a rose, that has become ill because some invisible worm has
attacked it. But why is the worm "invisible"? This worm seems quite
imaginary. In fact, the rose itself sleeps in a secret bed of "crimson" (or
red) joy. What is all this? The worm seems to love the rose with a "dark
secret love" that somehow destroys the happiness, the life, of the rose.
The poem is definitely talking about more than real roses and real worms,
although the literal level of the poem cannot be denied. The very nature
of a literary symbol is to become less specific on some levels. We *do* have
a poem here in which a rose is being preyed upon by a worm, but we
are quickly asked to imagine a larger scene of invasion and destruction.
The rose may stand for anything that is lovely and hidden and joyful;
the worm may represent any form of evil on the prowl. The rose may
well be female, the worm male, though that isn't necessarily the case.
(Do not, like many readers after Freud, assume that everything longer
than it is wide is a phallic symbol!)

EXERCISE

In one paragraph, come up with your own ideas of what the rose and worm
could "stand for." Allow your mind to associate freely. Even the most distant
association may still retain an element of truth.

At this juncture, it is important to recognize that a good symbol
should *not* encourage such free association that ridiculous connections
occur. Poets use symbols to control a reader's imagination, to stimulate
specific areas of the brain so as to call up a definite range of emotions.
Blake's poem, for instance, does limit us to associations of invasion and
sickness, to feelings of dread and terror. There's no way the poem could
be interpreted as a model for a healthy relationship. Poor readers often
let a poem set off a chain of thoughts unrelated to the poem itself.
Always make sure that your associations key into the poem's language
and relate to the poet's specific references. Although the symbol is by
definition indefinite, casting a wide net, it is not unspecific.

Metaphors and symbols are often called **figures of speech**. Think
of an ice skater, who makes an extraordinary and graceful figure in the
ice, perhaps the figure eight. A metaphor, then, is an elaborate turn in

language, a fancy shuffle. Many of the turns language can take have been given names. Metaphor itself is one such name; the different ways in which a phrase is metaphorical have been isolated and named as well. **Personification** is an obvious one: The poet gives human characteristics, like weeping or laughing, to an inanimate object, like a tree. Two other terms closely associated with metaphor are *metonomy* and *synecdoche*. In **metonomy**, the poet talks about something in terms of something associated with it. We do this every day when we say things like "The kettle is boiling." The kettle isn't boiling, but the water in the kettle is. This is metonomy. In a sense, we might think of metonomy as "guilt by association," as in a poem by D. H. Lawrence (1885–1930) called "Bavarian Gentians," where he says:

> Reach me a gentian, give me a torch
> let me guide myself with the blue, forked touch of this flower
> down the darker and darker stairs . . .

The gentian, a flower, is associated here with the finger of death.

Synecdoche—naming the part for the whole—is more common and easily isolated. We use it quite often, as when we say "Let's count noses" when we mean "Let's see how many people are here." In poetry, synecdochal metaphors are commonplace. Robert Frost once said, "If I must be classified as a poet, I might be called a Synecdochist, for I prefer the synecdoche in poetry—that figure of speech in which we use a part for the whole." In another place, Frost referred to synecdoche as an instance when "a little thing touches a larger thing." In other words, when an image is meant to imply a larger concept, it is synecdochal, as in "The Silken Tent," in which the cedar pole that supports the superstructure "signifies the sureness of the soul." (Frost brings the synechdochal metaphor out in the open here, forcing the reader to read beyond the simple description of a tent.)

A larger point, one that Frost would endorse, is that consciousness itself, our perception of the world, operates in a synecdochal fashion. Every little piece of the universe relates, mysteriously, to every other piece. Thomas Hardy once described this synecdochal quality in nature in a notebook entry. "The human race," he wrote, was to be pictured as "one great network or tissue which quivers in every part when one part is shaken, like a spider's web if touched." This sense of the interrelatedness of all life goes a long way toward explaining the force of poetry and its power to resonate in the mind and, as Hardy says, cause the fabric or "web" of society to "quiver." Indeed, a poem like "The Silken Tent" owes much of its power to its synechdochal suggestiveness. Think of it, for instance, as a poem about the use of poetic forms in writing.

Then, making a leap of the imagination, think of it as a poem about humanity and about how humanity must operate within the bounds of certain parameters, such as space and time. As you begin to contemplate poems in these terms, the possibilities widen; any poem, if it is a great one, makes the whole web of reality quiver by having touched one significant point.

Let's examine a contemporary poem that uses metaphors in a way that might be thought of as synecdochal.

ELIZABETH BISHOP   (1911–1980)

Seascape

This celestial seascape, with white herons got up as angels,
flying as high as they want and as far as they want sidewise
in tiers and tiers of immaculate reflections;
the whole region, from the highest heron
down to the weightless mangrove island   5
with bright green leaves edged neatly with bird-droppings
like illumination in silver,
and down to the suggestively Gothic arches of the mangrove roots
and the beautiful pea-green back-pasture
where occasionally a fish jumps, like a wild-flower   10
in an ornamental spray of spray;
this cartoon by Raphael for a tapestry for a Pope:
it does look like heaven.
But a skeletal lighthouse standing there
in black and white clerical dress,   15
who lives on his nerves, thinks he knows better.
He thinks that hell rages below his iron feet,
that that is why the shallow water is so warm,
and he knows that heaven is not like this.
Heaven is not like flying or swimming,   20
but has something to do with blackness and a strong glare
and when it gets dark he will remember something
strongly worded to say on the subject.

QUESTIONS

1. The sea is obviously meant to call our attention to something beyond a body of water. What?
2. The poet mentions white herons "got up as angels." How does this phrase affect our sense of the developing metaphor?
3. Why is the adjective "mangrove" in the fifth line so appropriate?
4. Analyze the image of the lighthouse, explaining in detail its range and suggestiveness as a symbol.

"Seascape" has much in common with a form of writing the French call *paysage moralisé,* or "moralized landscape." In this kind of poem, the landscape itself becomes a symbol; it embodies or parallels a condition of the soul. The next poem, "Rocky Acres," illustrates this concept.

ROBERT GRAVES (1895–1985)

Rocky Acres

This is a wild land, country of my choice,
With harsh craggy mountain, moor ample and bare.
Seldom in these acres is heard any voice
But voice of cold water that runs here and there
Through rocks and lank heather growing without care.   5
No mice in the heath run, no song-birds fly
For fear of the buzzard that floats in the sky.

He soars and he hovers, rocking on his wings,
He scans his wide parish with a sharp eye,
He catches the trembling of small things,   10
He tears them in pieces, dropping from the sky;
Tenderness and pity the heart will deny,
Where life is but nourished by water and rock—
A hardy adventure, full of fear and shock.

Time has never journeyed to this lost land,   15
Crakeberry and heather bloom out of date,
The rocks jut, the streams flow singing on either hand,
Careless if the season be early or late,
The skies wander overhead, now blue, not slate;
Winter could be known by his cutting snow   20
If June did not borrow his armour also.

Yet this is my country, beloved by me best,
The first land that rose from Chaos and the Flood,
Nursing no valleys for comfort and rest,
Trampled by no shod hooves, bought with no blood.   25
Sempiternal country whose barrows have stood
Stronghold for demigods when on earth they go,
Terror for fat burghers on far plains below.

When he wrote this poem, Graves had recently come home from World War I, and he was in no way ready to accept the soft life of the "fat burghers" or merchant class who occupied towns in "far plains below." Graves chose a language equivalent to his mood and attitude to describe the bare Welsh hills that he loved.

QUESTIONS

1. How would you describe the diction of "Rocky Acres"? Pick out specific words and phrases and characterize them.
2. What is the tone of the first line?
3. The "buzzard that floats in the sky" is a bird obviously beloved of the poet (his own metaphor for himself, perhaps). What are the buzzardly qualities that this poet seems to admire?
4. What about this poem strikes you as "symbolic" or metaphorical?
5. Look carefully at the formal aspects of the poem. How does the highly formal pattern affect the meaning of the poem?

POEMS FOR FURTHER READING

Read the following poems carefully and answer the questions on each.

SIR THOMAS WYATT   (1503–1542)

My Galley Charged with Forgetfulness

My galley charged° with forgetfulness	*loaded or accused, possibly both*
Thorough° sharp seas in winter nights doth pass	*through*
'Tween rock and rock; and eke° mine enemy, alas,	*also*
That is my lord, steereth with cruelness;	
And every oar a thought in readiness,	*5*
As though that death were light in such a case.	
An endless wind doth tear the sail apace	
Of forced sighs, and trusty fearfulness.	
A rain of tears, a cloud of dark disdain,	
Hath done the wearied cords great hinderance;	*10*
Wreathed with error and eke with ignorance,	
The stars be hid that led me to this pain;	
Drowned is reason that should me consort,	
And I remain despairing of the port.	

QUESTIONS

1. In this poem Wyatt compares a despairing lover to a ship in a storm at sea, "charged with forgetfulness" (which means laden with neglect). His lover or "lord" is also—or "eke"—his enemy. How does the poet develop this conceit?
2. What does Wyatt mean when he writes, "The stars be hid that led me to this pain"?

WILLIAM SHAKESPEARE   (1564–1616)

Sonnet 6
Like as the Waves Make Towards the Pebbled Shore

Like as the waves make towards the pebbled shore,
  So do our minutes hasten to their end;
Each changing place with that which goes before,
  In sequent toil all forwards do contend.
Nativity, once in the main of light,   5
  Crawls to maturity, wherewith being crowned,
Crooked eclipses 'gainst his glory fight,
  And Time that gave doth now his gift confound.
Time doth transfix the flourish set on youth
  And delves the parallels in beauty's brow,   10
Feeds on the rarities of nature's truth,
  And nothing stands but for his scythe to mow.
    And yet to times in hope my verse shall stand,
    Praising thy worth, despite his cruel hand.

QUESTIONS

1. Why is Shakespeare's simile for time so appropriate in this context?
2. Notice how the poet finds examples to illustrate the conceit or metaphor developed in the first four lines. What are these illustrations? How do they reinforce the first four lines?
3. How many references to strife, battle, contention, and such, can you discover in this poem? How do they complicate the simile?
4. Look at the word "parallels" in line 10. To what does it refer?
5. What is the final couplet about the poet's verse doing there? How does it derive from the central theme?

WILLIAM WORDSWORTH   (1770–1850)

Daffodils

I wandered lonely as a cloud
  That floats on high o'er vales and hills,
When all at once I saw a crowd,
  A host, of golden daffodils;
Beside the lake, beneath the trees,   5
Fluttering and dancing in the breeze.

Continuous as the stars that shine
  And twinkle on the Milky Way,
They stretched in never-ending line
  Along the margin of a bay: *10*
Ten thousand say I at a glance,
Tossing their heads in sprightly dance.
The waves beside them danced, but they
  Out-did the sparkling waves in glee:
A poet could not but be gay,   *15*
  In such a jocund company:
I gazed—and gazed—but little thought
What wealth the show to me had brought:

For oft, when on my couch I lie
  In vacant or in pensive mood,   *20*
They flash upon that inward eye
  Which is the bliss of solitude;
And then my heart with pleasure fills,
And dances with the daffodils.

QUESTIONS

1. The initial simile, in which the poet compares himself to a wandering cloud, is soon abandoned. Is it lost? What impression of the speaker does it give to the reader?

2. How does the comparison between the daffodils and the stars enrich our sense of each?

3. What examples of personification can you find in this poem?

4. Does the final stanza add anything to the poem? Would Wordsworth have done better to leave us with a present vision of the daffodils and not have told us how, later, he enjoyed thinking about them?

WALT WHITMAN (1819–1892)

The Dismantled Ship

  In some unused lagoon, some nameless bay,
On sluggish, lonesome waters, anchor'd near the shore,
An old, dismasted, gray and batter'd ship, disabled, done,
  After free voyages to all the seas of earth, haul'd up at last
    and hawser'd tight,
  Lies rusting, mouldering.

QUESTIONS

1. Is there anything metaphorical about this poem? Anything symbolic? Look carefully at all the adjectives.

2. What effect does the word "free" in the fourth line have on our sense of the ship's current situation?

SEAMUS HEANEY (1939–   )

Digging

Between my finger and my thumb
The squat pen rests; snug as a gun.

Under my window, a clean rasping sound
When the spade sinks into gravelly ground:
My father, digging, I look down   5

Till his straining rump among the flowerbeds
Bends low, comes up twenty years away
Stooping in rhythm through potato drills
Where he was digging.

The coarse boot nestled on the lug, the shaft   10
Against the inside knee was levered firmly.
He rooted out tall tops, buried the bright edge deep
To scatter new potatoes that we picked
Loving their cool hardness in our hands.

By God, the old man could handle a spade.   15
Just like his old man.

My grandfather cut more turf in a day
Than any other man on Toner's bog.
Once I carried him milk in a bottle
Corked sloppily with paper. He straightened up   20
To drink it, then fell to right away

Nicking and slicing neatly, heaving sods
Over his shoulder, going down and down
For the good turf. Digging.

The cold smell of potato mould, the squelch and slap   25
Of soggy peat, the curt cuts of an edge
Through living roots awaken in my head.
But I've no spade to follow men like them.

Between my finger and my thumb
The squat pen rests.   30
I'll dig with it.

QUESTIONS

1. The analogy here is between digging with a shovel and writing with a pen. In what ways does the poet conceive of these two activities as being similar?

2. Is the phrase "snug as a gun" in the first line appropriate?

3. What is the relationship between the speaker of the poem, the writer, and the digger's father in the sixth stanza, the one who could "cut more turf in a day / Than any other man on Toner's bog"?

4. What does the poet mean when he says, in the next to last stanza, that things "awaken" in his head?

5. How does the shape of the poem, the way the "story" of the poem proceeds, relate to the subject itself?

ROSANNA WARREN (1953–   )

Lily

The highway forever draws away
day and night in a whine and purr of trucks,
and your face recedes, as time
accumulates between us,

but I remember a morning when we lay   5
together on a flat rock
in a brown, unwinding stream
and the sun spread gloss

of gold across the water, and sparrows came
to dabble in the shallows. A stray cloud   10
shadowed us, vanished,
shadowed us again

and in the fluttered light we were the same
as stone and ripple. Water played out loud
twisting in harness;   15
one leaf ran

swivelling down the current, green canoe
side-tracked in eddies, released, then lost
for good. In this strange
space we invent   20

separately day by day between us, you
can't hear me breathing, touch me, taste
the sun's change
on my cheek, can't

hold me, tell me to hush. The wasps crawl   25
over their paper palace cell by cell
where pupae sleep
and swell toward their brief

flight and the end of summer. Wind riffles tall
pines' sleeves. Beyond, the highway still   *30*
trails away, but deep
in its own life

the pond lies motionless. From frog scum
and cloud reflection fractured, the lily blooms,
a white-fleshed star   *35*
with dab of sun at heart.

It holds its peace against the tires' hum,
hot miles of fleeing where the asphalt screams,
summer uncoiling in which we are
farther and farther apart.   *40*

QUESTIONS

1. What does the lily in this poem represent? Why did Warren choose it for the title?
2. When the poet asks of a "whine and purr of trucks," what does she call up in your mind? (Look at the implicit metaphor.)
3. In this poem nature seems more than an inanimate backdrop to the human scene. What little metaphors bring nature to life? What is nature like here?
4. Is the highway a symbol? What does it suggest?

IRONY

Any poem is most valuable for its ulterior meaning. I have developed an ulteriority complex.

—*ROBERT FROST*

Few terms in a critic's vocabulary are trickier than **irony**, which may be defined as saying one thing and meaning another, or speaking slant. Irony occurs commonly in everyday life. When someone steps outside into a rainstorm and says, "Ah, what a lovely day!" we recognize immediately a species of irony. When someone tells a friend that he could climb Mount Everest if he wanted, the friend might well say, ironically, "I'll bet." In both these examples, we hear a dry, almost mocking, tone—a quality often present when someone is being "ironic."

The term was first used by the Greek philosopher, Plato, to describe his great teacher, Socrates, who had a dry, witty manner of speaking. Socrates would often begin questioning someone by saying that he had "high hopes" of learning something crucial from that person. The reader, of course, would recognize that Socrates—one of the wisest men who ever lived—did *not* really entertain such high hopes. Indeed, he was using irony to mock the person in question. (In keeping with his great wisdom, Socrates was careful to reserve his most biting ironies for those who deserved and could handle it!)

Irony may take many forms, such as *verbal irony, situational irony,* or *dramatic irony.* **Verbal irony** covers all remarks or comments wherein the speaker says one thing while meaning another (usually its opposite). The tone of such remarks can be scathing, humorous, sarcastic, or merely wry. **Situational irony** applies to inherently ironic situations. Obviously, a link exists between these two forms, since a state of affairs can only be thought "ironic" by somebody possessed of an ironic sense. If you say to a seven-foot tall basketball player, "Hi, little fella!" you are using verbal irony. If you send the same basketball player a cassette recording of a song about short people, the situation itself represents an instance of situational irony. **Dramatic irony,** the third form mentioned, usually occurs in plays, when the audience knows something that a character on stage doesn't know. This discrepancy in knowledge inevitably results in irony of a very special kind.

We rarely encounter dramatic irony in poetry except in dramatic poems or verse plays. Verbal and situational irony occur everywhere, in all kinds of literature. In good writing, in fact, verbal and situational irony often work together. Here is a nicely ironic passage from Lytton Strachey's study of several Victorian heroes and heroines, called (ironically) *Eminent Victorians*. The passage is about the famous nurse, Florence Nightingale.

> With statesmen and governors at her beck and call, with her hands on a hundred strings, with mighty provinces at her feet, with foreign governments agog for her counsel, building hospitals, training nurses—she still felt that she had not enough to do. She sighed for more worlds to conquer—more, and yet more. She looked about her—and what was there left? Of course! Philosophy! After the world of action, the world of thought. Having set right the health of the British Army, she would now do the same good service for the religious convictions of mankind. She had long noticed—with regret—the growing tendency towards free-thinking among artisans. With regret, but not altogether with surprise: the current teaching of Christianity was sadly to seek; nay, Christianity itself was not without its defects. She would rectify these errors. She would correct the mistakes of the Churches; she would point out just where Christianity was wrong; and she would explain to the artisans what the facts of the case really were.

Strachey clearly takes a dim view of Miss Nightingale's ambition. He lays out her plans in an ironic fashion, pretending in a tone that we are meant to see straight through that he approves of her grandiose plans. The situation itself appears ridiculous, because Nightingale was not going to override the mistakes of the churches just like that.

Most irony is meant to be seen through quite easily. It betrays a particular stance taken toward a writer's given subject. The following ironic passage is from A. E. Housman's *Selected Prose:*

> The average man . . . believes that the text of ancient authors is generally sound, not because he has acquainted himself with the elements of the problem, but because he would feel uncomfortable if he did not believe

it; just as he believes, on the same cogent evidence, that he is a fine fellow, and that he will rise again from the dead.

EXERCISE

Analyze the preceding passage carefully, describing exactly Housman's attitude toward the "average man."

Irony, in all its various forms, plays an important role in poetry because ironic language always has a double edge. It allows poets to pack as much meaning as possible into their language. Situational irony and, of course, dramatic irony form the essence of drama, and playwrights from Shakespeare to Neil Simon or Sam Shepherd use them extensively. Lyric poets, too, depend on situational irony for certain effects. Note how George Herbert does so in the following poem:

GEORGE HERBERT   (1593–1633)

Virtue

Sweet day, so cool, so calm, so bright,
The bridal of the earth and sky:
The dew shall weep thy fall tonight,
For thou must die.

Sweet rose, whose hue angry and brave   5
Bids the rash gazer wipe his eye:
Thy root is ever in its grave,
And thou must die.

Sweet spring, full of sweet days and roses,
A box where sweets compacted lie: 10
My music shows ye have your closes,
And all must die.

Only a sweet and virtuous soul,
Like seasoned timber never gives;
But though the whole world turn to coal,   15
Then chiefly lives.

That things in nature bloom in spite of death presents an ironic situation that poets have always seen fit to exploit. Herbert, as a Christian, makes use of an ironic situation to preach the virtues of virtue itself.

EXERCISE

Trace the situational irony in "Virtue" as it develops in each stanza, moving from "day" to "rose" to "spring" to the "virtuous soul" that is finally the main subject of Herbert's poem.

Poets—who often possess a wicked sense of humor—love to employ verbal irony in wry, undiluted forms. This is evident in the following poem by Sir John Suckling:

SIR JOHN SUCKLING   (1609–1642)

The Constant Lover

Out upon it!° I have lov'd	*Implies abhorrence*
Three whole days together;	
And am like to love three more,	
If it prove fair weather.	
Time shall moult away his wings,	5
Ere he shall discover	
In the whole wide world again	
Such a constant° lover.	*faithful*
But the spite on't is, no praise	
Is due at all to me:	10
Love with me had made no stays,°	*Love is at a standstill*
Had it any been but she.	
Had it any been but she,	
And that very face,	
There had been at least ere this	15
A dozen dozen in her place.	

Even the title, "The Constant Lover," uses words in an ironic way. How constant is the lover in this poem? He has managed to remain faithful to the woman in question only three days. He is even willing to promise three more days of faithfulness if the weather holds "fair" between them! The third stanza says, Don't praise me, readers. I know I'm wonderful, but it's the woman who deserves the praise. Continuing this line of argument in the final stanza, he points to that "very face" which is responsible for his marvelous show of "constancy." Had she not been so attractive, there would already have been "A dozen dozen in her place," that is, at least 144 other lovers! Notice the deadpan tone of this poem, in which outrageous statements masquerade as banalities.

William Blake uses irony less slyly in "Mock On, Mock On, Voltaire, Rousseau."

WILLIAM BLAKE   (1757–1827)

Mock On, Mock On, Voltaire, Rousseau

Mock on, mock on, Voltaire, Rousseau,
   Mock on, mock on, 'tis all in vain;
You throw the sand against the wind
   And the wind blows it back again.

And every sand becomes a gem   5
   Reflected in the beams divine;
Blown back, they blind the mocking eye,
   But still in Israel's paths they shine.

The atoms of Democritus
   And Newton's particles of light   10
Are sands upon the Red Sea shore,
   Where Israel's tents do shine so bright.

Blake contrasts the French philosophers, who represent cold-hearted reason, and the Israelites, who represent the powers of the imagination. The Frenchmen scatter the sand, representing the natural world, only to find it blown back in their eyes. Likewise, Democritus and Newton tried to break the world into separate, quantifiable parts, only to find this world reconstituted as "sands upon the Red Sea shore." We are left with the enduring image of Israel's tents shining on the beach. The irony here is subtle and scathing, and is used by Blake to undercut the scientific view of life. (Of course, Blake is only attacking a certain kind of science, one that reduces life to "particles" and fails to see people in a larger, more humane, context.)

Poets often employ different kinds of irony in the same poem to create a complex effect. Separating the various strands of irony can be difficult, because there is a lot of "overlap" among them. In "Janet Waking," a poem by John Crowe Ransom, the poet keeps the strands fairly distinct.

JOHN CROWE RANSOM   (1888–1974)

Janet Waking

Beautifully Janet slept
Till it was deeply morning. She woke then
And thought about her dainty-feathered hen,
To see how it had kept.

One kiss she gave her mother.   5
Only a small one gave she to her daddy
Who would have kissed each curl of his shining baby;
No kiss at all for her brother.

"Old Chucky, old Chucky!" she cried,
Running across the world upon the grass   10
To Chucky's house, and listening. But alas,
Her Chucky had died.

It was a transmogrifying bee
Came droning down on Chucky's old bald head
And sat and put the poison. It scarcely bled,   15
But how exceedingly

And purply did the knot
Swell with the venom and communicate
Its rigor! Now the poor comb stood up straight
But Chucky did not.   20

So there was Janet
Kneeling on the wet grass, crying her brown hen
(Translated far beyond the daughters of men)
To rise and walk upon it.

And weeping fast as she had breath   25
Janet implored us, "Wake her from her sleep!"
And would not be instructed in how deep
Was the forgetful kingdom of death.

From the outset, the diction of this poem suggests Janet's own childlike
sense of herself and her feeling of self-importance. Like all children,
she imagines herself at the center of the universe. We also see her self-
dramatization, another form of childlike egoism. The poet then subjects
that sense of self to death, to utter destruction. Look carefully at the
poem's diction, the choice of specific words. Ransom's tone varies con-
siderably from stanza to stanza as he meditates on the action of the
poem.

Ransom's initial attitude toward Janet seems affectionate. After all, Janet slept "beautifully." That's the first word in the poem, so we have to take it seriously! Yet one begins to suspect that Ransom is not being altogether "straight" with us in the second stanza, when Janet begins kissing everyone. The syntax of the second line clues us in that something is amiss: "Only a small one gave she to her daddy" is an odd line. Too cute for words, it actually reveals a mild disdain, if not contempt, in the tone. The third stanza seems almost cruel: Contrasting the innocence of the girl ("Running across the world upon the grass" sounds like something from a fairy tale) with the last sentence, "But alas, / Her Chucky had died," is remarkably nasty. The "alas" is overtly, embarrassingly, ironic. It can also be confusing. The reader doesn't know whether to cry or laugh.

The next stanza introduces a new world of irony: "It was a transmogrifying bee. . . ." The word "transmogrify," meaning "to transform magically," is utterly incongruous, and incongruity often makes us laugh. The bee has "transmogrified" Chucky from a live to a dead chicken. It has killed the animal, not really "transmogrified" it. Ransom's words say one thing while meaning another, which is what ironic statements do. The way the highly formal tone of these stanzas contrasts with the subject matter is also ironic. There is a severe discordance here:

> But how exceedingly
> And purply did the knot
> Swell with the venom and communicate
> Its rigor!

The word "communicate" appears ludicrously out of keeping with the topic—the venom communicates its "rigor," a cruel pun (consider rigor as in *rigor mortis*). Puns, which by definition imply a doubling, a saying of one thing and meaning another, comprise one of the most common forms of irony. Ransom concludes the fifth stanza by employing a shockingly simple kind of situational irony (which is also, of course, verbal!): "Now the poor comb stood up straight / But Chucky did not."

The tone, however, becomes entirely nonironic in the final two stanzas, which bring the poem to its moving conclusion. It is quite difficult to change tones so radically in midflight, but Ransom is able to bring this off. His change of tone implies a deepening of the poem's meaning, a widening of its theme, as the language becomes quite suddenly biblical: "So there was Janet / Kneeling in the wet grass. . . ." Notice that strange verb in the parenthesis: "translated." The poet uses the word to suggest a great deal. Janet is lifted up out of her limited world of childhood; she becomes one of the "daughters of men" now (with further biblical intonations). He concludes the poem with high, consciously beautiful, nonironic diction. The word "instructed" is crucial to our understanding of the poem, which is meant to instruct.

Because the reader has, with Ransom, mocked the little girl in the early stanzas (or at least smiled at her with a bit of condescension), the ending seems especially powerful. The poet summons broad feelings of poignancy as the reader, suddenly, identifies with the little girl. The reader mourns his or her own mortality, which seems intimately bound up with that of every other creature in the world, from Janet to Chucky.

It is not easy in our deeply cynical, "ironic" times to write a poem about the death of a little girl's hen. It is not easy to write about death in a way that moves us deeply. Ransom begins his poem with great layers of irony, which he then proceeds to peel away. He works his way *through* irony to "straight" talk. That eerie last phrase, "the forgetful kingdom of death," is made powerful by the fact that the poet has set us up, carefully, for such a line. He has been *so* ironic that we get tired of irony and can accept a nonironic remark.

POEMS FOR FURTHER READING

Read the following poems carefully and answer the questions on each.

W. H. AUDEN   (1907–1973)

Fleet Visit

The sailors come ashore
Out of their hollow ships,
Mild-looking middle class boys
Who read the comic strips;
One baseball game is more   5
To them than fifty Troys.

They look a bit lost, set down
In this unamerican place
Where natives pass with laws
And futures of their own;   10
They are not here because
But only just-in-case.

The whore and ne'er-do-well
Who pester them with junk
In their grubby ways at least   15

Are serving the Social Beast;
They neither make nor sell—
No wonder they get drunk.

But their ships on the vehement° blue   *powerful*
Of this harbour actually gain   20
From having nothing to do;
Without a human will
To tell them whom to kill
Their structures are humane

And, far from looking lost,   25
Look as if they were meant
To be pure abstract design
By some master of pattern and line,
Certainly worth every cent
Of the billions they must have cost.

QUESTIONS

1. How would you describe Auden's attitude toward the "mild-looking middle class boys" who get off the ship in the first stanza?
2. How does he regard the "whore and ne'er-do-well" of the third stanza in comparison with the sailors?
3. Why are the last lines, which state that the battle ships must be worth "every cent / of the billions they must have cost," deeply ironic?
4. Can you find any other instances of ironic statement in "Fleet Visit"?

EMILY DICKINSON   (1830–1886)

Because I Could Not Stop for Death

Because I could not stop for Death—
He kindly stopped for me—
The Carriage held but just Ourselves—
And Immortality.

We slowly drove—He knew no haste   5
And I had put away
My labor and my leisure too,
For His Civility—

We passed the School, where Children strove
At Recess—in the Ring—   10
We passed the Fields of Gazing Grain—
We passed the Setting Sun—

Or rather—He passed Us—
The Dews drew quivering and chill—
For only Gossamer,° my Gown—   *15*
My Tippet°—only Tulle°—

We paused before a House that seemed
A Swelling of the Ground—
The Roof was scarcely visible—
The Cornice—in the Ground—   *20*

Since then—'tis Centuries—and yet
Feels shorter than the Day
I first surmised the Horses' Heads
Were toward Eternity—

QUESTIONS

1. How is the word "kindly" in the first stanza ironic? What about the word "Civility" in the next stanza? What do these words convey of the poet's attitude toward death?
2. How does the narrator's traveling with Death contrast, in the third stanza, with the school children, who "strove / At Recess—in the Ring"?
3. Go back to the beginning of this chapter and reread the definition of situational irony. Where is the situational irony in Dickinson's poem?

GWENDOLYN BROOKS (1917–   )

We Real Cool

The Pool Players.
Seven at the Golden Shovel.

We real cool. We
Left school. We

Lurk late. We
Strike straight. We

Sing sin. We   *5*
Thin gin. We

Jazz June. We
Die soon.

---

[15]*gossamer:* a very thin fabric.

[16]*tippet:* cape; *tulle:* thin silk.

QUESTIONS

1. How is the poet's attitude here different from that of the speakers, the "We" who talk?
2. Where does the irony lie in this poem? How would you describe it?

WILLIAM BUTLER YEATS   (1865–1939)

The Scholars

Bald heads forgetful of their sins,
Old, learned, respectable bald heads
Edit and annotate the lines
That young men, tossing on their beds,
Rhymed out in love's despair   5
To flatter beauty's ignorant ear.

All shuffle there; all cough in ink;
All wear the carpet with their shoes;
All think what other people think;
All know the man their neighbour knows.   10
Lord, what would they say
Did their Catullus walk that way?

QUESTIONS

1. Why does Yeats repeat the word "bald" in the first two lines?
2. Does the contrast between old and young men in the first stanza create an ironic situation? How?
3. Yeats becomes overtly sarcastic in the second stanza, ridiculing scholars. How does he characterize them?
4. What does he mean to imply in the last two lines about Catullus?

ROBIN MORGAN   (1941–   )

The Mermaid

(a lullaby, for Blake)

Once there was a mermaid
who lived in the sea.
She was as happy
as a mermaid can be,
as happy as you and me.   5

One day a fisherman came by
and caught her in his net.
He dragged her back to land
and
there she sat.   *10*

He laughed at her and said that he
a wealthy man would be,
for people they would pay to watch
a mermaid from the sea.

He laughed at her and then he turned   *15*
and went a little way;
wrapping his cloak about himself,
down on the sand he lay.

The sun went down, the moon came up
over the silver beach.   *20*
The mermaid strained to touch the tide
ebbing beyond her reach.

The fisherman slept.
The mermaid wept.

She called out to her Mother Sea   *25*
and to her sister fish.
She cried to them, "Come rescue me,
that is my only wish."

The foam heard her, the fish heard her,
the creatures of the sea: *30*
dolphin and whales, shrimp, squid, clams, crabs,
and sea anemone.

The waves and creatures heard her cry;
they swept onto the land.
They drowned the fisherman where he lay   *35*
sleeping on the sand.
He never saw a richer day.

The creatures came and gnawed the net
and set their sister free.
Then mermaid, waves, and fish were swept   *40*
back to their Mother Sea.

The mermaid lives within the waves,
happy as she can be,
happy as you and me.
And if you chance to see her there,   *45*
smile and go away,

for great the Wrath and wild the Rage
on any who would dare
to tear
a mermaid from her Mother Sea,   *50*
or you
from me.

QUESTIONS

1. How would you distinguish between the subject and theme of "The Mermaid"?

2. Is there any irony in "The Mermaid"? How is it used?

3. What does the poet mean when she says that the fisherman "never saw a richer day"?

THE POEM AS STORY

Better the rudest work that tells a story or relates a fact, than the richest without meaning.

—JOHN RUSKIN

Narrative Poetry

We all love stories. Evidence for this is everywhere: Television networks flourish, movie theaters are crowded with patrons, and bookstores are jammed with new novels in hardback and paperback. But *why* do we love stories? The answer probably has much to do with the human need to escape, as well as the desire for *useful* fictions—stories that help us to lead our lives by showing us how other people do it. No doubt plain old curiosity plays some parts in the popularity of stories, too. We like to catch glimpses of how other people live, think, and behave in various circumstances. Stories allow us to look into other lives.

Most written stories appear in the form of novels, but the novel is a relatively recent form of literature, in English less than three hundred years old. But stories written in poetry go back to ancient times, to Greece and Rome, India, and other ancient cultures. Some of these story-poems, such as Homer's *Iliad* and *Odyssey,* are among the crown jewels of world literature. In English, the earliest works of any literary value are long narratives in verse, such as *Beowulf,* written in the eighth century.

Beowulf was written in Anglo-Saxon, an early version of English that looks, on the page, more like German than the language we now speak. Middle English is more comprehensible to the modern reader.

It was the language used by English writers in the Middle Ages, such as Geoffrey Chaucer (1343–1400), author of the *Canterbury Tales,* a series of 22 stories in verse, each told by one of a group of pilgrims who were making their way to Canterbury, where the Church of England has always had its headquarters. These tales remain among the finest examples of narrative poetry in English. One of the most popular is "The Miller's Tale," which follows in a modern translation by Neville Coghill.

GEOFFREY CHAUCER   (1343–1400)

The Miller's Tale

Words Between the Host and the Miller

When we had heard the tale the Knight had told,
Not one among the pilgrims, young or old,
But said it was indeed a noble story
Worthy to be remembered for its glory,
And it especially pleased the gentlefolk.   5
Our Host began to laugh and swore in joke:
'It's going well, we've opened up the bale;
Now, let me see. Who'll tell another tale?
Upon my soul the game was well begun!
Come on, Sir Monk, and show what can be done;   10
Repay the Knight a little for his tale!'
   The Miller, very drunk and rather pale,
Was straddled on his horse half-on half-off
And in no mood for manners or to doff
His hood or hat, or wait on any man   15
But in a voice like Pilate's he began
To huff and swear. 'By blood and bones and belly,
I've got a noble story I can tell 'ee,
I'll pay the Knight his wages, not the Monk.'
   Our Host perceived at once that he was drunk   20
And said, 'Now hold on, Robin, dear old brother;
We'll get some better man to tell another;
You wait a bit. Let's have some common sense,'
'God's soul, I won't!' said he. 'At all events
I mean to talk, or else I'll go my way.'   25
Our Host replied, 'Well, blast you then, you may.
You're just a fool; your wits are overcome.'
   'Now listen,' said the Miller, 'all and some,
'To what I have to say. But first I'm bound
To say I'm drunk, I know it by my sound.   30
And if the words get muddled in my tale
Just put it down to too much Southwark ale.

I mean to tell a legend and a life
Of an old carpenter and of his wife,
And how a student came and set his cap . . .'   *35*
   The Reeve looked up and shouted, 'Shut your trap!
Give over with your drunken harlotry.
It is a sin and foolishness,' said he,
'To slander any man or bring a scandal
On wives in general. Why can't you handle   *40*
Some other tale? There's other things beside.'
   To this the drunken Miller then replied,
'My dear old brother Oswald, such is life.
A man's no cuckold if he has no wife.
For all that, I'm not saying you are one;   *45*
There's many virtuous wives, all said and done,
Ever a thousand good for one that's bad,
As well you know yourself, unless you're mad.
What's biting you? Can't I tell stories too?   *50*
I've got a wife, Lord knows, as well as you,
Yet for the oxen in my plough, indeed,
I wouldn't take it on me, more than need,
To think myself a cuckold, just because.
I'm pretty sure I'm not, and never was.   *55*
One shouldn't be too inquisitive in life
Either about God's secrets or one's wife.
You'll find God's plenty all you could desire;
Of the remainder, better not enquire.'
   What can I add? The Miller had begun,
He would not hold his peace for anyone,   *60*
But told his churl's tale his own way, I fear.
And I regret I must repeat it here,
And so I beg of all who are refined
For God's love not to think me ill-inclined
Or evil in my purpose. I rehearse   *65*
Their tales as told, for better or for worse,
For else I should be false to what occurred.
So if this tale had better not be heard,
Just turn the page and choose another sort;
You'll find them here in plenty, long and short;   *70*
Many historical, that will profess
Morality, good breeding, saintliness.
Do not blame me if you should choose amiss.
The Miller was a churl, I've told you this,
So was the Reeve, and other some as well,   *75*
And harlotry was all they had to tell.
Consider then and hold me free of blame;
And why be serious about a game?
Your love (unless his sufferings deceive me)
He would be worth considering, believe me.   *80*

A noble mercy should surpass a right,'
  And then he said to Palamon the knight,
'I think there needs but little sermoning
To gain your own assent to such a thing.
Come near, and take your lady by the hand.'   85
And they were joined together by the band
That is called matrimony, also marriage,
By counsel of the Duke and all his peerage.
  And thus with every bliss and melody
Palamon was espoused to Emily,   90
And God that all this wide, wide world has wrought,
Send them his love, for it was dearly bought!
Now Palamon's in joy, amid a wealth
Of bliss and splendour, happiness and health.
He's tenderly beloved of Emily   95
And serves her with a gentle constancy,
And never a jealous word between them spoken
Or other sorrow in a love unbroken.
Thus ended Palamon and Emily,
And God save all this happy company!   100
Amen.

The Miller's Tale

Some time ago there was a rich old codger
Who lived in Oxford and who took a lodger.
The fellow was a carpenter by trade,
His lodger a poor student who had made   105
Some studies in the arts, but all his fancy
Turned to astrology and geomancy,°   geometry
And he could deal with certain propositions
And make a forecast under some conditions
About the likelihood of drought or showers   110
For those who asked at favourable hours,
Or put a question how their luck would fall
In this or that, I can't describe them all.
  This lad was known as Nicholas the Gallant,
And making love in secret was his talent,   115
For he was very close and sly, and took
Advantage of his meek and girlish look.
He rented a small chamber in the kip
All by himself without companionship.
He decked it charmingly with herbs and fruit   120
And he himself was sweeter than the root
Of liquorice, or any fragrant herb.
His astronomic text-books were superb,
He had an astrolabe to match his art

And calculating counters laid apart   *125*
On handy shelves that stood above his bed.
His press was curtained coarsely and in red;
Above there lay a gallant harp in sight
On which he played melodiously at night
With such a touch that all the chamber rang;   *130*
It was *The Virgin's Angelus°* he sang,
And after that he sang *King William's Note,°*
And people often blessed his merry throat.
And that was how this charming scholar spent
His time and money, which his friends had sent.   *135*

    This carpenter had married a young wife
Not long before, and loved her more than life.
She was a girl of eighteen years of age.
Jealous he was and kept her in the cage,
For he was old and she was wild and young;   *140*
He thought himself quite likely to be stung.

    He might have known, were Cato on his shelf,
A man should marry someone like himself;
A man should pick an equal for his mate.
Youth and old age are often in debate.   *145*
His wits were dull, he'd fallen in the snare
And had to bear his cross as others bear.

    She was a pretty creature, fair and tender,
And had a weasel's body, softly slender.
She used to wear a girdle of striped silk,   *150*
Her apron was as white as morning milk
To deck her loins, all gusseted and pleated.
Her smock was white; embroidery repeated
Its pattern on the collar front and back,
Inside and out; it was of silk, and black.   *155*
And all the ribbons on her milky mutch
Were made to match her collar, even such.
She wore a broad silk fillet rather high,
And certainly she had a lecherous eye.
And she had plucked her eyebrows into bows,   *160*
Slenderly arched they were, and black as sloes.
And a more truly blissful sight to see
She was than blossom on a cherry-tree,
And softer than the wool upon a wether.
And by her girdle hung a purse of leather,   *165*
Tasselled in silk, with metal droplets, pearled.
If you went seeking up and down the world
The wisest man you met would have to wrench
His fancy to imagine such a wench.

[131,132]*The Virgin's Angelus, King William's Note:* two popular religious songs.

She had a shining colour, gaily tinted,   170
And brighter than a florin newly minted,
And when she sang it was as loud and quick
As any swallow perched above a rick.
And she would skip or play some game or other
Like any kid or calf behind its mother.   175
Her mouth was sweet as mead or honey—say
A hoard of apples lying in the hay.
Skittish she was, and jolly as a colt,
Tall as a mast and upright as a bolt
Out of a bow. Her collaret revealed   180
A brooch as big as boss upon a shield.
High shoes she wore, and laced them to the top.
She was a daisy, O a lollypop
For any nobleman to take to bed
Or some good man of yeoman stock to wed.   185
   Now, gentlemen, this Gallant Nicholas
Began to romp about and make a pass
At this young woman, happening on her one day,
Her husband being out, down Osney way.
Students are sly, and giving way to whim,   190
He made a grab and caught her by the quim
And said, 'O God, I love you! Can't you see
If I don't have you it's the end of me?'
Then held her haunches hard and gave a cry
'O love-me-all-at-once or I shall die!'   195
She gave a spring, just like a skittish colt
Boxed in a frame for shoeing, and with a jolt
Managed in time to wrench her head away,
And said, 'Give over, Nicholas, I say!
No, I won't kiss you! Stop it! Let me go   200
Or I shall scream! I'll let the neighbours know!
Where are your manners? Take away your paws!'
   Then Nicholas began to plead his cause
And spoke so fair in proffering what he could
That in the end she promised him she would,   205
Swearing she'd love him, with a solemn promise
To be at his disposal, by St Thomas,
When she could spy an opportunity.
'My husband is so full of jealousy,
Unless you watch your step and hold your breath   210
I know for certain it will be my death,'
She said, 'So keep it well under your hat.'
'Oh, never mind about a thing like that,'
Said he; 'A scholar doesn't have to stir
His wits so much to trick a carpenter.'   215
   And so they both agreed to it, and swore
To watch their chance, as I have said before,

When things were settled thus as they thought fit,
And Nicholas had stroked her loins a bit
And kissed her sweetly, he took down his harp   220
And played away, a merry tune and sharp.
　It happened later she went off to church,
This worthy wife, one holiday, to search
Her conscience and to do the works of Christ.
She put her work aside and she enticed   225
The colour to her face to make her mark;
Her forehead shone. There was a parish clerk
Serving the church, whose name was Absalon.
His hair was all in golden curls and shone;
Just like a fan it strutted outwards, starting   230
To left and right from an accomplished parting.
Ruddy his face, his eyes as grey as goose,
His shoes cut out in tracery, as in use
In old St Paul's. The hose upon his feet
Showed scarlet through, and all his clothes were neat 235
And proper. In a jacket of light blue,
Flounced at the waist and tagged with laces too,
He went, and wore a surplice just as gay
And white as any blossom on the spray.
God bless my soul, he was a merry knave!   240
He knew how to let blood, cut hair and shave,
And draw up legal deeds; at other whiles
He used to dance in twenty different styles
(After the current school at Oxford though,
Casting his legs about him to and fro)   245
He played a two-stringed fiddle, did it proud,
And sang a high falsetto rather loud;
And he was just as good on the guitar.
There was no public-house in town or bar
He didn't visit with his merry face   250
If there were saucy barmaids round the place.
He was a little squeamish in the matter
Of farting, and satirical in chatter.
This Absalon, so jolly in his ways,
Would bear the censer round on holy days   255
And cense the parish women. He would cast
Many a love-lorn look before he passed,
Especially at this carpenter's young wife;
Looking at her would make a happy life
He thought, so neat, so sweet, so lecherous.   260
And I dare say if she had been a mouse
And he a cat, she'd have been pounced upon.
　In taking the collection Absalon
Would find his heart was set in such a whirl
Of love, he would take nothing from a girl,   265

For courtesy, he said, it wasn't right.
   That evening, when the moon was shining bright
He ups with his guitar and off he tours
On the look-out for any paramours.
Larky and amorous, away he strode   *270*
Until he reached the carpenter's abode
A little after cock-crow, took his stand
Beside the casement window close at hand
(It was set low upon the cottage-face)
And started singing softly and with grace,   *275*
    'Now dearest lady, if they pleasure be
    In thoughts of love, think tenderly of me!'
On his guitar he plucked a tuneful string.
   This carpenter awoke and heard him sing
And turning to his wife said, 'Alison!   *280*
Wife! Do you hear him? There goes Absalon
Chanting away under our chamber wall.'
And she replied, 'Yes, John, I hear it all.'
If she thought more of it she didn't tell.
   So things went on. What's better than 'All's well'?   *285*
From day to day this jolly Absalon,
Wooing away, became quite woe-begone;
He lay awake all night, and all the day
Combed his thick locks and tried to pass for gay,
Wooed her by go-between and wooed by proxy,   *290*
Swore to be page and servant to his doxy,
Trilled and rouladed° like a nightingale,   *sang*
Sent her sweet wine and mead and spicy ale,
And wafers piping hot and jars of honey,
And, as she lived in town, he offered money.°   *295*
For there are some a money-bag provokes
And some are won by kindness, some by strokes.
   Once, in the hope his talent might engage,
He played the part of Herod on the stage.
What was the good? Were he as bold as brass,   *300*
She was in love with gallant Nicholas;
However Absalon might blow his horn
His labour won him nothing but her scorn.
She looked upon him as her private ape
And held his earnest wooing all a jape.   *305*
   There is a proverb—and it is no lie—
You'll often hear repeated: *'Nigh and Sly*
Wins against Fair and Square who isn't there.'
For much as Absalon might tear his hair
And rage at being seldom in her sight,   *310*

<hr>

[295]As you would to a whore.

Nicholas, nigh and sly, stood in his light.
Now, show your paces, Nicholas you spark!
And leave lamenting to the parish clerk.
 And so it happened that one Saturday,   *315*
When the old carpenter was safe away
At Osney, Nicholas and Alison
Agreed at last in what was to be done.
Nicholas was to exercise his wits
On her suspicious husband's foolish fits,   *320*
And, if so be the trick worked out all right,
She then would sleep with Nicholas all night,
For such was his desire and hers as well;
And even quicker than it takes to tell,
Young Nicholas, who simply couldn't wait,   *325*
Went to his room on tip-toe with a plate
Of food and drink, enough to last a day
Or two, and Alison was told to say,
In case her husband asked for Nicholas,
That she had no idea where he was,   *330*
And that she hadn't set eyes on him all day
And thought he must be ill, she couldn't say;
And more than once the maid had given a call
And shouted but no answer came at all.
 So things went on the whole of Saturday   *335*
Without a sound from Nicholas, who lay
Upstairs, and ate or slept as pleased him best
Till Sunday when the sun went down to rest.
 This foolish carpenter was lost in wonder
At Nicholas; what could have got him under?   *340*
He said, 'I can't help thinking, by the Mass,
Things can't be going right with Nicholas.
What if he took and died? God guard his ways!
A ticklish place the world is, nowadays.
I saw a corpse this morning borne to kirk   *345*
That only Monday last I saw at work.
Run up,' he told the serving-lad, 'be quick,
Shout at his door, or knock it with a brick.
Take a good look and tell me how he fares.'
 The serving-boy went sturdily upstairs.   *350*
Stopped at the door and, standing there, the lad
Shouted away and, hammering like mad,
Cried, 'Ho! What's up? Hi! Master Nicholay!
How can you lie up there asleep all day?'
 But all for nought, he didn't hear a soul.   *355*
He found a broken panel with a hole
Right at the bottom, useful to the cat
For creeping in; he took a look through that,
And so at last by peering through the crack

He saw this scholar gaping on his back
As if he'd caught a glimpse of the new moon.   360
Down went the boy and told his master soon
About the state in which he found the man.
   On hearing this the carpenter began
To cross himself and said, 'St Frideswide bless us!
We little know what's coming to distress us.   365
The man has fallen, with this here astromy,
Into a fit, or lunacy maybe.
I always thought that was how it would go.
God has some secrets that we shouldn't know.
How blessed are the simple, aye, indeed,   370
That only know enough to say their creed!
Happened just so with such another student
Of astromy and he was so imprudent
As to share upwards while he crossed a field,
Busy foreseeing what the stars revealed;   375
And what should happen but he fell down flat
Into a marl-pit. He didn't foresee that!
But by the Saints we've reached a sorry pass;
I can't help worrying for Nicholas.
He shall be scolded for his studying   380
If I know how to scold, by Christ the King!
Get me a staff to prise against the floor.
Robin, you put your shoulder to the door.
We'll shake the study out of him, I guess!'
   The pair of them began to heave and press   385
Against the door. Happened the lad was strong
And so it didn't take them very long
To heave it off its hinges; down it came.
Still as a stone lay Nicholas, with the same
Expression, gaping upwards into air.   390
The carpenter supposed it was despair
And shook him by the shoulders with a stout
And purposeful attack, and gave a shout:
'What, Nicholas! Hey! Look down! Is that a fashion
To act? Wake up and think upon Christ's passion.   395
I sign you with the cross from elves and sprites!'
And he began the spell for use at nights
In all four corners of the room and out
Across the threshold too and round about:
   Jesu Christ and Benedict Sainted   400
   Bless this house from creature tainted,
   Drive away night-hags, white Pater-noster,
   Where did you go St Peter's soster?°
And in the end the dandy Nicholas

---

[403]*soster:* a medieval chant used to drive away evil spirits.

Began to sigh, 'And must it come to pass?'   *405*
He said, 'Must all the world be cast away?'
The carpenter replied, 'What's that you say?
Put trust in God as we do, working men.'
    Nicholas answered, 'Fetch some liquor then,   *410*
And afterwards, in strictest secrecy,
I'll speak of something touching you and me,
But not another soul must know, that's plain.'
    This carpenter went down and came again
Bringing some powerful ale—a largeish quart.
When each had had his share of this support   *415*
Young Nicholas got up and shut the door
And, sitting down beside him on the floor,
Said to the carpenter, 'Now, John, my dear,
My excellent host, swear on your honour here
Not to repeat a syllable I say,   *420*
For here are Christ's intentions, to betray
Which to a soul puts you among the lost,
And vengeance for it at a bitter cost
Shall fall upon you. You'll be driven mad!'
'Christ and His holy blood forbid it, lad!'   *425*
The silly fellow answered. 'I'm no blab,
Though I should say it, I'm not given to gab.
Say what you like, for I shall never tell
Man, woman or child by Him° that harrowed Hell!   *Christ*
    'Now, John,' said Nicholas, 'believe you me,   *430*
I have found out by my astrology,
And looking at the moon when it was bright,
That Monday next, a quarter way through night,
Rain is to fall in torrents, such a scud
It will be twice as bad as Noah's Flood.   *435*
This world,' he said, 'in just about an hour,
Shall all be drowned, it's such a hideous shower,
And all mankind, with total loss of life,'
    The carpenter exclaimed, 'Alas, my wife
My little Alison! Is she to drown?'   *440*
And in his grief he very near fell down.
'Is there no remedy,' he said, 'for this?'
'Thanks be to God,' said Nicholas, 'there is,
If you will do exactly what I say
And don't start thinking up some other way.   *445*
In wise old Solomon you'll find the verse
"Who takes advice shall never fare the worse,"
And so if good advice is to prevail
I undertake with neither mast nor sail
To save her yet, and save myself and you.   *450*
Haven't you heard how Noah was saved too
When God forewarned him and his sons and daughters

That all the world should sink beneath the waters?'
'Yes,' said the carpenter, 'a long time back.'
'Haven't you heard,' said Nicholas, 'what a black   455
Business it was, when Noah tried to whip
His wife (who wouldn't come) on board the ship?
He'd have been better pleased, I'll undertake,
With all that weather just about to break,
If she had had a vessel of her own.   460
Now, what are we to do? We can't postpone
The thing; it's coming soon, as I was saying,
It calls for haste, not preaching or delaying.
    'I want you, now, at once, to hurry off
And fetch a shallow tub or kneading-trough   465
For each of us, but see that they are large
And such as we can float in, like a barge.
And have them loaded with sufficient victual
To last a day—we only need a little.
The waters will abate and flow away   470
Round nine o'clock upon the following day.
Robin the lad mayn't know of this, poor knave,
Nor Jill the maid, those two I cannot save.
Don't ask me why; and even if you do
I can't disclose God's secret thoughts to you.   475
You should be satisfied, unless you're mad,
To find as great a grace as Noah had.
And I shall save your wife, you needn't doubt it,
Now off you go, and hurry up about it.
    'And when the tubs have been collected, three,   480
That's one for her and for yourself and me,
Then hang them in the roof below the thatching
That no one may discover what we're hatching.
When you have finished doing what I said
And stowed the victuals in them overhead,   485
Also an axe to hack the ropes apart,
So, when the water rises, we can start,
And, lastly, when you've broken out the gable,
The garden one that's just above the stable,
So that we may cast free without delay   490
After the mighty shower has gone away,
You'll float as merrily, I undertake,
As any lily-white duck behind her drake.
And I'll call out, "Hey, Alison! Hey, John!
Cheer yourselves up! The flood will soon be gone."   495
And you'll shout back, "Hail, Master Nicholay!
Good morning! I can see you well. It's day!"
We shall be lords for all the rest of life
Of all the world, like Noah and his wife.
    'One thing I warn you of; it's only right.   500

We must be very careful on the night,
Once we have safely managed to embark,
To hold our tongues, to utter no remark,
No cry or call, for we must fall to prayer.
This is the Lord's dear will, so have a care.   505
    'Your wife and you must hang some way apart,
For there must be no sin before we start,
No more in longing looks than in the deed.
Those are your orders. Off with you! God speed!
To-morrow night when everyone's asleep   510
We'll all go quietly upstairs and creep
Into our tubs, awaiting Heaven's grace.
And now be off. No time to put the case
At greater length, no time to sermonize;
The proverb says, "Say nothing, send the wise."   515
You're wise enough, I do not have to teach you.
Go, save our lives for us, as I beseech you.'
    This silly carpenter then went his way
Muttering to himself, 'Alas the day!'
And told his wife in strictest secrecy.   520
She was aware, far more indeed than he,
What this quaint stratagem might have in sight,
But she pretended to be dead with fright.
'Alas!' she said. 'Whatever it may cost,
Hurry and help, or we shall all be lost.   525
I am your honest, true and wedded wife,
Go, dearest husband, help to save my life!'
    How fancy throws us into perturbation!
People can die of mere imagination,
So deep is the impression one can take.   530
This silly carpenter began to quake,
Before his eyes there verily seemed to be
The floods of Noah, wallowing like the sea
And drowning Alison his honey-pet.
He wept and wailed, his features were all set   535
In grief, he sighed with many a doleful grunt.
He went and got a tub, began to hunt
For kneading-troughs, found two, and had them sent
Home to his house in secret; then he went
And, unbeknowns, he hung them from a rafter.   540
With his own hands he made three ladders after,
Uprights and rungs, to help them in their scheme
Of climbing where they hung upon the beam.
He victualled tub and trough, and made all snug
With bread and cheese, and ale in a large jug,   545
Enough for three of them to last the day,
And, just before completing this array,
Packed off the maid and his apprentice too

To London on a job they had to do.
And on the Monday when it drew to night   550
He shut his door and dowsed the candle-light
And made quite sure all was as it should be
And shortly, up they clambered, all the three,
Silent and separate. They began to pray
And '*Pater Noster*° mum', said Nicholay,   *Our Father* 555
And 'mum' said John, and 'mum' said Alison.
The carpenter's devotions being done,
He sat quite still, then fell to prayer again
And waited anxiously to hear the rain.
    The carpenter, with all the work he'd seen,   560
Fell dead asleep—round curfew, must have been,
Maybe a little later on the whole.
He groaned in sleep for travail of his soul
And snored because his head was turned awry.
    Down by their ladders, stalking from on high   565
Came Nicholas and Alison, and sped
Softly downstairs, without a word, to bed,
And where this carpenter was wont to be
The revels started and the melody.
And thus lay Nicholas and Alison   570
At busy play in eager quest of fun,
Until the bell for lauds had started ringing
And in the chancel Friars began their singing.
    This parish clerk, this amorous Absalon,
Love-stricken still and very woe-begone,   575
Upon the Monday was in company
At Osney with his friends for jollity,
And chanced to ask a resident cloisterer
What had become of John the carpenter.
The fellow drew him out of church to say,   580
'Don't know; not been at work since Saturday.
I can't say where he is; I think he went
To fetch the Abbot timber. He is sent
Often enough for timber, has to go
Out to the Grange° and ston a day or so;   *farm* 585
If not he's certainly at home to-day,
But where he is I can't exactly say,'
    Absalon was a jolly lad and light
Of heart; he thought, 'I'll stay awake to-night;
I'm certain that I haven't seen him stirring   590
About his door since dawn; it's safe inferring
That he's away. As I'm alive I'll go
And tap his window softly at the crow
Of cock—the sill is low-set on the wall.
I shall see Alison and tell her all   595

My love-longing, and I can hardly miss
Some favour from her, at the least a kiss.
I'll get some satisfaction anyway;
There's been an itching in my mouth all day
And that's a sign of kissing at the least.　　　　　600
And all last night I dreamt about a feast.
I think I'll go and sleep an hour or two,
Then wake and have some fun, that's what I'll do,'
　The first cock crew at last, and thereupon
Up rose this jolly lover Absalon　　　　　605
In gayest clothes, garnished with that and this;
But first he chewed a grain of liquorice
To charm his breath before he combed in hair.
Under his tongue the comfit nestling there
Would make him gracious. He began to roam　　　610
To where old John and Alison kept home
And by the casement window took his stand.
Breast-high it stood, no higher than his hand.
He gave a cough, no more than half a sound:
'Alison, honey-comb, are you around?　　　　　615
Sweet cinnamon, my little pretty bird,
Sweetheart, wake up and say a little word!
You seldom think of me in all my woe,
I sweat for love of you wherever I go!
No wonder if I do, I pine and bleat　　　　　620
As any lambkin hungering for the teat,
Believe me, darling, I'm so deep in love
I croon with longing like a turtle-dove,
I eat as little as a girl at school.'
'You go away,' she answered, 'you Tom-fool!　　　625
There's no come-up-and-kiss-me here for you.
I love another and why shouldn't I too?
Better than you, by Jesu, Absalon!
Take yourself off or I shall throw a stone.
I want to get some sleep. You go to Hell!'　　　630
'Alas!' said Absalon. 'I knew it well;
True love is always mocked and girded at;
So kiss me, if you can't do more than that,
For Jesu's love and for the love of me!'
'And if I do, will you be off?' said she.　　　635
'Promise you, darling,' answered Absalon.
'Get ready then; wait, I'll put something on,'
She said and then she added under breath
To Nicholas, 'Hush . . . we shall laugh to death!'
　This Absalon went down upon his knees;　　　640
'I am a lord!' he thought, 'And by degrees
There may be more to come; the plot may thicken.'

'Mercy, my love!' he said, 'Your mouth, my chicken!'
   She flung the window open then in haste
And said, 'Have done, come on, no time to waste,   *645*
The neighbours here are always on the spy.'
   Absalon starting wiping his mouth dry.
Dark was the night as pitch, as black as coal,
And at the window out she put her hole,
And Absalon, so fortune framed the farce,   *650*
Put up his mouth and kissed her naked arse
Most savorously before he knew of this.
   And back he started. Something was amiss;
He knew quite well a woman had no beard,
Yet something rough and hairy had appeared.   *655*
'What have I done?' he said. 'Can that be you?'
'Teehee!' she cried and clapped the window to.
Off went poor Absalon sadly through the dark.
'A beard! a beard!' cried Nicholas the Spark.
'God's body, that was something like a joke!'   *660*
And Absalon, overhearing what he spoke,
Bit on his lips and nearly threw a fit
In rage and thought, 'I'll pay you back for it!'
   Who's busy rubbing, scraping at his lips
With dust, with sand, with straw, with cloth, with chips, *665*
But Absalon? He thought, 'I'll bring him down!
I wouldn't let this go for all the town.
I'd take my soul and sell it to the Devil
To be revenged upon him! I'll get level.
O God, why did I let myself be fooled?'   *670*
   The fiery heat of love by now had cooled,
For from the time he kissed her hinder parts
He didn't give a tinker's° curse for tarts;°   *gypsy's; whores*
His malady was cured by this endeavour
And he defied all paramours whatever.   *675*
   So, weeping like a child that has been whipped,
He turned away; across the road he slipped
And called on Gervase. Gervase was a smith;
His forge was full of things for ploughing with
And he was busy sharpening a share.   *680*
   Absalon knocked, and with an easy air
Called, 'Gervase! Open up the door, come on!'
'What's that? Who's there?' 'It's me, it's Absalon.'
'What, Absalon? By Jesu's blessed tree
You're early up! Hey, *benedicite*,°   *a blessing* *685*
What's wrong? Some jolly girl as like as not
Has coaxed you out and set you on the trot.
Blessed St Neot! You know the thing I mean.'
   But Absalon, who didn't give a bean

For all his joking, offered no debate.   *690*
He had a good deal more upon his plate
Than Gervase knew, and said, 'Wout it be fair
To borrow that coulter° in the chimney there,   *plow blade*
The hot one, see it? I've a job to do;
It won't take long, I'll bring it back to you.'   *695*
Gervase replied, 'Why, if you asked for gold,
A bag of sovereigns or for wealth untold,
It should be yours, as I'm an honest smith.
But, Christ, why borrow that to do it with?'
'Let that,' said Absalon, 'be as it may;   *700*
You'll hear about it all some other day.'
    He caught the coulter up—the haft was cool—
And left the smithy softly with the tool,
Crept to the little window in the wall
And coughed. He knocked and gave a little call   *705*
Under the window as he had before.
    Alison said, 'There's someone at the door.
Who's knocking there? I'll warrant it's a thief.'
'Why, no,' said he, 'my little flower-leaf,
It's your own Absalon, my sweety-thing!   *710*
Look what I've brought you—it's a golden ring
My mother gave me, as I may be saved.
It's very fine, and prettily engraved;
I'll give it to you, darling, for a kiss.'
    Now Nicholas had risen for a piss,   *715*
And thought he could improve upon the jape
And make him kiss his arse ere he escape,
And opening the window with a jerk,
Stuck out his arse, a handsome piece of work,
Buttocks and all, as far as to the haunch.   *720*
    Said Absalon, all set to make a launch,
'Speak, pretty bird, I know not where thou art!'
This Nicholas at once let fly a fart
As loud as if it were a thunder-clap.
He was near blinded by the blast, poor chap,   *725*
But his hot iron was ready; with a thump
He smote him in the middle of the rump.
    Off went the skin a hand's-breadth round about
Where the hot coulter struck and burnt it out.
Such was the pain, he thought he must be dying   *730*
And, mad with agony, he started crying,
'Help! Water! Water! Help! For Heaven's love!'
    The carpenter, startled from sleep above,
And hearing shouts for water and a thud,
Thought, 'Heaven help us! Here comes Nowel's Flood!'°   *Noah's Flood*   *735*
And up he sat and with no more ado

He took his axe and smote the ropes in two
And down went everything. He didn't stop
To sell his bread and ale, but came down flop
Upon the floor and fainted right away.   *740*
   Up started Alison and Nicholay
And shouted, 'Help!' and 'Murder!' in the street.
The neighbours all came running up in heat
And stook there staring at the wretched man.
He lay there fainting, pale beneath his tan;   *745*
His arm in falling had been broken double.
But still he was obliged to face his trouble,
For when he spoke he was at once borne down
By Nicholas and his wife. They told the town
That he was mad, there'd got into his blood   *750*
Some sort of nonsense about 'Nowel's Flood',
That vain imaginings and fantasy
Had made him buy the kneading-tubs, that he
Had hung them in the rafters up above
And that he'd begged them both for heaven's love   *755*
To sit up in the roof for company.
   All started laughing at this lunacy
And streamed upstairs to gape and pry and poke,
And treated all his sufferings as a joke.
No matter what the carpenter asserted   *760*
It went for nothing, no one was converted;
With powerful oaths they swore the fellow down
And he was held for mad by all the town;
Even the learned said to one another,
'The fellow must be crazy, my dear brother.'   *765*
So to a general laughter he succumbed.
   That's how the carpenter's young wife was plumbed
For all the tricks his jealousy could try,
And Absalon has kissed her nether eye
And Nicholas is branded on the bum.   *770*
And God bring all of us to Kingdom Come.

QUESTIONS

1. Chaucer takes great care with the portrayal of characters. Look again at his
   early description of Nicholas the Gallant (lines 114–135). What clues to his
   character do we find in the objects that Chaucer associates with him?

2. Look closely, too, at the poet's descriptions of Alison. Are there any
   clues to her true nature in the way Chaucer initially describes her? Pay
   attention to her clothing, her interests, any details to which value might
   be assigned.

3. With whom does Chaucer hope the reader will sympathize in this tale?—the clever Nicholas, the steadfast husband, John, the pretty Alison? Why?

4. How does Chaucer's depiction of woman in the character of Alison differ from contemporary views of women?

5. The tale develops on two fronts: the joke being played on poor John, concerning the coming flood, and the outwitting of Absalon. Is there any connection between these two plots?

6. Look at the concluding five lines of the tale, which sum up the moral of the story. How can the last line be reconciled with the previous four?

The Ballad

The **ballad** or **folk ballad,** another common form that narrative poetry took in the Middle Ages, persists to the present day. Folk ballads were anonymous, and they were passed on from generation to generation by ordinary people who enjoyed reciting stories. You can't just sit down and "make up" folk ballads, because only already existing stories warrant the adjective *folk.* Anyone can, of course, use the ballad form. It consists of any number of four-line stanzas in which the first and third lines and the second and fourth lines rhyme. Ballad-makers stick to a metrical pattern known as **common measure** that occurs frequently in popular songs and church hymns. ("Amazing Grace" is written in common measure.) Ballads also adhere to certain well-known conventions. Usually an anonymous narrator relates a tale of woe (lust, frustration, revenge, and domestic crime figure prominently in the traditional ballad, much as they do in today's popular TV "soap operas"). The supernatural also seems to attract ballad-makers, as do instances of exceptional courage or virtue. One expects to see a fair number of **stock epithets** or adjectival tags, too, such as "lily white" for a young girl's hands or "rosy red" for her cheeks. Such language lends a certain mythic quality to the ballad and its use probably dates back to the ballad's origins in the peasant class of medieval Europe.

Most of the well-known folk ballads written in English were collected by Francis J. Child, an industrious American scholar of the last century, in a book called *The English and Scottish Popular Ballads.* Sir Walter Scott, the novelist, had done a good deal of leg work himself a few decades before Child, gathering ballads from village to village in the Scottish Borders. Among the finest of these ballads is "Sir Patrick Spence," written in Scottish dialect by an anonymous poet during the fifteenth century.

ANONYMOUS

Sir Patrick Spence

The king sits in Dumferling toune,
 Drinking the blude-reid wine:°   *blood-red wine*
"O whar will I get guid sailor,
 To sail this schip° of mine?"   *ship*

Up and spak an eldern knicht,   *5*
 Sat at the kings richt kne:
"Sir Patrick Spence is the best sailor,
 That sails upon the se."

The king has written a braid° letter,   *broad* *10*
 And signd it wi his hand,
And sent it to Sir Patrick Spence,
 Was walking on the sand.

The first line that Sir Patrick red,
 A loud lauch lauchèd° he;   *laughed*
The next line that Sir Patrick red,   *15*
 The teir blinded his ee.°   *eye*

"O wha is this has don this deid,
 This ill deid don to me,
To send me out this time o' the yeir,
 To sail upon the se!   *20*

"Mak hast, mak haste, my mirry men all
 Our guid schip sails the morne:"
"O say na sae, my master deir,
 For I feir a deadlie storme.

"Late, late yestreen I saw the new moone,
 Wi the auld° moone in hir arme,   *25*
                  old
And I feir, I feir, my deir master,
 That we will cum to harme."

O our Scots nobles wer richt laith°   *loath*
 To weet their cork-heild schoone;°   *cork-heeled shoes* *30*
Bot lang owre a'° the play wer playd,   *before all*
 Thair hats they swam aboone.

O lang, lang may their ladies sit,
 Wi thair fans into their hand,
Or eir they se Sir Patrick Spence   *35*
 Cum sailing to the land.

O lang, lang may the ladies stand,
 Wi thair gold kems° in their hair   *combs*

Waiting for thar ain deir lords,
  For they'll se thame na mair.   *40*

Haf owre,° haf owre to Aberdour,   *half over*
  It's fiftie fadom deip,
And thair lies guid Sir Patrick Spence,
  Wi the Scots lords at his feit.°   *feet*

QUESTIONS

1. This ballad proceeds by small scenes. First, we see the king in his court. Given the story that follows, why does this scene appear ironic in retrospect?
2. The second scene occurs by the sea. How would you describe Sir Patrick's response to his king's request? What details support this?
3. The anonymous poet has left out the details of the shipwreck. Does this enhance or detract from the poem's overall effect? In what ways?
4. The stanza which begins at line 29 brings the poem into its concluding phase, picturing the "ladies" who sit around with "their fans into their hand" and their "gold kems in their hair." How does the poet expect us to regard these women? What leads us to believe this?
5. In the last stanza, a moral occurs. The poet opposes Sir Patrick with the other nobles, who were superior to him in life but not in death. What phrases in this stanza suggest that Sir Patrick was (in the poet's estimation) *morally* superior to the others? Was he? Why or why not?

Contemporary poets, too, have found poetry a useful medium for story telling, though few, with some important exceptions, have actually written in strict ballad form. Three narrative poems by contemporary poets follow.

JAMES DICKEY   (1923–   )

Cherrylog Road

Off Highway 106
At Cherrylog Road I entered
The '34 Ford without wheels,
Smothered in kudzu,
With a seat pulled out to run   *5*
Corn whiskey down from the hills,

And then from the other side
Crept into an Essex
With a rumble seat of red leather
And then out again, aboard   *10*

A blue Chevrolet, releasing
The rust from its other color,

Reared up on three building blocks.
None had the same body heat;
I changed with them inward, toward   *15*
The weedy heart of the junkyard,
For I knew that Doris Holbrook
Would escape from her father at noon

And would come from the farm
To seek parts owned by the sun   *20*
Among the abandoned chassis,
Sitting in each in turn
As I did, leaning forward
As in a wild stock-car race

In the parking lot of the dead.   *25*
Time after time, I climbed in
And out the other side, like
An envoy or movie star
Met at the station by crickets.
A radiator cap raised its head,   *30*

Become a real toad or a kingsnake
As I neared the hub of the yard,
Passing through many states,
Many lives, to reach
Some grandmother's long Pierce-Arrow   *35*
Sending platters of blindness forth

From its nickel hubcaps
And spilling its tender upholstery
On sleepy roaches,
The glass panel in between   *40*
Lady and colored driver
Not all the way broken out,

The back-seat phone
Still on its hook.
I got in as though to exclaim,   *45*
"Let us go to the orphan asylum,
John; I have some old toys
For children who say their prayers."

I popped with sweat as I thought
I heard Doris Holbrook scrape   *50*
Like a mouse in the southern-state sun
That was eating the paint in blisters
From a hundred car tops and hoods.
She was tapping like code,

Loosening the screws,   *55*
Carrying off headlights,
Sparkplugs, bumpers,
Cracked mirrors and gear-knobs,
Getting ready, already
To go back with something to show   *60*

Other than her lips' new trembling
I would hold to me soon, soon,
Where I sat in the ripped back seat
Talking over the interphone,
Praying for Doris Holbrook   *65*
To come from her father's farm

And to get back there
With no trace of me on her face
To be seen by her red-haired father
Who would change, in the squalling barn,   *70*
Her back's pale skin with a strop,
Then lay for me

In a bootlegger's roasting car
With a string-triggered 12-gauge shotgun
To blast the breath from the air.   *75*
Not cut by the jagged windshields,
Through the acres of wrecks she came
With a wrench in her hand,

Through dust where the blacksnake dies
Of boredom, and the beetle knows   *80*
The compost has no more life.
Someone outside would have seen
The oldest car's door inexplicably
Close from within:

I held her and held her and held her,   *85*
Convoyed at terrific speed
By the stalled, dreaming traffic around us,
So the blacksnake, stiff
With inaction, curved back
Into life, and hunted the mouse   *90*

With deadly overexcitement,
The beetles reclaimed their field
As we clung, glued together,
With the hooks of the seat springs
Working through to catch us red-handed   *95*
Amidst the gray breathless batting

That burst from the seat at our backs.
We left by separate doors
Into the changed, other bodies
Of cars, she down Cherrylog Road
And I to my motorcycle
Parked like the soul of the junkyard

Restored, a bicycle fleshed
With power, and tore off
Up Highway 106, continually
Drunk on the wind in my mouth,
Wringing the handlebar for speed,
Wild to be wreckage forever.

QUESTIONS

1. Compare the details of the first and last stanzas of this poem. What seems different?
2. The old cars, the Essex, the Chevrolet and, especially, the Pierce-Arrow, provide a remarkable contrast to the gradually unfolding narrative. How so?
3. Doris Holbrook and the narrator are compared several times to animals. What animals? To what effect?
4. Are any lines of this poem especially funny? Which lines? Why?
5. This poem *seems* like a contemporary ballad. What qualities give it this aura?

GALWAY KINNELL   (1927–   )

The Bear

1

In late winter
I sometimes glimpse bits of steam
coming up from
some fault in the old snow
and bend close and see it is lung-colored   5
and put down my nose
and know
the chilly, enduring odor of bear.

2

I take a wolf's rib and whittle
it sharp at both ends   10
and coil it up
and freeze it in blubber and place it out
on the fairway of the bears.

And when it has vanished
I move out on the bear tracks,   *15*
roaming in circles
until I come to the first, tentative, dark
splash on the earth.

And I set out
running, following the splashes   *20*
of blood wandering over the world.
At the cut, gashed resting places
I stop and rest,
at the crawl-marks
where he lay out on his belly   *25*
to overpass some stretch of bauchy ice
I lie out
dragging myself forward with bear-knives in my fists.

3

On the third day I begin to starve,
at nightfall I bend down as I knew I would   *30*
at a turd sopped in blood,
and hesitate, and pick it up,
and thrust it in my mouth, and gnash it down,
and rise
and go on running.   *35*

4

On the seventh day,
living by now on bear blood alone,
I can see his unturned carcass far out ahead, a scraggled,
steamy hulk,
the heavy fur riffling in the wind.   *40*

I come up to him
and stare at the narrow-spaced, petty eyes,
the dismayed
face laid back on the shoulder, the nostrils
flared, catching   *45*
perhaps the first taint of me as he
died.

I hack
a ravine in his thigh, and eat and drink,
and tear him down his whole length   *50*
and open him and climb in
and close him up after me, against the wind
and sleep.

5

And dream
of lumbering flatfooted   *55*
over the tundra,
stabbed twice from within,
splattering a trail behind me,
splattering it out no matter which way I lurch,
no matter which parabola of bear-transcendence,   *60*
which dance of solitude I attempt,
which gravity-clutched leap,
which trudge, which groan.

6

Until one day I totter and fall—
fall on this   *65*
stomach that has tried so hard to keep up,
to digest the blood as it leaked in,
to break up
and digest the bone itself: and now the breeze
blows over me, blows off   *70*
the hideous belches of ill-digested bear blood
and rotted stomach
and the ordinary, wretched odor of bear.

blows across
my sore, lolled tongue a song   *75*
or screech, until I think I must rise up
and dance. And I lie still.

7

I awaken I think. Marshlights
reappear, geese
come trailing again up the flyway.   *80*
In her ravine under old snow the dam-bear
lies, licking
lumps of smeared fur
and drizzly eyes into shapes

with her tongue. And one   *85*
hairy-soled trudge stuck out before me,
the next groaned out,
the next,
the next,
the rest of my days I spend   *90*
wandering: wondering
what, anyway,
was that sticky infusion, that rank flavor of blood, that poetry, by which I lived?

QUESTIONS

1. How would you characterize the "I" who narrates this poem? Pick out specific words or phrases which typify the narrator's way of looking at the world.
2. Why do you think Kinnell divided the poem into separate sections?
3. Think of this poem as a dream. Where does the story leave the arena of "normal" or everyday reality and enter the sense of a dream-world?
4. This poem might well have been included under the chapter that dealt with literary symbols. Think of the bear as a symbol. In what way is it symbolic? What are some of the things it might represent? (Look carefully at the final line but don't feel bound to use it.)

W. H. AUDEN   (1907–1973)

Miss Gee. A Ballad

Let me tell you a little story
   About Miss Edith Gee;
She lived in Clevedon Terrace
   At Number 83.

She'd a slight squint in her left eye,   5
   Her lips they were thin and small,
She had narrow sloping shoulders
   And she had no bust at all.

She'd a velvet hat with trimmings,
   And a dark grey serge costume;   10
She lived in Clevedon Terrace
   In a small bed-sitting room.

She'd a purple mac for wet days,
   A green umbrella too to take,
She'd a bicycle with shopping basket   15
   And a harsh back-pedal brake.

The Church of Saint Aloysius
   Was not so very far;
She did a lot of knitting,
   Knitting for that Church Bazaar.   20

Miss Gee looked up at the starlight
   And said: 'Does anyone care
That I live in Clevedon Terrace
   On one hundred pounds a year?'

She dreamed a dream one evening   *25*
   That she was the Queen of France
And the Vicar of Saint Aloysius
   Asked Her Majesty to dance.

But a storm blew down the palace,
   She was biking through a field of corn,   *30*
And a bull with the face of the Vicar
   Was charging with lowered horn.

She could feel his hot breath behind her,
   He was going to overtake;
And the bicycle went slower and slower   *35*
   Because of that back-pedal brake.

Summer made the trees a picture,
   Winter made them a wreck;
She bicycled to the evening service
   With her clothes buttoned up to her neck.   *40*

She passed by the loving couples,
   She turned her head away;
She passed by the loving couples
   And they didn't ask her to stay.

Miss Gee sat down in the side-aisle,   *45*
   She heard the organ play;
And the choir it sang so sweetly
   At the ending of the day,

Miss Gee knelt down in the side-aisle,
   She knelt down on her knees: *50*
'Lead me not into temptation
   But make me a good girl, please.'

The days and nights went by her
   Like waves round a Cornish wreck;
She bicycled down to the doctor   *55*
   With her clothes buttoned up to her neck.

She bicycled down to the doctor,
   And rang the surgery bell:
'O, doctor, I've a pain inside me,
   And I don't feel very well.'   *60*

Doctor Thomas looked her over,
   And then he looked some more;
Walked over to his wash-basin,
   Said, 'Why didn't you come before?'

Doctor Thomas sat over his dinner,   *65*
 Though his wife was waiting to ring;
Rolling his bread into pellets,
 Said, 'Cancer's a funny thing.'

His wife she rang for the servant,
 Said, 'Don't be so morbid, dear.'   *70*
He said: 'I saw Miss Gee this evening
 And she's a goner, I fear.'

They took Miss Gee to the hospital,
 She lay there a total wreck,
Lay in the ward for women   *75*
 With the bedclothes right up to her neck.

They laid her on the table,
 The students began to laugh;
And Mr Rose the surgeon
 He cut Miss Gee in half.   *80*

Mr Rose he turned to his students,
 Said, 'Gentlemen, if you please,
We seldom see a sarcoma
 As far advanced as this.'

They took her off the table,   *85*
 They wheeled away Miss Gee
Down to another department
 Where they study Anatomy.

They hung her from the ceiling,
 Yes, they hung up Miss Gee;   *90*
And a couple of Oxford Groupers
 Carefully dissected her knee.

QUESTIONS

1. Look carefully at the description of Miss Gee in stanza two. What tone does Auden adopt here?

2. "Miss Gee" has its cruel side, of course. Does the traditional form of the poem accentuate or modify the poem's cruelty? How?

3. What is Edith Gee's relation to the "loving couples" that appear in lines 41 and 43? What is the poet's attitude to these couples?

4. Miss Gee dreams that she is Queen of France at one point. What stereotypical view of woman does Auden express here? Do you find the poem demeaning of Miss Gee? Of women in general?

5. Can you locate parts of the poem where Auden shows sympathy for the plight of a woman like Miss Gee?

6. How are the doctors and medical students characterized, and what attitude does the narrator take toward the knee dissection in the final stanza? ("Oxford Groupers" are students who fit well into the elite "group" admired by other students.)

8

DRAMATIC MONOLOGUE

Our intonations contain our philosophy of life, what each of us is constantly telling himself about things.

—MARCEL PROUST

Rather than tell a whole story, as in a long poem or ballad, poets often give readers a small piece of a story and let them infer the rest. To do this, they often create a character, a *persona* or speaker, who plays some part in the larger narrative, either as participant or observer. This kind of poem is called a **dramatic monologue**—a poem written as a speech by one character caught in a significant ("dramatic") moment. The speaker addresses another character, who does not speak. We call this person the **implied listener**. Reading a dramatic monologue is like dropping in on one little scene in a play, a *crucial* scene upon which much depends. Because readers have access only to what is in front of them, they must infer the rest of the drama by figuring out what has already happened and why the character is talking in such a way. As ever, subtle intonations of voice reveal a great deal about people and their situations. Close reading means paying close attention to the details that give clues to this larger situation.

As a form, the dramatic monologue has been popular since the middle of the nineteenth century, when plays went out of fashion. Not surprisingly, the rise of the dramatic monologue as a **genre** or type of English poem occurred at the same time that drama as a whole declined. The great Victorian poets, Robert Browning and Alfred Lord Tennyson, became masters of the form, and their monologues have served as models for a number of modern poets, such as T. S. Eliot and Robert Frost. It has also been used widely by contemporary poets (note the distinction between *modern* and *contemporary*. The former refers to poets involved in the cultural movement known as *Modernism,* which began in the early decades of this century and continued as a major influence on poets until, roughly, the 1950s. Contemporary poets are alive and well and still writing poems!)

The dramatic monologue also has much in common with the play **soliloquy**—a scene in which a major character struts out onto the stage and delivers a long speech. The play soliloquies of Shakespeare remain the best known; his characters often walk up into the footlights, alone, and meditate aloud on the action of the drama, sometimes addressing the audience itself. Hamlet's "To Be, or Not To Be" soliloquy is probably the most famous monologue ever written in English.

WILLIAM SHAKESPEARE (1564–1616)

To Be, or Not To Be . . .

(Soliloquy from Hamlet*)*

To be, or not to be, that is the question:	
Whether 'tis nobler in the mind to suffer	
The slings and arrows of outrageous fortune,	
Or to take arms against a sea of troubles,	
And by opposing end them. To die, to sleep—	*5*
No more; and by a sleep to say we end	
The heartache, and the thousand natural shocks	
That flesh is heir to. 'Tis a consummation	
Devoutly to be wished—to die, to sleep—	
To sleep, perchance to dream, ay there's the rub;	*10*
For in that sleep of death what dreams may come	
When we have shuffled off this mortal coil°	*this flesh*
Must give us pause—there's the respect°	*consideration*
That makes calamity of so long life.	
For those who would bear the whips and scorns of time	*15*
Th' oppressor's wrong, the proud man's contumely,°	*insulting behavior*
The pangs of despised love, the law's delay,	
The insolence of office, and the spurns°	*rejections*
That patient merit of th' unworthy takes,	
When he himself might his quietus° make	*settlement 20*
With a bare bodkin?° Who would fardels° bear,	*dagger; burdens*
To grunt and sweat under a weary life,	
But that the dread of something after death,	
The undiscovered country, from whose bourn°	*boundary*
No traveller returns, puzzles the will,	*25*

And makes us rather bear those ills we have
Than fly to others that we know not of?
Thus conscience does make cowards of us all;
And thus the native° hue of resolution   *natural*
Is sicklied o'er with the pale cast of thought,   30
And enterprises of great pitch and moment°   *importance*
With this regard their currents turn awry
And lose the name of action.

EXERCISE

Go back and read the quotation from Marcel Proust that heads this chapter.
How does this apply to Hamlet? How would you characterize Hamlet's philosophy of life as it appears in these lines? Be specific, making sure you back up
every assertion you make by something Hamlet actually says.

Several characteristics set the dramatic monologue apart from other
poems, such as the lyric, in which the poet *must still be thought of as someone
other than the speaker.* The dramatic monologue implies a dramatic situation. In Hamlet's soliloquy, for example, a young man is trying to decide
whether or not to commit suicide. The speech of the monologist becomes
an example of thought *in progress,* and with the reader takes the role of
voyeur or Peeping Tom. This opportunity to observe intimate thoughts
in motion attracts many readers to this form which, more than most,
demands the closest kind of attention. As Proust has said, a person's
intonations inevitably reveal much about that person's situation and view
of life, though intonations also require of the listener a good ear. Sher-
lock Holmes was doubtless the ideal reader of the dramatic monologue,
since a good deal of detective work goes into the reading of this form!
The speakers let out the details of the dramas gradually, bit by bit, and
thus increase the drama by tantalizing the readers. Novelists, of course,
have used the technique of letting the cat out of the bag *slowly* for
centuries. This trick works well in poems, too. Ideally, the whole picture
shouldn't become clear until the end, if then. The following monologue,
by Robert Browning, has become a classic instance of the genre:

ROBERT BROWNING   (1812–1889)

My Last Duchess

FERRARA

That's my last Duchess painted on the wall,
Looking as if she were alive. I call
That piece a wonder, now: Frà Pandolf's hands
Worked busily a day, and there she stands.

Will't please you sit and look at her? I said   5
"Frà Pandolf" by design, for never read
Strangers like you that pictured countenance,
The depth and passion of its earnest glance,
But to myself they turned (since none puts by
The curtain I have drawn for you, but I)   10
And seemed as they would ask me, if they durst,
How such a glance came there; so, not the first
Are you to turn and ask thus. Sir, 'twas not
Her husband's presence only, called that spot
Of joy into the Duchess' cheek: perhaps   15
Fra Pandolf chanced to say, "Her mantle laps
Over my lady's wrist too much," or "Paint
Must never hope to reproduce the faint
Half-flush that dies along her throat." Such stuff
Was courtesy, she thought, and cause enough   20
For calling that spot of joy. She had
A heart—how shall I say?—too soon made glad,
Too easily impressed; she liked whate'er
She looked on, and her looks went everywhere.
Sir, 'twas all one! My favour at her breast,   25
The dropping of the daylight in the West,
The bough of cherries some officious fool
Broke in the orchard for her, the white mule
She rode with round the terrace—all and each
Would draw from her alike the approving speech,   30
Or blush, at least. She thanked men,—good! but thanked
Somehow—I know not how—as if she ranked
My gift of a nine-hundred-years-old name
With anybody's gift. Who'd stoop to blame
This sort of trifling? Even had you skill   35
In speech—(which I have not)—to make your will
Quite clear to such an one, and say, "Just this
"Or that in you disgusts me; here you miss,
"Or there exceed the mark"—and if she let
Herself be lessoned so, nor plainly set   40
Her wits to yours, forsooth, and made excuse,
—E'en then would be some stooping; and I choose
Never to stoop. Oh sir, she smiled, no doubt,
Whene'er I passed her; but who passed without
Much the same smile? This grew; I gave commands;   45
Then all smiles stopped together. There she stands
As if alive. Will't please you rise? We'll meet
The company below, then. I repeat,
The Count your master's known munificence
Is ample warrant that no just pretense   50
Of mine for dowry will be disallowed;
Though his fair daughter's self, as I avowed

As starting, is my object. Nay, we'll go
Together down, sir. Notice Neptune, though,
Taming a sea-horse, thought a rarity,   55
Which Claus of Innsbruck cast in bronze for me!

QUESTIONS

1. The poet transmits considerable information about the speaker and his "last
   duchess" in the striking first sentence: "That's my last Duchess painted on
   the wall, / Looking as if she were alive." What details of the dramatic situation
   can you infer from those lines alone?
2. When in the poem do we see that the narrator, the Duke, held certain ominous
   reservations about his last Duchess?
3. Why might the lines "I choose / Never to stoop" chill the blood of the reader?
   What further lines increase the depth of this chill?
4. Who is the implied speaker? What is the situation in which the monologue
   takes place?
5. Think of the final image, the bronze sculpture of the Duke as Neptune, god
   of the sea, who tames a sea-horse in this particular pose. How is this symbolic?

Contemporary poets have found the dramatic monologue especially attractive as a form, perhaps because it allows them to experience
many of the pleasures normally reserved for novelists, such as the creation of character and story. The monologue form depends heavily on
character portrayal and narrative, though the story itself may be "buried"
or hidden and revealed gradually, often in a syndecdochal fashion—that
is, with the part revealing the whole. In a recent monologue written in
epistolary or letter form by Anne Stevenson, a young bride in the nineteenth century, Mrs. Reuben Chandler, writes home from Cincinnati to
her mother in New Orleans to explain how things are going now that
she is an "adult," a "married lady."

ANNE STEVENSON   (1930–   )

A Daughter's Difficulties as a Wife: Mrs. Reuben Chandler
to her Mother in New Orleans

SEPTEMBER 3, 1840   CINCINNATI, OHIO

Now that I've been married for almost four weeks, Mama,
    I'd better drop you and Papa dear a line.
        I guess I'm fine.

Ruby has promised to take me to the Lexington
    buggy races Tuesday, if the weather cools.   5
        So far we've not been out much.

Just stayed here stifling in hot Cincinnati.
  Clothes almost melt me, Mama, so I've not got out
    my lovely red velvet-and-silk pelisse yet,

or that sweet little lambskin coat with the fur hood.   *10*
  The sheets look elegant!
    I adore the pink monogram on the turnover

with exactly the same pattern on the pillowcases!
  Darlings!
    How I wish you could breeze in and admire them!   *15*

And the table linen,
  and the bone china,
    and the grand silver candlesticks,

and especially those
  long-stemmed Venetian wine glasses   *20*
    with the silver rims.

My, didn't your little daughter
  play the queen the other day
    serving dinner to a whole bevy of bachelors!

To tell the truth, Mama,   *25*
  Reuben was a silly to ask them,
    just image me, tiny wee me,

hostess to fourteen dragons
  and famished monsters,
    doing battle with fuming pipes and flying plugs.   *30*

Poor Rube!
  He doesn't chew and hardly ever smokes.
    He must have felt out of place.

I was frantic, naturally,
  for fear of wine stains and   *35*
    tobacco juice on the table cloth,

so I set Agatha to dart in and dab with a towel,
  and told Sue in the kitchen, to brew up some coffee
    quick, before they began speechmaking.

But it was no use.   *40*
  They would put me up on a chair after the ices,
    and one of them—Big Tom they call him—

(runs a sizable drygoods business here)
  well, this Tom pulled off my shoe,
    tried to drink wine out of it while   *45*

I was dying of laughter,
   and Tom was laughing too, when suddenly
      I slipped, and fell on the Flemish decanter!

It broke.
   Such a terrible pity.   *50*
      And so funny at the same time.

I must admit the boys were bricks,
   carrying the tablecloth out to the kitchen,
      holding it out while I

poured hot water from a height,   *55*
   just as you always said to.
      Everything would have been all right.

The party could have gone on.
   Then Reuben had to nose in and spoil things,
      sending me to bed!   *60*

So the boys went off, kind of sheepish.

Later Reuben said I had disgraced us
   and where was I brought up anyway,
      to behave like a bar maid!

But it wasn't my fault, Mama,   *65*
   They were his friends. He invited them.
      I like to give men a good time!

I'm writing this in bed because
   my head thumps and drums every time I move
      and I'm so dog tired!   *70*

The only time I sleep is in the morning
   when Reuben has left for the office.
      Which brings up a *delicate* subject, Mama.

I've been thinking and thinking,
   wondering whether I'll *ever* succeed in being   *75*
      the tender, devoted little wife you wanted me to be.

Because . . . oh, Mama,
   why didn't you tell me or warn me before I was married
      that a wife is expected to do it *every night!*

But how could we have guessed?   *80*
   Ruby came courting so cool and fine and polite,
      while beneath that gentlemanly, educated exterior . . .

well! I don't like to worry you, Mama.
   You know what men are like!
      I remember you once said the dears couldn't help it.   *85*

I try to be brave.
  But if you *did* have a chance to speak to Papa,
    mightn't you ask him to slip a word,

sort of man to man to Reuben . . .
  about how delicate I am
    and how sick I am every month,   *90*

not one of those cows
  who can be used and used?
    Someone's at the door.

I forgot,   *95*
  I asked Fanny Daniels to come up this morning
    to help fix a trim for my hat.

I'll have to hustle!
  Give all my love to dear Spooky and Cookie!
    How I miss them, the doggy darlings!   *100*

Oceans of hugs and kisses for you, too,
  and for precious Papa,

        From your suffering and loving daughter,

                    Marianne

QUESTIONS

1. Why do you think the poet chose to write this poem as a dramatic monologue?
2. Compare the way Ruby treats his wife to the way his friends treat her? What discrepancies exist?
3. Follow Mrs. Chandler's changing response to the dinner party as it develops, paying special attention to the language she uses to write about this dinner party to her mother.
4. We never really meet Reuben Chandler, but we hear a great deal about his attitude toward women, especially toward his wife and how he expects her to behave, by what his wife tells us. How would you characterize his view of his wife's role in society and within the marriage, judging from what Mrs. Chandler says?
5. The tone of the letter changes drastically at several specific points. Can you isolate these points and describe the shifts of tone? (Where Mrs. Chandler compares herself to a cow who is "used and used" the tone seems to alter drastically. Focus on that change in particular.)
6. What expectations does Mrs. Chandler's mother in New Orleans have for her daughter? How can you infer these expectations from what her daughter says?

POEMS FOR FURTHER READING

Read each poem carefully and answer the questions.

ROBERT FROST   (1874–1965)

Home Burial

He saw her from the bottom of the stairs
Before she saw him. She was starting down,
Looking back over her shoulder at some fear.
She took a doubtful step and then undid it
To raise herself and look again. He spoke   *5*
Advancing toward her: 'What is it you see
From up there always—for I want to know.'
She turned and sank upon her skirts at that,
And her face changed from terrified to dull.
He said to gain time: 'What is it you see,'   *10*
Mounting until she cowered under him.
'I will find out now—you must tell me dear.'
She, in her place, refused him any help
With the least stiffening of her neck and silence.
She let him look, sure he wouldn't see,   *15*
Blind creature; and awhile he didn't see.
But at last he murmured, 'Oh,' and again, 'Oh.'

'What is it—what?' she said.

                            'Just that I see.'
'You don't,', she challenged. 'Tell me what it is.'   *20*

'The wonder is I didn't see at once.
I never noticed it from here before.
I must be wonted to it—that's the reason.
The little graveyard where my people are!
So small the window frames the whole of it.   *25*
Not so much larger than a bedroom, is it?
There are three stones of slate and one of marble,
Broad-shouldered little slabs there in the sunlight
On the sidehill. We haven't to mind *those.*
But I understand: it is not the stones,   *30*
But the child's mound—'

                  'Don't, don't, don't, don't,' she cried.

She withdrew shrinking from beneath his arm
That rested on the bannister, and slid downstairs;
And turned on him with such a daunting look,   *35*
He said twice over before he knew himself:
'Can't a man speak of his own child he's lost?'

'Not you! Oh, where's my hat? Oh, I don't need it!
I must get out of here. I must get air.
I don't know rightly whether any man can.'   *40*

'Amy! Don't go to someone else this time.
Listen to me. I won't come down the stairs.'
He sat and fixed his chin between his fists.
'There's something I should like to ask you, dear.'

'You don't know how to ask it.'   45

                        'Help me, then.'
Her fingers moved the latch for all reply.

'My words are nearly always an offense.
I don't know how to speak of anything
So as to please you. But I might be taught   50
I should suppose. I can't say I see how.
A man must partly give up being a man
With women-folk. We could have some arrangement
By which I'd bind myself to keep hands off
Anything special you're a-mind to name.   55
Though I don't like such things 'twixt those that I love
Two that don't love can't live together without them.
But two that do can't live together with them.'
She moved the latch a little. 'Don't—don't go.
Don't carry it to someone else this time.   60
Tell me about it if it's something human.

Let me into your grief. I'm not so much
Unlike other folks as your standing there
Apart would make me out. Give me my chance.
I do think, though, you overdo it a little.   65
What was it brought you up to think it the thing
To take your mother-loss of a first child
So inconsolably—in the face of love.
You'd think his memory might be satisfied—'

'There you go sneering now!'   70

                        'I'm not, I'm not!
You make me angry. I'll come down to you.
God, what a woman! And it's come to this,
A man can't speak of his own child that's dead.'

'You can't because you don't know how to speak.   75
If you had any feelings, you that dug
With your own hand—how could you?—his little grave;
I saw you from that very window there,
Making the gravel leap and leap in air,
Leap up, like that, like that, and land so lightly   80
And roll back down the mound beside the hole.
I thought, Who is that man? I didn't know you.
And I crept down the stairs and up the stairs
To look again, and still your spade kept lifting.

Then you came in. I heard your rumbling voice   *85*
Out in the kitchen, and I don't know why,
But I went near to see with my own eyes.
You could sit there with the stains on your shoes
Of the fresh earth from your own baby's grave   *90*
And talk about your everyday concerns.
You had stood the spade up against the wall
Outside there in the entry, for I saw it.'

'I shall laugh the worst laugh I ever laughed.
I'm cursèd. God, if I don't believe I'm cursed.'

'I can repeat the very words you were saying.   *95*
"Three foggy mornings and one rainy day
Will rot the best birch fence a man can build."
Think of it, talk like that at such a time!
What had how long it takes a birch to rot
To do with what was in the darkened parlor.   *100*
You *couldn't* care! The nearest friends can go
With anyone to death, comes so far short
They might as well not try to go at all.
No, from the time when one is sick to death,
One is alone, and he dies more alone.   *105*
Friends make pretense of following to the grave,
But before one is in it, their minds are turned
And making the best of their way back to life
And living people, and things they understand.
But the world's evil. I won't have grief so   *110*
If I can change it. Oh, I won't, I won't!'

'There, you have said it all and you feel better.
You won't go now. You're crying. Close the door.

The heart's gone out of it: why keep it up.
Amy! There's someone coming down the road!'   *115*

'You—oh, you think the talk is all. I must go—
Somewhere out of this house. How can I make you—'

'If—you—do!' She was opening the door wider.
'Where do you mean to go? First tell me that.
I'll follow and bring you back by force. I *will!*—'   *120*

QUESTIONS

1. This poem incorporates many aspects of the dramatic monologue form, though
   it isn't one exactly. In what ways does it differ from the monologues you've
   already read?

2. Frost was well known for adapting everyday speech to poetry. He was especially good at catching the particular cadences of New England farmers. Can you find several phrases that illustrate his use of colloquial speech?

3. What does the husband mean to imply when he says in lines 96 and 97, "Three foggy mornings and one rainy day / Will rot the best birch fence a man can build"? Is he being heartless?

4. The position of husband and wife on the stairs and in relation to each other changes throughout the poem. Track their different *physical* positions throughout the poem and decide how these changes affect their *emotional* positions toward one another.

5. "The nearest friends can go / With anyone to death, comes so far short / They might as well not try to go at all," says Amy to her husband in lines 101 to 103. To what extent does this poem imply a fear of death in her that goes well beyond her grief over the loss of a child?

6. What is Amy's husband's response to her need to run away? Have we been prepared for this response by anything that precedes it in the poem?

ROBERT PACK   (1929–   )

Prayer for Prayer

   Darling, splitting the wood can wait until
the wind dies down. I want to try to say
what's troubling me, although we vowed before
we married that we'd keep our own beliefs
and let the children choose. They've left home now;   *5*
there's not much more that we can do for them;
it's you and me together, only us,
and I'm afraid you won't get into heaven,
not having turned to God. Without you, how
could I be happy there, unless God wills   *10*
that I forget this life? I don't want that!
The March sun hasn't thawed those icicles
gleaming along the edges of our roof;
perhaps this constant wind has numbed my faith.
   I've never had to ask you this before,   *15*
but would you try to pray? Make up the words
if only for my sake; start thanking God
for daily things like breakfast oranges
heaped in the yellow bowl your mother painted—
a couple bathing in a waterfall—   *20*
our wedding gift of thirty years ago;
thank Him for your routine: feeding the birds
in winter, pruning apple trees in spring;
thank Him for splitting wood. You know I know
that even when you grumble, still it's work   *25*

you love. Nothing I do will feel complete
until I've given thanks for doing it,
so that I'm not alone: like thanking you
for thanking me when I prepare a meal
adds grace to grace. That's not a phrase you'd use;   30
you would prefer to hold some meanings back:
"Grace is not fattening, how can it hurt?"
but what we feel is not so far apart,
though maybe it's the very space God wants
to test us with? My mother used to say: 35
"You cannot cling to what you love with all
your strength; God made some special part of us
for letting go." I understood her when
our children left, and I can almost hear
the spaces where they were. Maybe sorrow   40
is allowed in heaven, so God won't have to
cancel human love by making us forget?
      I won't forget, not willingly; one day
in paradise, watching the clouds, I'd think
of you standing beside the frozen stream,   45
eyeing the wood still to be split and stacked,
and I'd be back on earth—at least at heart.
God means for marriages to end with death,
but after that the Bible isn't clear.
Perhaps God's love begins where human love   50
completes itself, and yet I'll never tire
of the past we've shared. I know you'll promise me
you'll try to pray, and then you'll ask the Lord
to help me find the strength to give up prayer—
as if God would enjoy your joke; you'll swear: 55
"By yonder icicle, I'll love the world until
it does me in" Thinking is the problem;
we can't escape the sorrow of an end
without an end, death going on and on.
Although you never speak of it, I know   60
your father died while he was splitting wood;
your mother's telling always starts the same:
"Some snow had fallen on his knitted hat . . ."
as if for her all time had stopped. Maybe
that is what heaven's like? She seems to smile,   65
but then the age-lines darken in her face.
      Darling, I know you know something in me
approves your laughing at my need to pray.
By yonder icicle, what human love
allows, we have! But don't stand grinning with   70
that orange in your mouth as if you were
some sacrificial pig! Go split more wood
while I put dinner on; listen to God's

silences even as the wind blows through
the icicles and piles snow by our shed;
we may be in for quite a night of it.

QUESTIONS

1. Who is speaking to whom? What is the situation that might be called "dramatic" here?

2. The speaker seems to have an obsession with the past. How would you characterize this obsession? Point to specific phrases in the poem.

3. How does splitting wood relate to the husband's sense of the world and his attitude toward prayer?

4. What role does the weather play in this poem? Is it merely a backdrop to the action of the poem, or does it inhabit a symbolic role that makes it central to the poem's meaning?

5. Compare this poem with Robert Frost's "Home Burial." Are there important similarities or differences?

PAMELA WHITE HADAS (1947–   )

The Ballad of Baseball Annie

For Ron Powers

Don't ask me why a passion starts
   Or how, just let me say
It clobbered me two years ago,
   When I first saw Swat play.

The way he swaggers to the box   5
   And waggles in his stance . . .
The way he strokes the sweet horsehide . . .
   He makes the diamond dance.

My room, my heart's all cluttered up—
   Clips, scraps, diary.
I study my gospel scorecards, pray   10
   And litter, order, sigh.

I hang around the stadium,
   I hang around the bars.
It's full-blown now—but can he see?—   15
   I am all eyes, all ears.

Annie Burns is the name I give,
   It is my baseball name,
And this diamond life is a life apart,
   and everything but tame.   20

It's not like where you type all day
  And never score a point.
Its home is not all up-in-the-air.
  Either you're safe of you ain't.

My story . . . I go over it   25
  Again and again, as if
I could make madness plain to you,
  Just plain garden stuff.

The fated field, the devil't pitch,
  The globe, its spin, the sun . . .   30
It's here we get a glimpse of gods.
  I'm not the only one

I know, but all of us cockeyed gals
  Glued to the diamond tilt,
I am the only one I know   35
  Who feels this thunderbolt

As Swat whams the apple over the fence,
  Or at any move he makes:
He shifts his feet, my belly writhes,
  All twisted up with snakes.   40

A diamond is a girl's best friend.
  Ha Ha—I told you so.
We were engaged at Wrigley Field.
  You are the last to know

How I was the pull behind your whack,   45
  My hand the one inside
Your mitt, my keen eyes on your balls . . .
  Good luck, my love, God-speed.

Some Whiz Kid, you, to ditch the Cubs
  And me, your secret Annie.   50
My room, my heart's still cluttered up
  With you. Why don't you die?

In the loony-bin I ponder you
  All twisted up with snakes,
Shot down—is that face mine or yours?   55
  I guess I've got what it takes.

I make the meaning of my life
  That night at the Edgewater Beach:
I send that note, you answer it.
  At the door, I'm about to reach   60

For my paring knife, but you slip past.
   I reach my gun. You say
I'm a silly honey to think of this,
   You're such a decent guy.

Point-blank. It's done, and I kneel down   *65*
   And hold your hand, your eyes.
I mess my hem in the spill of blood,
   Safe on your sacrifice.

It's here you get this glimpse of gods.
   And here come the flashbulbs, fuzz.   *70*
Annie Burns is the name I give,
   Nineteen, and why is because.

I'm finally in on your headlines, Swat,
   Closer than any wife.
That's just why I got that hotel room,   *75*
   That's why I brought the knife.

The bullet was for me, I swear.
   According to my plan,
First I'd open you, then blast
   Myself—we'd die as one.   *80*

I missed your heart by just an inch—
   How lucky—just enough
To make a miracle, beyond
   Just plain garden stuff.

I wasn't safe 'til you filled me up   *85*
   Like God fills up a saint.
The game's much like. You're in or out.
   Either you're safe or you ain't.

My diamond life may be fouled away,
   But my split-skinned heart's still fair.   *90*
Who doesn't know that Annie Burns,
   When this cursed play is over,

Will rise right up from Kankakee
   And start all over again,
With hits and catch-as-catch-can and breaks   *95*
   For home, as some light-fingered man?

Or anything, to bring me back,
   To all my fans out there
Who love to watch me, win or lose,
   My heart completely bare   *100*

In court, the way it was that day,
  And in the papers, too.
This is America—it's love
  And war and hullabaloo.

It's bang-bang plays, split-second affairs,   *105*
  Putting a spin on the globe.
It's tenderness and violence,
  All that jazz and sob . . .

My story . . . I go over it
  Again and again like a game   *110*
I put on *your* glamour with my crime.
  But I won't accept no shame.

For she's a jolly good fellow
  Who can say to passion: die.
A diamond is a girl's best friend   *115*
  That nobody can deny.

QUESTIONS

1. Although Pamela White Hadas has written a poem based on a "true" story—there was a woman to whom the press referred as "Baseball Annie," and she did stab a famous baseball player—we can assume that much of this poem is fiction, because all poems are fiction. Examine the language of this poem carefully. What kind of person is Annie, judging from what she actually says, the way she uses words? Are there any signs that she is crazy?

2. The poet puts some lines in italics. How are these lines different from the other lines in the poem and what purpose do they serve?

3. The game of baseball is often used metaphorically. How so?

4. This poem represents a cross between two genres: the ballad and the dramatic monologue. Why do you think Hadas chose to graft these two forms together? What advantages derive from the ballad form, especially?

5. Puns are words with two or more meanings that are often contradictory. What puns can you find in "The Ballad of Baseball Annie" and how do these puns work to reveal something important about the speaker's mental condition?

6. "I'm finally in on your headlines, Swat, / Closer than any wife," says Annie. Examine the complex tone of that remark in lines 73 and 74 as a key to the overall tone of the poem. What is Annie's attitude toward the situation as she describes it? How does the poet's attitude differ from Annie's?

9

THE LYRIC POEM

The Poet is most the Poet when he is preponderantly lyrical, when he speaks, laughing or crying, most directly from his individual heart, which throbs under the impressions of life.

—HENRY JAMES

The **lyric** is a brief, intensely personal poem with a strong musical quality. "Western Wind," an anonymous medieval English lyric, is a good example:

> Western wind, when will thou blow,
> The small rain down can rain?
> Christ, if my love were in my arms,
> and I in my bed again!

Partly owing to its brevity, this lyric makes a strong, unified impression. (The second line is easier to understand if you read it: "So that a little rain can come again.") As in most lyrics, the "I" in the poem purports to *be* the poet, though a word of caution is in order: Never mistake the lyric "I" for the poet. As in all fiction (and poetry *is* fiction), the narrator must be kept separate in the reader's mind from the writer; a reader who identifies writer and narrator too closely will almost certainly make naive assumptions about the work in question. The lyric "I" is an invention, a fiction, however much it helps while reading to assume that the poet is speaking *in propria persona* (a fancy Latin phrase which means, simply, "in his or her own voice").

From the earliest times, poets have adored the lyric. The Greeks, to whom we owe so much for our culture, were among the pioneers of the form. Indeed, the word *lyric* comes from a Greek word, *lurikos*, which referred to songs written to accompany the lyre, a seven-stringed instrument resembling a small harp that was invented in the seventh century B.C. by a man called Terpander of Lesbos. A woman on the island of Lesbos, Sappho, was among the earliest and greatest lyric poets in the West.

Poems of Celebration and Love

In many lyrics, the poet celebrates his or her romantic affections, as in this poem by Sappho:

SAPPHO   (620–550 B.C.)

Untitled

Some there are who say that the fairest thing seen
on the black earth is an array of horsemen;
some, men marching; some would say ships; but I say
she whom one loves best

is the loveliest. Light were the work to make this   *5*
plain to all, since she, who surpassed in beauty
all mortality, Helen, once forsaking her lordly husband,

fled away to Troy-land across the water.
Not the thought of child nor beloved parents
was remembered, after the Queen of Cyprus won her at first sight.   *10*

Since young brides have hearts that can be persuaded
easily, light things, palpitant to passion
as am I, remembering Anaktória who has gone from me

and whose lovely walk and the shining pallor
of her face I would rather see before my   *15*
eyes than Lydia's chariots in all their glory armored for battle.

—translated by Richmond Lattimore

This poem requires some explanation for many reasons. First, notice that the poet is a woman. The history of poetry includes relatively few "major" women poets. Feminist critics and historians suggest many reasons for this howling gap because, clearly, something has gone wrong. The point is not that men simply have a "knack" for writing poems and women do not. One basic fact explains a lot: Women were rarely taught to read and write in ancient times. Only men were literate; indeed, only a tiny percentage of men who belonged to the upper echelons of society— nobles and "free" citizens (property owners)—had anything beyond the most rudimentary education. This positioning of women "below" men had enormous historical consequences. Women were excluded from the literary **canon**—the body of literature that has the approval of authority, the "namebrand" poems and novels—from the beginning. Traditions were established that made it hard for women, once they did manage to educate themselves, to become writers in the same way that men could become writers. To give you a small example of the kind of problem facing women, let's consider the idea of nature. Men who wrote poetry usually cast nature into a feminine role. The "male" spirit thus engaged—metaphorically—with Mother Nature. The nature poems of, say, William Wordsworth owe their underlying structure to this longstanding tradition. So how do women write about nature? Obviously, they can't write as "male" spirits longing to connect with Mother Nature. Women had to form, with great effort, their own traditions. The natural tendency of male critics has been to exclude women poets from the canon *because* they don't fit in.

That one of the best and earliest lyric poets was a woman, then, is in itself a fact worth noting. Perhaps the male tradition hadn't yet established itself sufficiently to derail Sappho, who as a lesbian was forced to start pretty much from scratch in any case. From the contents of the poem itself, we can assume that the relationship between the speaker, who says she is easily persuaded, "palpitant to passion" like a young bride, is homosexual. (Note: The island of Lesbos was known for homosexuality—hence, the origin of the word *lesbian*.) Sappho makes an **allusion** or reference to the most famous and beautiful woman of all Greek mythology, Helen of Troy. She celebrates the beauty and attractiveness of the woman in the poem, her friend or lover, praising her "lovely walk and the shining pallor / of her face."

It's fascinating that one of the earliest important American lyric poets was also a woman, Anne Bradstreet. Bradstreet wrote during the eighteenth century, before most of the traditions that we think of as especially "American" were established. In the following poem, Bradstreet celebrates her love for her husband:

ANNE BRADSTREET   (1612?–1672)

To My Dear and Loving Husband

If ever two were one, then surely we.
If ever man were lov'd by wife, then thee;
If ever wife was happy in a man,
Compare with me ye women if you can.
I prize the love more than whole Mines of gold,   5
Or all the riches that the East doth hold.
My love is such that Rivers cannot quench,
Nor ought but love from thee, give recompence.
Thy love is such I can no way repay,
The heavens reward thee manifold I pray.   10
Then while we live, in love let's so persever,
That when we live no more, we may live ever.

EXERCISE

Read Bradstreet's poem again and compare it to Sappho's. What differences between the two poems can you point to? What similarities can you find?

Shakespeare, of course, was also a master of the love poem. Here is one of his sonnets from his famous series of 154 sonnets:

WILLIAM SHAKESPEARE   (1564–1616)

Sonnet 18
Shall I Compare Thee to a Summer's Day

Shall I compare thee to a summer's day?
   Thou art more lovely and more temperate:
Rough winds do shake the darling buds of May,
   And summer's lease hath all too short a date:
Sometime too hot the eye of heaven shines,   *5*
   And often is his gold complexion dimmed;
And every fair from fair sometime declines,
   By chance, or nature's changing course untrimmed;
But thy eternal summer shall not fade,
   Nor lose possession of that fair thou owest,   *10*
Nor shall Death brag thou wanderest in his shade,
   When in eternal lines to time thou growest;
     So long as men can breathe, or eyes can see,
     So long lives this, and this gives life to thee.

Notice that Shakespeare makes repeated comparisons. The speaker's lover, to whom the poem is addressed, is specifically compared to aspects of a summer's day. To facilitate his analysis by comparison, he breaks the day down into parts, thus allowing him to compare each aspect of his lover to the day in turn. "Thou are more lovely and more temperate," says the speaker to his lover, with reference to the summer day. Throughout, he resorts to every form of extravagance, and extravagance that borders on **hyperbole** or willful exaggeration for effect. Read the poem again carefully and answer the following questions:

QUESTIONS

1. Shakespeare's poem is full of metaphors and conceits. One of them, beloved of Shakespeare, was the "legal" comparison. How does he employ it here? To what effect?

2. Personification also plays an important part in the poem, beginning with the fifth line: "the hot eye of heaven shines." Does Shakespeare continue to use this figure of speech? Where?

3. If we think of this poem as an argument which develops through comparison, how does the final couplet (the last two lines) resolve the argument?

4. In many ways, the extravagance of the speaker's comparisons tell us more about him than about the woman addressed. Cite individual phrases and show how they reflect back on the speaker as much as or more than on the woman whom they are meant to describe.

Not all love lyrics are secular, addressed to a person. Often, in fact, poets have written in praise of God or some natural object or set of objects, such as a beautiful scene. Let's examine a poem in praise of God by Gerard Manley Hopkins, a Jesuit poet who took seriously the motto of his religious order: *ad majoram dei gloriam*—"to the greater glory of God."

GERARD MANLEY HOPKINS   (1844–1889)

Pied Beauty°

Glory be to God for dappled things—
   For skies of couple-colour as a brinded cow;
     For rose-moles all in stipple upon trout that swim;
Fresh-firecoal chestnut-falls; finches' wings;
   Landscape plotted and pieced—fold, fallow, and plough;   5
     And áll trádes, their gear and tackle and trim.

All things counter, original, spare, strange;
   Whatever is fickle, freckled (who knows how?)
     With swift, slow; sweet, sour; adazzle, dim;
He fathers-forth whose beauty is past change: 10
                   Praise him

°*pied:* scrambled. When a printer drops the tray in which a page of print has been carefully composed, the work is said to be "pied."

QUESTIONS

1. Hopkins loved unusual words. Make a list of the words in "Pied Beauty" that you don't know and look up their definitions. How do these words *sound?* What effect does Hopkins's use of these words have on the poem as a whole?

2. Compare the first and second stanzas. What difference can you find between them with regard to the nature of things being praised?

3. How does the last full line—"He fathers-forth whose beauty is past change"— relate to what goes before it?

4. How does the pattern of this poem differ form the love lyrics by Sappho, Bradstreet, and Shakespeare?

POEMS FOR FURTHER READING

Read the following poems and answer the questions on each.

WALT WHITMAN   (1819–1892)

From *Song of Myself*

1

I celebrate myself,
And what I assume you shall assume,
For every atom belonging to me as good belongs to you.

I loafe and invite my soul,
I lean and loafe at my ease . . . . observing a spear of summer grass.   *5*

2

Houses and rooms are full of perfumes . . . . the shelves are crowded
    with perfumes,
I breathe the fragrance myself, and know it and like it,
The distillation would intoxicate me also, but I shall not let it.

The atmosphere is not a perfume . . . . it has no taste of the
    distillation . . . . it is odorless,
It is for my mouth forever . . . . I am in love with it,   *10*
I will go to the bank by the wood and become undisguised and naked,
I am mad for it to be in contact with me.

The smoke of my own breath,
Echoes, ripples, and buzzed whispers . . . . loveroot, silkthread,
    crotch and vine,
My respiration and inspiration . . . . the beating of my heart *15*
    the passing of blood and air through my lungs,
The sniff of green leaves and dry leaves, and of the shore and
    darkcolored sea-rocks, and of hay in the barn,
The sound of the belched words of my voice . . . . words loosed to the
    eddies of the wind,

A few light kisses . . . . a few embraces . . . . a reaching around of arms,
The play of shine and shade on the trees as the supple boughs wag,
The delight alone or in the rush of the streets, or along the fields   *20*
    and hillsides,

The feeling of health . . . . the full-noon trill . . . . the song of me
    rising from bed and meeting the sun.

Have you reckoned a thousand acres much? Have you reckoned the
    earth much?
Have you practiced so long to learn to read?
Have you felt so proud to get at the meaning of poems?

Stop this day and night with me and you shall possess the origin of   25
    all poems,
You shall possess the good of the earth and sun . . . . there are millions
    of suns left,
You shall no longer take things at second or third hand . . . . nor look
    through the eyes of the dead . . . . nor feed on the spectres in books,
You shall not look through my eyes either, nor take things from me,
You shall listen to all sides and filter them from yourself.

QUESTIONS

1. There's something odd happening in this poem. Whitman is celebrating his
   love of *himself*. Is this love entirely egotistical? Why or why not? (Before you
   respond to this question, look carefully at the language Whitman invokes to
   describe himself.)
2. Whitman liked to "catalogue" or to list examples of things. How does he use
   lists of examples, and to what effect, in this excerpt?
3. Who is the "you" that Whitman seems to be addressing toward the end of
   the passage quoted? How does the existence of an implied reader or listener
   affect your reading of the poem?

D. H. LAWRENCE   (1885–1930)

Gloire de Dijon

When she rises in the morning
I linger to watch her;
Spreads the bath-cloth underneath the window
And the sunbeams catch her
Glistening white on the shoulders,   5
While down her sides the mellow
Golden shadow glows as
She stoops to the sponge, and the swung breasts
Sway like full-blown yellow
Gloire de Dijon roses.   10

She drips herself with water, and the shoulders
Glisten as silver, they crumple up
Like wet and falling roses, and I listen
For the sluicing of their rain-dishevelled petals.

In the window full of sunlight   *15*
Concentrates her golden shadow
Fold on fold, until it glows as
Mellow as the glory roses.

QUESTIONS

1. The title may be translated "The Glory of Dijon." Dijon is a region of France.
   How does this title relate to the poem as a whole?

2. This poem employs the figure of speech known as *metonymy*, whereby the
   name of one thing is substituted for that of something associated with it. How
   does it work in Lawrence's poem?

3. To what extent does Lawrence's characterization of the woman in this poem
   issue from stereotypical views of women? How does this poem differ from a
   similar poem that a woman might write in praise of a man? (Perhaps look
   back to Bradstreet for a parallel.)

ERICA JONG   (1942–   )

In Praise of Clothes

If it is only for the taking off—
        the velvet cloak,
        the ostrich feather boa,
        the dress which slithers to the floor
        with the sound of strange men sighing   *5*
        on imagined street corners . . .

If it is only for the taking off—
        the red lace bra
        (with rosewindows of breasts),
        the red lace pants   *10*
        (with dark suggestion
        of Venus' first name),
        the black net stockings
        cobwebby as fate,
        the black net stockings   *15*
        crisscrossed like our lives,
        the silver sandals
        glimmering as rain—

clothes are necessary.
Oh bulky barrier between soul & soul,   *20*
soul & self—
how it comforts us
to take you down!
How it heartens us to strip you off!

        & this is no matter of fashion.   *25*

QUESTIONS

1. "In Praise of Clothes" adopts a tone of celebration different from anything we've seen previously. How would you describe this tone?
2. Carefully examine the clothes mentioned. What aura do they suggest?
3. Look at the last line. How does this affect your reading of the rest of the poem?

Poems of Loss and Love

Many lyrics express an acute sense of loss. The speaker in the poem may mourn the death or removal of a lover, a husband, a wife, or a close friend. Quite often, he or she merely meditates in a melancholy way on some generalized feeling that accompanies the loss of seemingly insignificant things. A poet may, for instance, ostensibly write about autumn, with its falling leaves, but the "real" subject of the poem might be the speaker's own intimations of mortality. In "The Song of Wandering Aengus," William Butler Yeats wrote of loss and love; the dream-loss of a beautiful girl is transformed into a generalized sense of vacancy and despair that verges on nostalgia.

WILLIAM BUTLER YEATS   (1865–1939)

The Song of Wandering Aengus

I went out to the hazel wood,
Because a fire was in my head,
And cut and peeled a hazel wand,
And hooked a berry to a thread;
And when white moths were on the wing,   5
And moth-like stars were flickering out,
I dropped the berry in a stream
And caught a little silver trout.

When I had laid it on the floor
I went to blow the fire aflame,   10
But something rustled on the floor,
And some one called me by my name:
It had become a glimmering girl
With apple blossom in her hair
Who called me by my name and ran   15
And faded through the brightening air.

Though I am old with wandering
Through hollow lands and hilly lands,
I will find out where she has gone,

And kiss her lips and take her hands;   *20*
And walk among long dappled grass,
And pluck till time and times are done
The silver apples of the moon,
The golden apples of the sun.

The narrator in this poem—who is obviously not the poet, since the poem takes place in a strange mythical realm where fish become girls—is obsessed by his sense of loss. He was, first of all, "hungry" for a vision of beauty; he has gone off to a "hazel wood" (a wood full of hazel trees) because a "fire" was in his head—an uncomfortable longing, an unquenched desire. It's worth noticing how the scene is set with phrases implying transformations: The hazel wood becomes a hazel wand, the berry that is used for bait seems to become the fish, the white moths that flicker at this time of day are transformed, magically, into mothlike stars. The poet has well prepared us for an even greater transformation—the little silver trout turning into a "glimmering girl." When the girl gets up and runs away, in the second stanza, the poet is bereft. A huge jump ahead in time accompanies the third stanza, where the poet-narrator has now become old with wandering the valleys and mountains ("hollow lands and hilly lands"). He is left hopeless, dreamy, plucking at the "silver apples of the moon" and the "golden apples of the sun"—which represent night and day. The reader puts this poem down flooded with a vague nostalgia, a sense of loss, though specific grief is hardly at issue. The narrator wasn't in love with an actual woman with a name and date of birth. He was in love with the idea of Romantic love.

In the following poem, Theodore Roethke writes as himself (or, as we say, *in propria persona*). He is in a sense "in love" with a very specific woman, a student of his who was thrown from her horse and killed.

THEODORE ROETHKE   (1908–1963)

Elegy for Jane

(My Student, Thrown by a Horse)

I remember the neckcurls, limp and damp as tendrils;
And her quick look, a sidelong pickerel smile;
And how, once startled into talk, the light syllables leaped for her,
And she balanced in the delight of her thought,
A wren, happy, tail into the wind,   *5*
Her song trembling the twigs and small branches.
The shade sang with her;

The leaves, their whispers turned to kissing,
And the mould sang in the bleached valleys under the rose.

Oh, when she was sad, she cast herself down into such a pure depth,   10
Even a father could not find her:
Scraping her cheek against straw,
Stirring the clearest water.

My sparrow, you are not here,
Waiting like a fern, making a spiney shadow.   15
The sides of wet stones cannot console me,
Nor the moss, wound with the last light.

If only I could nudge you from this sleep,
My maimed darling, my skittery pigeon.
Over this damp grave I speak the words of my love: 20
I, with no rights in this matter,
Neither father nor lover.

QUESTIONS

1. Compare the natural associations in this poem—the way the girl is associated implicitly with natural objects—with the same kind of associations made by Yeats in "The Song of the Wandering Aengus." Are there differences?

2. Summarize what information is transmitted in each of the four stanzas.

3. What does Roethke mean to suggest by the last two lines? Throughout the poem, what kind of relationship between fathers and daughters does he project?

Ben Jonson, a friend of Shakespeare and himself a major figure in English Renaissance literature, wrote a beautiful, sad poem about the death of his 7-year-old son. The poet's emotions in this poem seem more controlled than Roethke's in the elegy for his student. But the very fact of the self-control seems only to increase the pain and the sense of loss felt by the reader.

BEN JONSON   (1572?–1637)

On My Son

Farewell, thou child of my right hand, and joy;
    My sin was too much hope of thee, loved boy.
Seven years thou wert lent to me, and I thee pay,
    Exacted by thy fate, on the just day.
O, cculd I lose all father now! For why   5
    Will man lament the state he should envy?
To have so soon 'scaped world's and flesh's rage,
    And, if no other misery, yet age?

Rest in soft peace, and, asked, say here doth lie
  Ben Jonson, his best piece of poetry.   *10*
For whose sake, henceforth, all his vows be such
  As what he loves may never like too much.

QUESTIONS

1. What does the poet mean to suggest by the phrase "thou child of my right hand"?
2. How does the metaphor of lease and payment work to control the emotion in lines 3 and 4?
3. What does the poet mean by the last two lines: "For whose sake, henceforth, all his vows be such / As what he loves may never like too much"?

    A contemporary poem that deals in an interesting way with the sense of loss as it relates to love is "Meditation at Lagunitas" by Robert Hass.

ROBERT HASS (1941–   )

Meditation at Lagunitas

All the new thinking is about loss.
In this it resembles all the old thinking.
The idea, for example, that each particular erases
the luminous clarity of a general idea. That the clown-
faced woodpecker probing the dead sculpted trunk   *5*
of that black birch is, by his presence,
some tragic falling off from a first world
of undivided light. Or the other notion that,
because there is in this world no one thing
to which the bramble of *blackberry* corresponds,   *10*
a word is elegy to what it signifies.
We talked about it late last night and in the voice
of my friend, there was a thin wire of grief, a tone
almost querulous. After a while I understood that,
talking this way, everything dissolves: *justice,*   *15*
pine, hair, woman, you and *I.* There was a woman
I made love to and I remembered how, holding
her small shoulders in my hands sometimes,
I felt a violent wonder at her presence
like a thirst for salt, for my childhood river   *20*
with its island willows, silly music from the pleasure boat,
muddy places where we caught the little orange-silver fish
called *pumpkinseed.* It hardly had to do with her.
Longing, we say, because desire is full
of endless distances. I must have been the same to her.   *25*

But I remember so much, the way her hands dismantled bread,
the thing her father said that hurt her, what
she dreamed. There are moments when the body is as numinous
as words, days that are the good flesh continuing.
Such tenderness, those afternoons and evenings,   *30*
saying *blackberry, blackberry, blackberry.*

The poem begins with an abstract statement of the kind one normally finds in a philosophical treatise: "All the modern thinking is about loss." This seems absurdly grand, however true. If the poet didn't see how ridiculous it was to think in such large and general terms, he would deserve our ridicule. But the second line suggests that he knows how empty such a statement is without the concrete addition of a context and examples. Note that the "new thinking" referred to merely "resembles the old thinking." The word "resembles"—tonally—is crucial; the speaker's attitude toward this word is ironic. The speaker in fact believes that all thinking is always about loss. From here, Hass goes on to explore loss and these "ideas" about loss in a more specific context. The lines that follow meditate on some common "old" ideas in linguistics and philosophy that date back to Plato, the most important of these being the notion of Platonic *forms* or ideal types. In Plato's understanding of the universe, the general class of any object, its *form* in heaven, is superior to any of the imperfect versions of this object that occur on earth (so that the ideal Woodpecker in heaven, for instance, becomes the model from which all imperfect woodpeckers have been constructed). This makes every instance of a thing a "falling off," less than perfect, and, therefore, lamentable. Hass becomes more particular as he meditates on language as it relates to this Platonic theory of reality. That "a word is elegy to what it signifies" seems to make fun of much of our current philosophical speech—"signifies" being such a pompous jargon word these days. But the word "elegy" coupled with the concept of signification seems to refresh the meaning of both terms. The perceived distance between the actual bramble and the word *bramble* has led the poet to his overall meditation on the lack of connections in the world and the sense of loss that plagues all human attempts to recover or hold onto reality with language. Notice how the tone suddenly changes and becomes personal in line 12: "We talked about it late last night"—implying both a real speaker and the presence of another person. A "thin wire of grief" ran through their conversation, a grief related to the sense of the actual, commonplace distance between language and reality. The poet himself, almost shockingly, becomes even more personal in line 16: "There was a woman / I made love to," he says. Suddenly, Hass throws all the philosophical talk into the context of real people, real experience, and real language. The sexual contact described, which occurred with a "real" woman (!), throws everything into the context of physical reality and reconnects the ideal with the real, the word with what it points to; *pumpkinseed* becomes the little orange-silver fish the word signifies. Similarly, the speaker can now reexperience a word like *blackberry* and, further, can narrow the gap between words and their objects, between language and the world. The movement of the poem, as a whole, is from abstract to concrete, with the concrete finally redeeming the abstract (and vice versa).

EXERCISE

Read the poem again and write your own summary of its meaning. Take care to examine all the phrases that stand out in your mind.

POEMS FOR FURTHER READING

Read each poem and answer the questions that follow.

JOHN KEATS (1795–1821)

La Belle Dame Sans Merci

O what can ail thee, Knight at arms,
   Alone and palely loitering?
The sedge has withered from the Lake
   And no birds sing!

O what can ail thee, Knight at arms,   *5*
   So haggard, and so woebegone?
The squirrel's granary is full
   And the harvest's done.

I see a lily on thy brow
   With anguish moist and fever dew,   *10*
And on thy cheeks a fading rose
   Fast withereth too.

I met a Lady in the Meads,
   Full beautiful, a faery's child,
Her hair was long, her foot was light   *15*
   And her eyes were wild.

I made a garland for her head,
   And bracelets too, and fragrant Zone;°   *girdle*
She looked at me as she did love
   And made sweet moan.   *20*

I set her on my pacing steed
   And nothing else saw all day long,
For sidelong would she bend and sing
   A faery's song.

She found me roots of relish sweet,   *25*
   And honey wild, and manna dew,
And sure in language strange she said,
   "I love thee true."

She took me to her elfin grot
   And there she wept and sighed full sore,   *30*
And there I shut her wild wild eyes
   With kisses four.

And there she lulléd me asleep,
   And there I dreamed, Ah Woe betide!
The latest° dream I ever dreamt   *last* *35*
   On the cold hillside.

I saw pale Kings, and Princes too,
   Pale warriors, death-pale were they all;
They cried, "La belle dame sans merci
   Thee hath in thrall!"   *40*

I saw their starved lips in the gloam
   With horrid warning gapéd wide,
And I awoke, and found me here
   On the cold hill's side.

And this is why I sojourn here,   *45*
   Alone and palely loitering;
Though the sedge is withered from the Lake
   And no birds sing.

QUESTIONS

1. "The sedge has withered from the Lake / And no birds sing!" the poet says. What atmosphere do these lines invoke? Why is this an appropriate atmosphere for this poem?

2. In the third stanza, the poet associates two flowers—a lily and a rose—with the pale, young knight. To what purpose?

3. Notice what, in his dream, the knight does for the lady and what she does for him. Why is this dream so disturbing?

4. The poem's title, which Keats borrowed from a medieval French poem, means "the lovely, merciless woman." Why do you think the poet kept the title in French?

5. What does the knight mean, in line 35, when he calls this the "latest dream" he has had?

6. Compare this poem, in detail and overall effect, to "The Song of the Wandering Aengus" by William Butler Yeats. What do the women in these poems

have in common? What do the men have in common? Can you find any differences?

7. Why did Keats, in the industrial nineteenth century, choose to write about the world of knights and ladies?

EDGAR ALLAN POE   (1809–1849)

Annabel Lee

It was many and many a year ago,
   In a kingdom by the sea,
That a maiden there lived whom you may know
   By the name of ANNABEL LEE;
And this maiden she lived with no other thought   5
   Than to love and be loved by me.

I was a child and *she* was a child,
   In this kingdom by the sea,
But we loved with a love that was more than love—
   I and my ANNABEL LEE—   10
With a love that the wingèd seraphs of heaven
   Coveted her and me.

And this was the reason that, long ago,
   In this kingdom by the sea,
A wind blew out of a cloud, chilling   15
   My beautiful ANNABEL LEE;
So that her high-born kinsmen came
   And bore her away from me,
To shut her up in a sepulchre
   In this kingdom by the sea.   20

The angels, not half so happy in heaven,
   Went envying her and me—
Yes!—that was the reason (as all men know,
   In this kingdom by the sea)
That the wind came out of the cloud by night,   25
   Chilling and killing my ANNABEL LEE.

But our love it was stronger by far than the love
   Of those who were older than we—
   Of many far wiser than we—
And neither the angels in heaven above,   30
   Nor the demons down under the sea,
Can ever dissever my soul from the soul
   Of the beautiful ANNABEL LEE:

For the moon never beams, without bringing me dreams
   Of the beautiful ANNABEL LEE;   35

And the stars never rise, but I feel the bright eyes
  Of the beautiful ANNABEL LEE:
And so, all the night-tide, I lie down by the side
Of my darling—my darling—my life and my bride,
  In the sepulchre there by the sea—   *40*
  In her tomb by the sounding sea.

QUESTIONS

1. Compare "Annabel Lee" with Keats's "La Belle Dame Sans Merci." What obvious points of comparison are there? What significant differences?
2. These two lyric poems by Keats and Poe might just as easily be called narrative poems. What is the relationship between the lyric and narrative aspects of these two poems? Do these aspects work together or against each other?
3. This poem was thought to have been written after the death of Poe's young wife, Virginia Clemm. Much is made of her youth, and the poet's youth, which creates a context of irony and opposition. How would you characterize this irony? What opposites can you find here?
4. Does "Annabel Lee" sound to you like a nursery rhyme? If so, why, and what effect does this have on the meaning of the poem?

THOMAS HARDY (1840–1928)

The Going

Why did you give no hint that night
That quickly after the morrow's dawn,
And calmly, as if indifferent quite,
You would close your term here, up and be gone
    Where I could not follow   *5*
    With wing of swallow
To gain one glimpse of you ever anon!

    Never to bid good-bye,
    Or lip me the softest call,
Or utter a wish for a word, while I   *10*
Saw morning harden upon the wall,
    Unmoved, unknowing
    That your great going
Had place that moment, and altered all.
Why do you make me leave the house   *15*
And think for a breath it is you I see
At the end of the alley of bending boughs
Where so often at dusk you used to be;
    Till in darkening dankness
    The yawning blankness   *20*
Of the perspective sickens me!

You were she who abode
By those red-veined rocks far West,
You were the swan-necked one who rode   25
Along the beetling Beeny Crest,
    And, reining nigh me,
    Would muse and eye me,
While Life unrolled us its very best.

Why, then, latterly did we not speak,
Did we not think of those days long dead,   30
And ere your vanishing strive to seek
That time's renewal? We might have said,
    'In this bright spring weather
    We'll visit together
Those places that once we visited.'   35

    Well, well! All's past amend,
    Unchangeable. It must go.
I seem but a dead man held on end
To sink down soon. . . . O you could not know
    That such swift fleeing   40
    No soul foreseeing—
Not even I—would undo me so!

QUESTIONS

1. "The Going" was written after the death of Hardy's first wife. How does it differ from Poe's poem on a similar theme?
2. How does Hardy characterize his relationship with his wife while she was alive? What effect does this have on the way he sees things now that she is dead?
3. Examine the final stanza carefully. How would you describe Hardy's tone here? Does this constitute a resolution of Hardy's problematic feelings about his marriage?
4. Are there any musical qualities in Hardy's language that help to reinforce the poem's meaning? (Pay attention to the combined effects of rhyme and rhythm.)

10

THE MEDITATIVE POEM

*Our meditation must proceed in due order. . . . It begins in the un-
derstanding, endeth in the affection; it begins in the brain, descends
to the heart; begins on earth, ascends to heaven; not suddenly, but
by certain stairs and degrees, till we come to the highest.*

—JOSEPH HALL

Keep in mind that a poem may fall into several categories at the same
time. A poem could be a dramatic monologue that celebrates God or a
love relationship of some kind. A poem of loss could also be a narrative
poem. These categories are rough but nonetheless useful when trying
to survey the terrain of poetry. The **meditative poem**—one in which the
poet focuses on some object, theme, or person in order to widen his or
her perspective—quite often overlaps with other kinds of poetry. For
this reason it rarely gets singled out, though its features are both distinct
and common.

In a meditative poem the poet begins narrow and ends wide. If
you are familiar with the techniques of meditation, you are probably
aware of this pattern. In Eastern forms of meditation, for instance, a
meditator is frequently given a *mantra* or special word to focus on. This
relieves the meditator of incidental thoughts and allows a higher consciousness to enter and possess the mind. In the Middle Ages, St. Ignatius
Loyola brought together many Western techniques of meditation in a
book called *The Spiritual Exercises* (1536). This handbook of Christian
meditation laid out a three-part system. First, the meditator was asked
to call up an image—a very concrete or visual image. The image often
called upon or referred to the human senses: sight, smell, sound, taste,
touch. In the second phase of the meditation, the meditator was asked

to contemplate his or her theme by using analogies or metaphors. Comparisons were the key to bringing the intellect or conscious mind into play. In the final phase, the meditator was ready to turn outward, to open his or her consciousness to God or the universe, to address God as a servant speaks to a master or as one friend speaks to another. This outward turning was crucial, because it represented a culmination of the meditation.

Techniques of meditation have long been used by poets, who have found it useful to contemplate a subject by starting with a concrete image. This provides a foundation for the intellectual and emotional work that follows. Meditation by analogy or comparison comes naturally to poets, because nearly all poetic "thinking" is metaphorical. The outward turning at the end occurs typically in nearly all poems that might be called "meditative." Let's look at a fairly early English poem, "To Daffodils" by Robert Herrick, focusing on its meditative aspects.

ROBERT HERRICK   (1591–1674)

To Daffodils

Fair daffodils, we weep to see
  You haste away so soon:
As yet the early-rising sun
  Has not attained his noon.
    Stay, stay,   5
  Until the hasting day
    Has run
  But to the evensong
And, having prayed together, we
  Will go with you along.   10

We have short time to stay as you;
  We have as short a spring;
As quick a growth to meet decay,
  As you or anything.
    We die,   15
  As your hours do, and dry
    Away
  Like to the summer's rain;
Or as the pearls of morning's dew,
  Ne'er to be found again.   20

The poem begins by addressing, therefore "calling up" to mind, the daffodils. Because most people know what daffodils look like, the word itself registers a specific image for contemplation. Meditation by comparison begins quickly: the maturing of the flower is compared to the unfolding of the day, which "Has not attained his noon," even though presumably, the flower has achieved and gone beyond its metaphorical "noon." A general address, using an unspecified "we," begins with the second stanza, in which the poet develops his larger point about decline from the peak of life into death itself. The poet finds a number of metaphors that help him contemplate the flower and the way this flower represents mortality: "Like to the summer's rain" and "as the pearls of morning's dew" both stand out as memorable comparisons. The poem ends with an overall sense of loss in the face of death, the poet suggesting that we, human beings, must die just as the daffodils do. Without strictly adhering to the Ignatian pattern of meditation, Herbert makes use of the scheme in his own way; the shape of the poem owes a great deal to the kind of thinking fostered by religious meditation.

John Donne, Herbert's contemporary (and, like Herbert, a Protestant minister), used the Ignatian form of meditation quite explicitly. In one of his "Holy Sonnets," the poet "calls up" to the mind's eye an image of the soul in thrall to Satan.

JOHN DONNE   (1572–1631)

Holy Sonnet 14
Batter My Heart, Three-Personed God

Batter my heart, three-personed God; for You
As yet but knock, breathe, shine, and seek to mend;
That I may rise and stand, o'erthrow me, and bend
Your force to break, blow, burn, and make me new.
I, like an usurped town, to another due,   5
Labor to admit You, but Oh, to no end;
Reason, Your viceroy in me, me should defend,
But is captived, and proves weak or untrue.
Yet dearly I love You, and would be loved fain,°   *gladly*
But am betrothed unto Your enemy.   10
Divorce me, untie or break that knot again;
Take me to You, imprison me, for I,
Except You enthrall me, never shall be free,
Nor ever chaste, except You ravish me.

The real "action" of this poem occurs during the final phase of the Ignation meditation, when the meditator is addressing God directly. Donne begins with a vivid image, that of a person crying out to be "battered" by God, who is "three-personed" because of the Trinity (Father, Son, and Holy Ghost). The idea of a heart being "battered" by God is, of itself, an interesting metaphor: The speaker's heart is *like* something, perhaps a door or wall, that can be battered. Consider the highly visual imagery of action: knock, breathe, break, blow, burn. The poet piles paradoxical verb on verb to make his point: God breaks a person to piece him or her back together in a "new" way. Further comparisons occur in the second phase of the poem, which—within itself—follows the three-part Ignatian structure. The soul of the speaker is compared to "an usurped town." Reason is compared to a "viceroy" or agent of the king. God is, implicitly, compared to a king. The reasoning soul, the part of the poet that creates analogies, is said to be held "captive." The final phase, the outward turning, occurs in the quite obvious final "conversation" with God, beginning "Yet dearly I love you." The speaker has moved from resistance to acceptance of God's love, from reserve and intellectual confinement to a full outward expression of emotion. In its general outline, the intellectual and emotional trajectory of the Ignatian meditation parallels Donne's sonnet.

It is interesting to see how poets use the meditative pattern within a secular context. The following poem by Wordsworth is a good example of this technique.

WILLIAM WORDSWORTH   (1770–1850)

The Solitary Reaper

Behold her, single in the field,
   Yon solitary Highland Lass!
Reaping and singing by herself;
   Stop here, or gently pass!
Alone she cuts and binds the grain,   *5*
And sings a melancholy strain;
O listen! for the vale profound
Is overflowing with the sound.

No nightingale did ever chaunt
   More welcome notes to weary bands   *10*
Of travellers in some shady haunt,
   Among Arabian sands:
A voice so thrilling ne'er was heard
In spring-time from the cuckoo-bird,
Breaking the silence of the seas   *15*
Among the farthest Hebrides.

Will no one tell me what she sings?—
   Perhaps the plaintive numbers flow

For old, unhappy, far-off things,
　　And battles long ago;   20
Or is it some more humble lay,
Familiar matter of to-day?
Some natural sorrow, loss, or pain,
That has been, and may be again?

Whate'er the theme, the maiden sang   25
　　As if her song could have no ending;
I saw her singing at her work,
　　And o'er the sickle bending;—
I listened, motionless and still;
And, as I mounted up the hill,   30
The music in my heart I bore,
Long after it was heard no more.

The first word of this poem is "Behold," a powerful injunction. The poet brings the reader's visual sense directly into play with one word, one image—that of a woman "single in the field" as she reaps and sows. The entire first stanza consists of what Ignatius Loyola would call a "composition of place," the recreation of a solid image in place and time. With the second stanza, Wordsworth begins the "meditation by comparison," the phase in any meditation in which the intellect comes into the picture. The poet compares the woman as she sings to the nightingale and the cuckoo-bird, two of the sweetest singing birds (and, not incidentally, two birds often associated with poetry by poets themselves). In the third and fourth stanzas, Wordsworth begins the outward turning that brings most meditations to a close, first by asking a rhetorical question (i.e., one that does not require an answer): "Will no one tell me what she sings?" The final stanza places the action of the poem in perspective, widening the lens of the poem further to include what Robert Frost called "after-images," all later recollections of the scene. The aim of any meditation, of course, is the deepening of vision, the activation of the meditator's whole mind. Wordsworth ᴜas accomplished just that in "The Solitary Reaper," taking an incidental scene and transforming it, making it representative of all moments when one sees into the heart of things and comes to experience that "peace which passeth all understanding."

POEMS FOR FURTHER READING

Read each poem and answer the questions that follow.

GERARD MANLEY HOPKINS   (1844–1889)

Spring and Fall

To a young child

Márgarét, áre you gríeving
Over Goldengrove unleaving?
Léaves, líke the things of man, you
With your fresh thoughts care for, can you?
Áh! ás the heart grows older   5
It will come to such sights colder
By and by, nor spare a sigh
Though worlds of wanwood leafmeal lie,
And yet you *will* weep and know why.
Now no matter, child, the name: 10
Sórrow's spríngs áre the same.
Nor mouth had, no nor mind, expressed
What heart heard of, ghost guessed:
It ís the blight man was born for,
It is Margaret you mourn for.   15

QUESTIONS

1. What does the title "Spring and Fall" suggest? (Note that, in British English, the term *fall* rarely refers to the season of autumn.)
2. "Léaves, like the things of man, you/With your fresh thoughts care for, can you?" asks the speaker. What is the metaphor he calls up? What is the import of his question at the end?
3. What is the tone of lines 5 and 6?
4. In line 8 ("Through worlds of wanwood leafmeal lie") the unique rhythm and syntax (word order) are intimately related to the poet's meaning. Explain how.
5. What are "sórrows spríngs . . . the same," as line 11 suggests?
6. How does this poem seem to fit the pattern of meditative poetry discussed so far? See if you can actually make a diagram that separates the poem into three parts.
7. Describe the tone of the last line: "It is Margaret you mourn for."

JOHN CROWE RANSOM   (1888–1974)

Blue Girls

Twirling your blue skirts, travelling the sward
Under the towers of your seminary,

Go listen to your teachers old and contrary
Without believing a word.

Tie the white fillets then about your hair   *5*
And think no more of what will come to pass
Than bluebirds that go walking on the grass
And chattering on the air.

Practise your beauty, blue girls, before it fail;
And I will cry with my loud lips and publish   *10*
Beauty which all our power shall never establish,
It is so frail.

For I could tell you a story which is true;
I know a woman with a terrible tongue,
Blear eyes fallen from blue,   *15*
All her perfections tarnished—yet it is not long
Since she was lovelier than any of you.

QUESTIONS

1. What picture does the first stanza raise in your mind? Fill in as many details
   as you can.
2. What is the attitude of the poet toward these "blue girls"? Is it patronizing
   or demeaning? Why or why not? Examine his diction carefully.
3. Look at the third stanza. What does the poet mean by "Practise your beauty"
   and what is the power that could possibly attempt to "establish" it?
4. How does the last stanza constitute an outward turning or widening of the
   theme?
5. How does the speaker's attitude toward youth and beauty compare to the
   speaker's attitude to the same things in "Spring and Fall" by Hopkins? What
   similar devices do Ransom and Hopkins rely on for their effects?

ROBERT PENN WARREN (1905–   )

Heart of Autumn

Wind finds the northwest gap, fall comes.
Today, under gray cloud-scud and over gray
Wind-flicker of forest, in perfect formation, wild geese
Head for a land of warm water, the *boom*, the lead pellet.

Some crumple in air, fall. Some stagger, recover control,   *5*
Then take the last glide for a far glint of water. None
Knows what has happened. Now, today, watching
How tirelessly *V* upon *V* arrows the season's logic,

Do I know my own story? At least, they know
When the hour comes for the great wing-beat. Sky-strider,   *10*

Star-strider—they rise, and the imperial utterance,
Which cries out for distance, quivers in the wheeling sky.

That much they know, and in their nature know
The path of pathlessness, with all the joy
Of destiny fulfilling its own name.   *15*
I have known time and distance, but not why I am here.

Path of logic, path of folly, all
The same—and I stand, my face lifted now skyward,
Hearing the high beat, my arms outstretched in the tingling
Process of transformation, and soon tough legs,   *20*

With folded feet, trail in the sounding vacuum of passage,
And my heart is impacted with a fierce impulse
To unwordable utterance—
Toward sunset, at a great height.

With folded feet, trail in the sounding vacuum of passage,   *25*
And my heart is impacted with a fierce impulse
To unwordable utterance—
Toward sunset, at a great height.

QUESTIONS

1. Find the places in this poem where the "story" seems to change course, where the "seams" of the cloth can be discovered. Do these suggest a meditative pattern of any kind?

2. A sudden outburst of questioning occurs at the beginning of the third stanza. Examine these questions closely. What do they tell us about the speaker in the poem and about the nature of his thought?

3. Why does the poet find the path of logic and the path of folly "all the same" in stanza five? Has Warren led the reader to a point where he or she might be willing to accept this conclusion?

4. Write a prose version of the two final stanzas, focusing on the visual imagery. Do these last two stanzas comprise an adequate ending for "Heart of Autumn"?

DON L. LEE   (1942–   )

Man Thinking About Woman

some thing is lost in me,
like
the way you lose old thoughts   that
somehow seemed unlost at the right time.

i've not known it or you many days;   *5*
we met as friends with an absence of strangeness.

it was the month
that my lines got longer & my metaphors softer.

it was the week   that
i felt the city's narrow breezes rush about   *10*
me
looking for a place to disappear
as   i walked the clearway,
sure footed in used sandals screaming to be replaced

your empty shoes (except for used stockings)   *15*
partially hidden beneath the dresser
looked at me,
as i sat thoughtlessly   waiting
for your touch.

that day,   *20*
as your body rested upon my chest
i saw the shadow of the
window blinds   beam
across the unpainted ceiling
going somewhere   *25*
like the somewhere i was going
when
the clearness of yr/teeth,
& the scars on yr/legs stopped me.

your beauty: un-noticed by regular eyes   is   *30*
like   a blackbird resting

QUESTIONS

1. To whom is this poem addressed? At what point does that become clear?
2. The speaker recollects a personal scene in some detail. What little details account for its vividness?
3. How does the final image, that of the blackbird resting, act as a consolidating or summarizing image?
4. Does this poem accomplish what a meditative poem sets out to accomplish? Does it take an image and deepen it? Does it activate and enlarge the speaker's awareness of what lies behind the image?

11

METER

As regarding rhythm: to compose in the sequence of the musical phrase, not in sequence of a metronome.

—EZRA POUND

Measuring Words: Meter as a Principle of Recurrence

We should all be familiar with **rhythm**, because music—rock music in particular—depends heavily on it for the effects we enjoy. A band without a drummer is like a sailboat without a rudder to keep it steady. That recurrent *boom boom boom* of the bass drum reminds us that a melody derives much of its power to satisfy listeners from the way it plays *against* something regular and recurring. Poems, like songs, have **rhythm**—a recurring beat—and that rhythm may or may not follow identifiable patterns (though to a trained ear most poems seem very regular compared to the language of ordinary speech.)

Meter offers us a way to identify certain recurring patterns of sound, what we may think of as beats. In English, rhythms are identified by **strong beats** and **weak beats**. Let's examine a few lines from English poetry. Alfred, Lord Tennyson once wrote:

> The woods decay, the woods decay and fall,
> The vapours weep their burthen to the ground.

Try this experiment. You put a mark above the words or syllables that seem "strong"; I'll put the stronger sounds in capital letters. See if our ears have anything in common.

> The WOODS deCAY, the WOODS deCAY and FALL,
> The VApours WEEP their BURthen TO the GROUND.

This meter is called *iambic pentameter*. Much of the poetry written in English—Shakespeare's plays, for instance, or Milton's *Paradise Lost*—employs this meter. What the term recognizes is a particular rhythm or sequence of "hard" and "soft" (what we call **stressed** and **unstressed beats**.) The *pentameter* part of the term means that there are five so-called "feet" to the line—that is, you isolate five stressed syllables in each line. If the line had only one stress per line, the term *monometer* would be used; for two stresses, *dimeter*, and so on—*trimeter, tetrameter, pentameter, hexameter*. (The prefixes before the word *meter* are simply Greek numbers—*tri* means "three," for instance.)

The *iambic* part of the term *iambic pentameter* refers to the pattern of the stresses within each separate foot. Again, the terminology comes from Greek words. Iambic means "unstressed, then stressed." The "foot" goes something like this: ka-BOOM. One crackpot theory of meter suggests that the iambic foot has proven so congenial to poets and readers because the iamb (the noun version of the word) sounds like a heart beat (lub-DUB, lub-DUB, lub-DUB). Critics traditionally mark stressed and unstressed syllables in a line like this:

> ˘ ´ ˘ ´ ˘ ´ ˘ ´ ˘ ´
> The woods decay, the woods decay and fall,
> ˘ ´ ˘ ´ ˘ ´ ˘ ´ ˘ ´
> The vapours weep their burthen to the ground.

They also often measure out the feet with slashes, as follows:

> The woods | decay, | the woods | decay | and fall, |
> The va | pours weep | their bur | then to | the ground. |

If you want to measure both *feet* and *stresses* at the same time, you just put it all together, like this:

> ˘ ´ ˘ ´ ˘ ´ ˘ ´ ˘ ´
> The woods | decay, | the woods | decay | and fall, |
> ˘ ´ ˘ ´ ˘ ´ ˘ ´ ˘ ´
> The va | pours weep | their bur | then to | the ground. |

The most common stress patterns in English poetry are:

iambic	˘ ´	*dactyllic*	´ ˘ ˘
trochaic	´ ˘	*spondaic*	´ ´ ´
anapestic	˘ ˘ ´		

Note that the spondaic pattern is rare, because the spondaic foot contains no unstressed syllables. The following line is an example of *spondaic pentameter:*

> ´   ´   ´   ´   ´
> Boom, boom, boom, boom boom.

Except maybe in a poem about the Fourth of July, that type of line would never occur. But poets often throw in an occasional spondaic foot to enliven a patch of verse.

This brings up a little understood but extremely important point: *Poetic meter is rarely perfectly regular.* If a poet stuck to one pattern throughout a poem, he or she would either bore readers or put them to sleep very quickly. Let's reconsider the lines of poetry quoted earlier, which are two of the *most* regular lines you'll ever see. There is only one obvious irregularity, at the end of the second line: "to the ground." A bad reader, reciting the poem aloud, might stress the TO just because the pattern has been established, but that wouldn't be natural. Never force poetry to sound like anything but ordinary speech. The poet's job is to make sure that the music is there already, in the arrangement of the words.

When we say, then, that a poem is written in iambic pentameter or trochaic trimeter or any combination of feet and stresses, we mean that it follows that pattern *in general* but with variations throughout. These variations account for individuality and style in good poetry. For instance, Robert Frost begins a poem called "The Oven Bird" like this:

> There is a singer everyone has heard,
> Loud, a mid-summer and a mid-wood bird,
> Who makes the solid tree trunks sound again.

The first line fits the pattern of iambic pentameter exactly. But the second line begins with "Loud," a firmly stressed syllable that calls attention to itself. The rhythm works together with the meaning of the words in the second line to emphasize Frost's point. Read it aloud and feel the difference between the first and second lines; then read it again and notice that it sounds different from the third line, which is regular. The quirkiness of the second line singles it out, just as Frost is singling out this unusual bird, the oven bird. As always, thoughtful variation of meter is a mark of a poet's excellence.

Another point is relevant here, too: *Not every stressed syllable is stressed the same.* Just as you can expect a ballet dancer's foot to clomp down hard sometimes and just graze the floor at others, you can expect poets to vary the "hardness" or "thump" of their stresses. Look at our sample lines once again. Which *stressed* words seem to carry more weight than others?

The process of dissecting poetry with regard to its stresses and feet is called **scansion**. Remember that you can't dissect a frog and expect it to hop. The same is true of poetry. Poets rarely sit down and count out the meter while they're in the act of creation. Readers of poetry rarely sit down and dissect the poem while they're enjoying the music that it makes. (Do you break a rock song into its parts while you're dancing to it at a party?) Nonetheless, scansion is useful to good readers. It makes their appreciation keener the next time they read the poem. By learning how poems are put together—how they work—we can become much better readers; we can learn to appreciate the subtle effects that create subtle meanings.

Aspects of Rhythm

Let's examine three very different poems and see how their rhythms affect meaning. Robert Frost's "Stopping by Woods on a Snowy Evening" employs the principle of metrical recurrence to good effect.

ROBERT FROST   (1874–1963)

Stopping by Woods on a Snowy Evening

Whose woods these are I think I know.
His house is in the village though;
He will not see me stopping here
To watch his woods fill up with snow.

My little horse must think it queer   5
To stop without a farmhouse near
Between the woods and frozen lake
The darkest evening of the year.

He gives his harness bells a shake
To ask if there is some mistake.   10
The only other sound's the sweep
Of easy wind and downy flake.

The woods are lovely, dark and deep,
But I have promises to keep,
And miles to go before I sleep,   15
And miles to go before I sleep.

Few other poems in the English language use the iambic foot so repetitiously as does this particular poem. If you blank out the meaning of the words, you find the rhythm almost lulling you to sleep: *ta-dum, ta-dum, ta-dum, ta-dum*. If you count them out, you'll find four strong beats in every line. Generally speaking, such extreme regularity of meter is narcotic; it's a great cure for insomnia but little else, as all readers of truly bad poetry (such as the stuff that appears on greeting cards) surely know. Frost wanted to write a poem that would suggest the hypnotic quality of snow falling in the woods, a quality that seduces the reader as much as the speaker in the poem, both of whom want to resist this hypnotic effect. The speaker seems terrified of giving up, of succumbing to the cold, the snow, the deathlike stillness; thus, he reminds himself, repeatedly, of the promises he has to keep and the miles he has to go before he sleeps. Sleep, of course, reminds one of death, which can be tempting in a situation like this one. The reader will probably feel that the civilization that lies out there, beyond these snowy woods, is too demanding. It would be easier just to lie down and sleep or die. The overall effect of eeriness and terror that infuses this poem derives in part from the powerful repetitions, such as the last two lines. The regularity of the meter, which in a bad poem is boring, here adds to the poem's seductive sway.

"The Windhover," by Gerard Manley Hopkins, is a very different kind of poem. No one would call it simple, though the idea behind it isn't especially complex. The speaker compares a falcon in flight to a prince, a "dauphin." An innovative poet, Hopkins conceived of a rhythm called "sprung rhythm." In "sprung rhythm," you count only the number of really strong beats per line. Any number of unstressed syllables are allowed to accumulate around the strong beats. This makes for enormous metrical flexibility. Read the following poem aloud and observe its unique rhythms, which mimic the falcon's flight.

GERARD MANLEY HOPKINS   (1844–1889)

The Windhover

To Christ Our Lord

I caught this morning morning's minion, kingdom of daylight's dauphin,
    dapple-dawn-drawn Falcon, in his riding
  Of the rolling level underneath him steady air, and striding
High there, how he rung upon the rein of a wimpling wing
In his ecstasy! then off, off forth on swing,   5
  As a skate's heel sweeps smooth on a bow-bend: the hurl and gliding
  Rebuffed the big wind. My heart in hiding
Stirred for a bird,—the achieve of, the mastery of thing!

Brute beauty and valour and act, oh, air, pride, plume, here
  Buckle! AND the fire that breaks from thee then, a billion   *10*
Times told lovelier, more dangerous, O my chevalier!

No wonder of it, shéer plód makes plough down sillion
Shine, and blue-bleak embers, ah my dear,
  Fall, gall themselves, and gash gold-vermilion.

At the outset, the poem's diction seems to fold out of itself like an accordion: "I caught this morning morning's minion." The poet "catches" sight of the bird in flight, which in turn is likened to morning's "minion" or knight, as if morning were a king and could have vassals. The metaphor of servitude stands at the center of this poem: God is, for Hopkins (a Catholic priest), the ultimate king, and even the writing of this poem is for him an act of service. As always in Hopkins's poetry, some difficult words appear: a "wimpling" wing is one that wrinkles like the "wimples" or hooding cowls that nuns wear. To "ring on the rein" is what a horse does when it circles around its master on a rein. The word "sillion" is an English dialect word for the furrow dug by a plough.

QUESTIONS

1. How does the rhythm of the first four lines work to suggest the flight of the falcon?
2. Comment on this line: "High there, how he rung upon the rein of a wimpling wing." What picture comes to mind? How does the metaphor of horse and master work?
3. Comment on the line about the skate's heel that "sweeps smooth on a bow-bend." How do rhythm and meaning interact?
4. Look at the last line of the first stanza, beginning with "Stirred for a bird." How does what follows ("—the achieve of, the mastery of the thing!") affect the rhythmical flow of the poem? How does this rhythmical flow relate to the meaning of these lines?
5. Why does Hopkins place the word "Buckle" where he does? (Think of the lines in terms of where stresses fall, and how sharply they fall.) How does it relate, rhythmically, to the previous line?
6. What does the subtitle of the poem, the dedication "To Christ Our Lord," suggest? (Think of the falcon as a symbol.)

Free Verse

Most contemporary poetry is written in **free verse**, a translation of the French phrase *vers libre*. As T. S. Eliot once said to his friend Ezra Pound, no verse is really free for the poet who wants to do a good job. Pound himself offered this advice on free verse to young poets:

> I think one should write *vers libre* only when one "must," that is to say, only when the "thing" builds up a rhythm more beautiful than that of set metres, or more real, more a part of the emotion of the "thing," more

germane, intimate, interpretative than the measure of regular accentual verse.

In other words, it's best for a poet to work in firm metrical verse except when a poem seems to cry out for a totally original (and therefore irregular) meter. Amateur poets ought to stick to the basics, which includes standard meter.

In a provocative remark, the sort he preferred, Robert Frost once took Pound's warning about free verse a different way. He said that writing free verse was like playing tennis with the net down. Unlike Pound, he believed that free verse was too *easy*, that it didn't present the necessary formal restraint and make the proper demands on the poet. Anyone could write free verse, so he assumed. What Frost really meant was that *bad* free verse can be written easily. No well-written verse (remember not to confuse free verse with **blank verse**, which is unrhymed iambic pentameter) is easy to compose, and free verse remains among the most difficult and demanding poetic forms to write properly. It's not that poets writing free verse simply avoid rhymes and meters altogether; rather, they vary the meter and rhythms according to the poem's internal demands. In a sense, the poem's subject dictates the form. The free verse line expands and contracts with the poet's pattern of thought, shaping itself to the delicate contours of the imagination. Unaccomplished poets *rarely* succeed at writing decent poems in free verse. You can't, then, just take some prose and chop it into lines and expect it to pass for free verse. The free verse poem has to grow out of itself, like a plant, and expand into a unique and unpredictable shape that, once discovered, seems inevitable. It has to achieve its own music, which doesn't come easily when there is no base line, no fixed thump of the base drum against which the "tune" of the poem is played out. The reader of a formal, metrical poem knows exactly what to expect, which means that the poet can surprise with irregularity. Where irregularity is the norm, how can there be surprises? The poet who would write free verse is forced to establish a rhythm, to create a tension, to invent his or her own rules. This takes talent, if not genius.

Read the following poem by A. R. Ammons, written in free verse; then answer the questions.

A. R. AMMONS   (1926–   )

So I Said I Am Ezra

So I said I am Ezra
and the wind whipped my throat
gaming for the sounds of my voice
   I listened to the wind

go over my head and up into the night   *5*
Turning to the sea I said
    I am Ezra
but there were no echoes from the waves
The words were swallowed up
    in the voice of the surf   *10*
or leaping over the swells
lost themselves oceanward
    Over the bleached and broken fields
I moved my feet and turning from the wind
    that ripped sheets of sand   *15*
    from the beach and threw them
    like seamists across the dunes
swayed as if the wind were taking me away.
and said
    I am Ezra   *20*
As a word too much repeated
falls out of being
so I Ezra went out into the night
like a drift of sand
and splashed among the windy oats   *25*
that clutch the dunes
of unremembered seas

QUESTIONS

1. Why does the subject of the poem seem especially well suited to free verse?
2. Are there any recurring elements in this poem that create a kind of structural regularity? If so, point them out.
3. "A word too much repeated / falls out of being," says Ezra, the speaker, in the last stanza of this poem. How does this observation relate to the poem's concluding lines?

POEMS FOR FURTHER STUDY

Read and scan the following poems, marking them up according to patterns of stress and feet per line. In a short paragraph, show how the rhythms enhance each poem's meaning.

EDMUND WALLER   (1606–1687)

Song

  Go, lovely rose,
Tell her that wastes her time and me,
  That now she knows,
When I resemble her to thee,
  How sweet and fair she seems to be.   *5*

Tell her that's young
And shuns to have her graces spied,
   That hadst thou sprung
In deserts where no men abide
   Thou must have uncommended died.   *10*

   Small is the worth
Of beauty from the light retired;
   Bid her come forth,
Suffer herself to be desired,
   And not blush so to be admired.   *15*

   Then die, that she
The common fate of all things rare
   May read in thee;
How small a part of time they share
   That are so wondrous sweet and fair.   *20*

SAMUEL TAYLOR COLERIDGE (1772–1834)

Kubla Khan°

Or a vision in a dream. A fragment

In Xanadu did Kubla Khan
A stately pleasure dome decree:
Where Alph, the sacred river, ran
Through caverns measureless to man
   Down to a sunless sea.   *5*

°The first *khan*, or chief, of the Mongol dynasty in thirteenth-century China. The geography is all invented. In a prefatory note to the poem, Coleridge said: "In the summer of the year 1797, the author, then in ill health, had retired to a lonely farmhouse between Porlock and Linton, on the Exmoor confines of Somerset and Devonshire. In consequence of a slight indisposition, an anodyne had been prescribed, from the effects of which he fell asleep in his chair at the moment that he was reading the following sentence, or words of the same substance, in *Purchas's Pilgrimage:* "Here the Khan Kubla commanded a palace to be built, and a stately garden thereunto. And thus ten miles of fertile ground were inclosed with a wall." The author continued for about three hours in a profound sleep, at least of the external sense, during which time he has the most vivid confidence that he could not have composed less than from two to three hundred lines; if that indeed can be called composition in which all the images rose up before him as *things*, with a parallel production of the correspondent expressions, without any sensation or consciousness to effort. On awaking he appeared to himself to have a distinct recollection of the whole, and taking his pen, ink, and paper, instantly and eagerly wrote down the lines that are here preserved. At this moment he was unfortunately called out by a person on business from Porlock, and detained by him above an hour, and on his return to his room, found, to his no small surprise and mortification, that though he still retained some vague and dim recollection of the general purport of the vision, yet, with the exception of some eight or ten scattered lines and images, all the rest had passed away like the images on the surface of a stream into which a stone has been cast, but, alas! without the after restoration of the latter!"

So twice five miles of fertile ground
With walls and towers were girdled round:
And there were gardens bright with sinuous rills,
Where blossomed many an incense-bearing tree;
And here were forests ancient as the hills,   *10*
Enfolding sunny spots of greenery.

But oh! that deep romantic chasm which slanted
Down the green hill athwart a cedarn cover!
A savage place! as holy and enchanted
As e'er beneath a waning moon was haunted   *15*
By woman wailing for her demon lover!
And from this chasm, with ceaseless turmoil seething,
As if this earth in fast thick pants were breathing,
A mighty fountain momently was forced:
Amid whose swift half-intermitted burst   *20*
Huge fragments vaulted like rebounding hail,
Or chaffy grain beneath the thresher's flail:
And 'mid these dancing rocks at once and ever
It flung up momently the sacred river.
Five miles meandering with a mazy motion   *25*
Through wood and dale the sacred river ran,
Then reached the caverns measureless to man,
And sank in tumult to a lifeless ocean:
And 'mid this tumult Kubla heard from far
Ancestral voices prophesying war!   *30*

　　The shadow of the dome of pleasure
　　Floated midway on the waves;
　　Where was heard the mingled measure
　　From the fountain and the caves.
It was a miracle of rare device,   *35*
A sunny pleasure dome with caves of ice!

　　A damsel with a dulcimer
　　In a vision once I saw:
　　It was an Abyssinian maid,
　　And on her dulcimer she played,   *40*
　　Singing of Mount Abora.
　　Could I revive within me
　　Her symphony and song,
　　To such a deep delight 'twould win me,
That with music loud and long,   *45*
I would build that dome in air,
That sunny dome! those caves of ice!
And all who heard should see them there,
And all should cry, Beware! Beware!
His flashing eyes, his floating hair!   *50*
Weave a circle round him thrice,

And close your eyes with holy dread,
For he on honey-dew hath fed,
And drunk the milk of paradise.

ALFRED, LORD TENNYSON   (1809–1892)

Break, Break, Break

Break, break, break,
   On thy cold gray stones, O Sea!
And I would that my tongue could utter
   The thoughts that arise in me.

O, well for the fisherman's boy,   5
   That he shouts with his sister at play!
O, well for the sailor lad,
   That he sings in his boat on the bay!

And the stately ships go on
   To their haven under the hill;   10
But O for the touch of a vanished hand,
   And the sound of a voice that is still!

Break, break, break,
   At the foot of thy crags, O Sea!
But the tender grace of a day that is dead   15
   Will never come back to me.

EZRA POUND   (1885–1972)

The Return

See, they return; ah, see the tentative
Movements, and the slow feet,
The trouble in the pace and the uncertain
Wavering!

See, they return, one, and by one,   5
With fear, as half-awakened;
As if the snow should hesitate
And murmur in the wind,
     and half turn back;
These were the "Wing'd-with-Awe,"   10
   Inviolable,

Gods of the wingèd shoe!
With them the silver hounds,
     sniffling the trace of air!

Haie! Haie!   *15*
  These were the swift to harry;
These the keen-scented;
These were the souls of blood.

Slow on the leash,
    pallid the leash-men!   *20*

EDNA ST. VINCENT MILLAY (1892–1950)

The Strawberry Shrub

Strawberry Shrub, old-fashioned, quaint as quinces,
Hard to find in a world where neon and noise
Have flattened the ends of the three more subtle senses;
And blare and magenta are all that a child enjoys.

More brown than red the bloom—it is a dense colour;   *5*
Colour of dried blood; colour of the key of F.
Tie it in your handkerchief, Dorcas, take it to school
To smell. But no, as I said, it is browner than red; it is duller
Than history, tinnier than algebra; and you are colour-deaf.

Purple, a little, the bloom, like musty chocolate;   *10*
Purpler than the purple avens of the wet fields;
But brown and red and hard and hiding its fragrance;
More like an herb it is: it is not exuberant.
You must bruise it a bit: it does not exude; it yields.

Clinker-built, the bloom, over-lapped its petals   *15*
Like clapboards; like a boat I had; like the feathers of a wing;
Not graceful, not at all Grecian, something from the provinces:
A chunky, ruddy, beautiful Boeotian thing.

Take it to school, knotted in your handkerchief, Dorcas,
Corner of your handkerchief, take it to school, and see   *20*
What your teacher says; show your pretty teacher the curious
Strawberry Shrub you took to school for me.

ELLEN BRYANT VOIGT (1943–   )

Jug Brook

Beyond the stone wall,
the deer should be emerging from their yard.
Lank, exhausted, they scrape at the ground
where roots and bulbs will send forth

new definitions. The creek swells in its ditch;   *5*
the field puts on a green glove.
Deep in the woods, the dead ripen,
and the lesser creatures turn to their commission.

Why grieve for the lost deer,
for the fish that clutter the brook,   *10*
the kingdoms of midge that cloud its surface,
the flocks of birds that come to feed.
The earth does not grieve.
It rushes toward the season of waste

On the porch the weather shifts,   *15*
the cat dispatches
another expendable animal from the field.
Soon she will go inside to cull her litter,
addressing each with a diagnostic tongue.
Have I learned nothing? God,   *20*
into whose deep pocket our cries are swept,
it is you I look for
in the slate face of the water.

12

RHYME

Rhyme as Echo

It is commonly supposed by people who haven't read many recent poems that poetry is language that rhymes. The truth is, most of the poems written since the dawn of literature *do not* rhyme. For instance, the great poetry of ancient Israel, Greece, India, Rome, and China did not rhyme. Even in English, rhyme was among the later effects poets sought. The anonymous author of *Beowulf,* the first major English poem, wrote in unrhymed meter. The most celebrated English epic, John Milton's *Paradise Lost* (1667), is written in **blank verse** or *unrhymed* iambic pentameter, as is William Wordsworth's long autobiographical poem, *The Prelude* (1850). Most contemporary poetry, good and bad alike, does not rhyme.

The point should be obvious: Rhyme has not always been a conspicuous element in poetry. Nevertheless, poetry has been well defined by Thomas Campion as "a system of linked sounds," and rhyme often plays a central part in the linking process that makes for good poetry.

Probably the best way to think of rhyme is not as a series of lock-stepping sound effects but as a *system of echoes.* Poets use rhyme to recall earlier words, to emphasize certain points, and to make their language memorable. It's a commonplace observation that nursery rhymes are memorable; their memorability has much to do with their rhyming. The delight that rhymes may give is best exemplified by the responsiveness of young children to words that sound alike. Adults, too, find words that chime or sound nearly alike somehow attractive: Pop songs are the most obvious example of the daily rhyming that comes into our lives as are TV and radio commercials. In fact, rhymes can be extremely effective in making language take hold in a reader's mind; they may even help to sell beer or panty hose!

When rhyming, poets most often follow a **rhyme scheme,** a pattern to which the rhymes adhere. Usually, this pattern is repeated in several stanzas, as it is in the following poem by Richard Lovelace:

RICHARD LOVELACE (1618–1657)

To Lucasta, Going to the Wars

Tell me not, sweet, I am unkind
That from the nunnery
Of thy chaste breast and quiet mind,
To war and arms I fly.

True, a new mistress now I chase,   5
The first foe in the field;
And with a stronger faith embrace
A sword, a horse, a shield.

Yet this inconstancy is such
As you too shall adore;   10
I could not love thee, dear, so much,
Loved I not honor more.

Rhyme words are each assigned a letter, so the rhyme scheme followed here is: ABAB CDCD EFEF. In other words, the first and third lines of each stanza always rhyme. The second and fourth lines rhyme, too. This is perhaps the most common rhyme scheme used in English poetry.

EXERCISE

Determine the rhyme scheme in the following poem by J. V. Cunningham:

J. V. CUNNINGHAM   (1911–1985)

For a College Yearbook

Somewhere on these bare rocks in some bare hall,
Perhaps unrecognized, wisdom and learning
Flash like a beacon on a sleeper's wall,
Ever distant and dark, ever returning.

Words like *house* and *mouse* and *bed* and *dead,* which we call **exact rhymes,** form the simplest kind of rhymes. But good poets also use **slant rhymes:** rhymes that might be called "near misses." These can be quite ingenious. The word *seek* can form a slant rhyme with words that use the same consonants, for instance, such as *sack* or *sick.* A poet may also choose to rhyme on vowels and ignore consonants; thus, *seek* can be rhymed with *leap* or *weed.* Another version of the slant rhyme is the **eye rhyme** or **sight rhyme,** in which the rhyme plays more to the eye of the reader than the ear; consider rhyming *tough* with *dough* or *plea* with *idea.* As Ezra Pound said, the element of surprise is essential in good rhyming; slant rhymes (and eye rhymes) offer endless possibilities for surprise.

Rhyme schemes only take into account **end rhymes,** the rhymes that occur at the ends of the lines. But poets often make use of **internal rhymes,** which is rhyming words within the lines themselves. This kind of rhyming helps to link the sounds that make the poem work. In many of the best poems, words echo and chime off each other, making the poem an enclosed system of melodic reverberation. Almost all poets make use of internal rhyming, whether consciously or not; they occasionally turn internal rhyming into a major stylistic effect.

EXERCISE

Langston Hughes, Gerard Manley Hopkins, and E. E. Cummings made rhyming an important aspect of their styles and poetic visions. Underline all echoes—regular rhymes, internal rhymes, and slant rhymes—that you can discover in the following poems. Try to find some very remote echoes, too.

LANGSTON HUGHES   (1902–1967)

The Weary Blues

Droning a drowsy syncopated tune,
Rocking back and forth to a mellow croon,
    I heard a Negro play.

Down on Lenox Avenue the other night
By the pale dull pallor of an old gas light   5
  He did a lazy sway. . . .
  He did a lazy sway. . . .
To the tune o' those Weary Blues.
With his ebony hands on each ivory key
He made that poor piano moan with melody.   10
  O Blues!
Swaying to and fro on his rickety stool
He played that sad raggy tune like a musical fool.
  Sweet Blues!
Coming from a black man's soul.   15
  O Blues!
In a deep song voice with a melancholy tone
I heard that Negro sing, that old piano moan—
  "Ain't got nobody in all this world,
  Ain't got nobody but ma self.   20
  I's gwine to quit ma frownin'
  And put ma troubles on the shelf."
Thump, thump, thump, went his foot on the floor.
He played a few chords then he sang some more—
  "I got the Weary Blues   25
  And I can't be satisfied.
  Got the Weary Blues
  And can't be satisfied—
  I ain't happy no mo'
  And I wish that I had died."   30
And far into the night he crooned that tune.
  The stars went out and so did the moon.
  The singer stopped playing and went to bed
  While the Weary Blues echoed through his head.
  He slept like a rock or a man that's dead.   35

GERARD MANLEY HOPKINS   (1844–1889)

Spring

Nothing is so beautiful as Spring—
  When weeds, in wheels, shoot long and lovely and lush;
  Thrush's eggs look little low heavens, and thrush
Through the echoing timber does so rinse and wring
The ear, it strikes like lightnings to hear him sing;   5
  The glassy peartree leaves and blooms, they brush
  The descending blue; that blue is all in a rush
With richness; the racing lambs too have fair their fling.

What is all this juice and all this joy?
   A strain of the earth's sweet being in the beginning   *10*
In Eden garden.—Have, get, before it cloy,

   Before it cloud, Christ, lord, and sour with sinning,
Innocent mind and Mayday in girl and boy,
   Most, O maid's child, thy choice and worthy the winning.

E. E. CUMMINGS (1894–1962)

anyone lived in a pretty how town

anyone lived in a pretty how town
(with up so floating many bells down)
spring summer autumn winter
he sang his didn't he danced his did.

Women and men (both little and small)   *5*
cared for anyone not at all
they sowed their isn't they reaped their same
sun moon stars rain

children guessed (but only a few
and down they forgot as up they grew   *10*
autumn winter spring summer)
that noone loved him more by more

when by now and tree by leaf
she laughed his joy she cried his grief
bird by snow and stir by still   *15*
anyone's any was all to her

someones married their everyones
laughed their cryings and did their dance
(sleep wake hope and then) they
said their nevers they slept their dream   *20*

stars rain sun moon
(and only the snow can begin to explain
how children are apt to forget to remember
with up so floating many bells down)

one day anyone died i guess   *25*
(and noone stooped to kiss his face)
busy folk buried them side by side
little by little and was by was

all by all and deep by deep
and more by more they dream their sleep   *30*
noone and anyone earth by april
wish by spirit and if by yes.

Women and men (both dong and ding)
summer autumn winter spring
reaped their sowing and went their came   *35*
sun moon stars rain

    Alliteration is similar to internal rhyming except for the fact that
the poet echoes or repeats consonantal sounds, as in these lines by Emily
Dickinson: "The Soul selects her own Society/Then shuts the Door."
(The echoing of vowel sounds is called **assonance.**) Alliteration, when
not overdone, can help in linking the sounds of a poem. Some poets
also employ a device called **onomatopoeia** that is, the use of words that
imitate sounds—for example, *pop* or *fizzle.*

EXERCISE

In a page, summarize and comment on the argument against rhyme (also spelled
rime—as in the poem that follows) as it is made by Ben Jonson in "A Fit of Rime
Against Rime." (Look up the word *rime* in a good dictionary to find its various
meanings.)

BEN JONSON   (1572?–1637)

A Fit of Rime Against Rime°

Rime the rack of finest wits,
That expresseth but by fits,
    True conceit.
Spoiling senses of their treasure,
Cozening° judgment with a measure,   *deceiving*   5
    But false weight.
Wresting words from their true calling;
Propping verse for fear of falling
    To the ground
Jointing syllables, drowning letters,   *10*
Fastening vowels, as with fetters
    They were bound!
Soon as lazy thou wert known
All good poetry hence was flown
    And art banished.   *15*
For a thousand years together,
All Parnassus'° green did wither   *mountain in Greece, abode of the Muses*
    And wit vanished.

°The title is a pun on the word "fit," which is also a type of poem.

Pegasus° did fly away,   *winged horse of mythology*
At the wells no Muse did stay,   *20*
    But bewailed,
So to see the fountain dry
And Apollo's music die,
    All light failed!
Starveling rimes did fill the stage,   *25*
Not a poet in an age
    Worth crowning.
Not a work deserving bays,°   *laurel leaves, used for crowns*
Nor a line deserving praise,
    Pallas° frowning;   *Athena, Greek goddess of beauty*   *30*
Greek was free from rime's infection,
Happy Greek by this protection!
    Was not spoiled.
Whilst the Latin, queen of tongues,
Is not free from rime's wrongs,   *35*
    But rests foiled.
Scarce the hill° again doth flourish,   *Parnassus*
Scarce the world a wit doth nourish,
    To restore
Phoebus° to his crown again;   *Apollo, as sun god*   *40*
And the Muses to their brain,
    As before.
Vulgar° languages that want   *common, popular, unrefined (such as English)*
Words, and sweetness, and be scant
    Of true measure,   *45*
Tyrant rime hath so abused,
That they long since have refused
    Other ceasure.°   *caesura or pause in a line of verse*
He that first invented thee,
May his joints tormented be,   *50*
    Cramped forever;
Still may syllables jar with time,
Still may reason war with rime,
    Resting never.
May his sense when it would meet   *55*
The cold tumor in his feet
    Grow unsounder.
And his title be long fool,
That in rearing such a school
    Was the founder.   *60*

POEMS FOR FURTHER READING

Read the following poems and answer the questions.

RICHARD LOVELACE   (1618–1657)

To Althea, from Prison°

When Love with unconfinèd wings
Hovers within my gates
And my divine Althea brings
To whisper at the grates;°   *prison bars*
When I lie tangled in her hair   5
And fettered to her eye:
The birds that wanton° in the air   *play freely*
Know no such liberty.

When flowing cups run swiftly round
With no allaying° Thames,   *diluting*   10
Our careless heads with roses bound,
Our hearts with loyal flames;
When thirsty grief in wine we steep,
When healths and draughts go free:°   *when toasts are liberally made*
Fishes that tipple in the deep   15
Know no such liberty.

When, like committed° linnets, I   *caged*
With shriller throat shall sing
The sweetness, mercy, majesty,
And glories of my King;   20
When I shall voice aloud, how good
He is, how great should be:
Enlargèd° winds that curl the flood°   *freely flowing; the sea*
Know no such liberty

Stone walls do not a prison make,   25
Nor iron bars a cage;
Minds innocent and quiet take
That for an hermitage.
If I have freedom in my love
And in my soul am free,   30
Angels alone that soar above
Enjoy such liberty.

°In 1642, just before the outbreak of the English Civil War, Lovelace was imprisoned because of his Royalist sympathies.

QUESTIONS

1. What is the rhyme scheme used in "To Althea, from Prison"? How does that scheme work to enhance the meaning of the poem?
2. What effect does the repetition of the word "liberty" have?
3. Does alliteration occur in this poem? To what effect?

ROBERT LOUIS STEVENSON   (1850–1894)

Requiem

Under the wide and starry sky,
Dig the grave and let me lie.
Glad did I live and gladly die,
   And I laid me down with a will.

This be the verse you grave for me:
Here he lies where he longed to be;
Home is the sailor, home from sea,
   And the hunter home from the hill.

QUESTIONS

1. Sketch out the rhyme scheme in "Requiem." Why do you think Stevenson chose this particular rhyme scheme for this poem?
2. How would you characterize the attitude of the speaker in this poem toward the subject?
3. In what ways does alliteration work to knit together the memorable three lines at the end, which are in italics?

ALASTAIR REID   (1926–   )

A Lesson in Music

Play the tune again: but this time
with more regard for the movement at the source of it
and less attention to time. Time falls
curiously in the course of it.

Play the tune again: not watching   5
your fingering, but forgetting, letting flow
the sound till it surrounds you. Do not count
or even think. Let go.

Play the tune again: but try to be
nobody, nothing, as though the pace   10
of the sound were your heart beating, as though
the music were your face.

Play the tune again. It should be easier
to think less every time of the notes, of the measure.
It is all an arrangement of silence. Be silent, and then   15
play it for your pleasure.

Play the tune again; and this time, when it ends,
do not ask me what I think. Feel what is happening
strangely in the room as the sound glooms over
you, me, everything.   *20*

Now,
play the the tune again.

QUESTIONS

1. What use does the poet make of repetition in "A Lesson in Music"?
2. How does alliteration help to link stanza to stanza?
3. Track the pattern of assonance (internal rhyming on vowels). Why does such heavy use of one poetical device seem justified in this poem, if indeed you think it justified.
4. Make a short paraphrase of this poem. What abstract lesson is the poet trying to convey to the person addressed? Does it relate to more than music?

MARK STRAND (1934–   )

Shooting Whales

For Judith and Leon Major

When the shoals of plankton
swarmed into St. Margaret's Bay,
turning the beaches pink,
we saw from our place on the hill
the sperm whales feeding,   *5*
fouling the nets
in their play,
and breaching clean
so the humps of their backs
rose over the wide sea meadows.   *10*

Day after day
we waited inside
for the rotting plankton to disappear.
The smell stilled even the wind,
and the oxen looked stunned,   *15*
pulling haw on the slope
of our hill.
But the plankton kept coming in
and the whales would not go.

That's when the shooting began.   *20*
The fishermen got in their boats
and went after the whales
and my father and uncle
and we children went, too.
The froth of our wake sank fast   *25*
in the wind-shaken water.

The whales surfaced close by.
Their foreheads were huge,
the doors of their faces were closed.
Before sounding, they lifted   *30*
their flukes into the air
and brought them down hard.
They beat the sea into foam,
and the path that they made
shone after them.   *35*

Though I did not see their eyes,
I imagined they were
like the eyes of mourning,
glazed with rheum,
watching us, sweeping along   *40*
under the darkening sheets of salt.

When we cut our engine and waited
for the whales to surface again,
the sun was setting,
turning the rock-strewn barrens a gaudy salmon.   *45*
A cold wind flailed at our skin.
When finally the sun went down
and it seemed like the whales had gone,
my uncle, no longer afraid,
shot aimlessly into the sky.   *50*

Three miles out
in the rolling dark
under the moon's astonished eyes,
our engine would not start
and we headed home in the dinghy.   *55*
And my father, hunched over the oars,
brought us in. I watched him,
rapt in his effort, rowing against the tide,
his blond hair glistening with salt.
I saw the slick spillage of moonlight   *60*
being blown over his shoulders,
and the sea and spindrift
suddenly silver.

He did not speak the entire way.
At midnight   65
when I went to bed,
I imagined the whales
moving beneath me,
sliding over the weed-covered hills of the deep;
they knew where I was;   70
they were luring me
downward and downward
into the murmurous
waters of sleep.

QUESTIONS

1. "Shooting Whales," like the previous poem, is written in free verse; nevertheless, the poet uses sound patterns in a repetitive way. Where are these
   repetitions?
2. How many instances of alliteration can you find? Make a list.
3. How would you describe the "sound" made by this poem? How does it compare to "A Lesson in Music"? Point to similarities and differences.
4. In what ways is the music of this poem—the cumulative effect of the meter
   and rhymes, the alliteration and assonance—appropriate to the poet's subject
   and theme?

13

POETIC SHAPES
AND FORMS

Rhythm is to time what symmetry is to space.

The sensitive reader must be aware of a poem's visual pattern—the effects of typography and stanza shapes used to enhance a poem's meaning, to create an effect. These effects, like those achieved by painters and sculptors, can be extremely powerful because of their physicality.

Typographical Patterns

In addition to the sound effects made by poetry, poets also have to consider the shapes of their poems on the page. Although poems are sometimes read aloud—and benefit greatly from being performed—the truth is that most readers experience a poem as a visual object, a series of black squiggles on a white page. Some poems seem to *ask* to be thought of as visual objects first; they could almost be hung on a wall like pictures.

Poetry that depends entirely on its "look" or shape is called **concrete poetry**. "Easter Wings" by George Herbert is a classic example of a concrete poem.

GEORGE HERBERT   (1593–1633)

Easter Wings

Lord, who createdst man in wealth and store,
    Though foolishly he lost the same,
        Decaying more and more
           Till he became
             Most poor.   5
             With thee
           O let me rise
        As larks, harmoniously,
    And sing this day thy victories:
Then shall the fall further the flight in me.   10

    My tender age in sorrow did begin:
      And still with sicknesses and shame
        Thou didst so punish sin,
           That I became
             Most thin.   15
             With thee
           Let me combine,
        And feel this day thy victory;
    For, if I imp my wing on thine,
Affliction shall advance the flight in me.   20

Poets in the seventeenth century liked to invent shapes for their poems that would contribute to their meaning. Crosses, chalices, and other obvious religious symbols were most popular. Herbert's poem is about Easter, which expresses the sense of joy in the Resurrection. The wings of the poem relate to the lark's wings, mentioned in the eighth line. The special word *imp* (a wing graft) that occurs in the next to last line, carries a great deal of meaning. A falconer repaired the wing of an injured falcon by grafting a feather onto the wing. The idea of the poet's grafting himself to God's wing is quite ingenious as an image and metaphor. Notice, too, that when the speaker talks about being "thin," in line 15, the poem physically narrows. The effect is oddly satisfying.

EXERCISE

Examine "Easter Wings" in detail. Find other examples in the poem where the poem's physical shape reinforces meaning. Consider especially the effect of the poem's shape on your expectations of rhyme and rhythm.

One modern poet, E. E. Cummings, has also made ingenious use

of the typographical aspects of poetry in the following poem about the
death of Buffalo Bill.

E. E. CUMMINGS   (1894–1962)

Buffalo Bill's

<pre>
Buffalo Bill's
defunct
         who used to
         ride a watersmooth-silver
                                    stallion   5
and break onetwothreefourfive pigeonsjustlikethat
                                    Jesus
he was a handsome man
                   and what i want to know is
how do you like your blueeyed boy   10
Mister Death
</pre>

Notice how Cummings varies his line lengths with the imagery as it breaks
under the eye. He forces the reader to speed up or slow down by employing certain typographical tricks, such as running the numbers one
through five together or dropping the exclamation "Jesus" down a line.
He forces us to think hard about the use of the word "defunct," which
means more than merely "dead," by putting it on one line. That single
word, "defunct," carries enormous freight in this poem, because it de-
termines the poet's attitude toward Buffalo Bill as a person and a culture
hero. The word emphasizes that this man, Buffalo Bill, was either more
or less than a real person. It has cold, clinical overtones that, in some
ways, seem at odds with the passion of the poem.

EXERCISE

Discuss other parts of the poem about Buffalo Bil' where the physical shape of
the poem affects the meaning.

Stanza Patterns

Although poets rarely make such heavy use of the visual sides of
their poems as do Cummings or Herbert in the preceding poems, the
shape of any poem has a bearing on its meaning. Most poems divide
into units or **stanzas**, as we have already seen. Usually the stanza acts to
delimit or contain a logical or intuitive step as the poem advances. Church

hymns are a good example of the stanza in its simplest manifestation. Church hymns, ballads, and popular songs—as we have already seen— often use the form called **common measure**, a simple, four-line rhyming stanza with alternating four and three beat lines. Emily Dickinson, the first American woman who might safely be called a "major" poet, wrote most of her poems in this form (which, incidentally, means that most of them can be sung to the tune of 'The Yellow Rose of Texas"). One of her eeriest poems follows.

EMILY DICKINSON   (1830–1886)

I Heard a Fly Buzz—When I Died

I heard a Fly buzz—when I died—
The Stillness in the Room
Was like the Stillness in the Air—
Between the Heaves of Storm—

The Eyes around—had wrung them dry— 5
And Breaths were gathering firm
For that last Onset—when the King
Be witnessed—in the Room—

I willed my Keepsakes—Signed away
What portion of me be 10
Assignable—and then it was
There interposed a Fly—

With Blue—uncertain stumbling Buzz—
Between the light—and me—
And then the Windows failed—and then 15
I could not see to see—

QUESTIONS

1. Dickinson's poem is written in the past tense. Why? Who is the speaker and in what situation do you imagine her now?
2. Examine the notion of a fly buzzing. What symbolic effects does Dickinson seem to strive for?
3. Make a paraphrase of the poem in which you summarize the information conveyed stanza by stanza. How does Dickinson use stanza divisions to gradually let out the information that the poem contains?
4. Common measure is most frequently associated with the type of hymns sung in orthodox Christian churches. This is hardly an orthodox poem, however. Does the fact that Dickinson wrote this strange poem in a form associated with church hymns matter? What effects does this produce?

5. Read the last stanza again. What does the adjective "Blue" modify? How is this possible? Why does Dickinson repeat the word "see"? To what effect? To what do the "Windows" in line 15 refer?

Stanzas come in all shapes and sizes, depending on the poet's inventiveness or whim. In the **ode**, a long lyric on a serious theme, the poet is free to invent intricate stanza patterns, which must then be applied consistently throughout the poem, as in the famous "Ode on a Grecian Urn."

JOHN KEATS   (1795–1821)

Ode on a Grecian Urn°

Thou still unravished bride of quietness,
  Thou foster-child of silence and slow time,
Sylvan historian, who canst thus express
  A flowery tale more sweetly than our rhyme:
What leaf-fringed legend haunts about thy shape   *5*
  Of deities or mortals, or of both,
    In Tempe or the dales of Arcady?°   *two beautiful valleys in Greece*
What men or gods are these? What maidens loath?
  What mad pursuit? What struggle to escape?
  What pipes and timbrels?° What wild ecstasy?   *a tambourine-like instrument* *10*

Heard melodies are sweet, but those unheard
  Are sweeter; therefore, ye soft pipes, play on;
Not to the sensual ear, but, more endeared,
  Pipe to the spirit ditties of no tone:
Fair youth, beneath the trees, thou canst not leave   *15*
  Thy song, nor ever can those trees be bare;
    Bold lover, never, never canst thou kiss,
Though winning near the goal—yet, do not grieve;
  She cannot fade, though thou hast not thy bliss,
    Forever wilt thou love, and she be fair!   *20*

Ah, happy, happy boughs! that cannot shed
  Your leaves, nor ever bid the spring adieu;
And, happy melodist, unwearied,
  Forever piping songs forever new;

More happy love! more happy, happy love!   *25*
  Forever warm and still to be enjoyed,
    Forever panting, and forever young;

°The urn is decorated with a lovely woodland scene.

All breathing human passion far above,
    That leaves a heart high-sorrowful and cloyed,
        A burning forehead, and parching tongue.   *30*

Who are these coming to the sacrifices?
    To what green altar, O mysterious priest,
Leadest thou that heifer lowing at the skies,
    And all her silken flanks with garlands dressed?
What little town by river or sea shore,   *35*
    Or mountain-built with peaceful citadel,°   *castle*
        Is emptied of this folk, this pious morn?
And, little town, thy streets forevermore
    Will silent be; and not a soul to tell
        Why thou art desolate, can e'er return.   *40*

O Attic shape! Fair attitude! with brede°   *border*
    Of marble men and maidens overwrought,
With forest branches and the trodden weed;
    Thou, silent form, dost tease us out of thought
As doth eternity: Cold Pastoral!   *45*
    When old age shall this generation waste,
        Thou shalt remain, in midst of other woe
Than ours, a friend to man, to whom thou sayest
    "Beauty is truth, truth beauty,"—that is all
        Ye know on earth, and all ye need to know.   *50*

QUESTIONS

1. How would you describe the stanzas with regard to rhyme and meter? Do these formal restraints have any bearing on the subject of the poem?
2. Write a very brief summary of what happens and what thoughts are expressed in each stanza.
3. Examine the three different ways the urn is addressed by the speaker in lines 1 to 3. Why does Keats use three different addresses?
4. A flurry of questions concludes the first stanza. What impression does this give of the poem's speaker? Are these questions answered?
5. The second stanza begins with the oxymoronic (or parodoxical) remark that "unheard melodies" are sweeter than heard ones! What can this mean? What does it tell us about the nature of the argument that the poet pursues?
6. "When old age shall this generation waste, / Thou shalt remain," the poet declares in the last stanza. How is this relevant to the poem as a whole? (Note that generation means "production" as well as its more common reference to a particular age group.)
7. Who says, "Beauty is truth, truth beauty"? What does this remark mean in the context of the poem?

The Sonnet

A poetic form may be thought of as a vase into which language, like clear water, is poured. The language depends upon the form to give it shape and beauty. Likewise, without language, the shape itself is empty. To use another metaphor, poetic forms may be thought of as musical instruments. They come in different shapes and sizes, and they differ in their range of tones. The ode may be compared to the viola, which has a deeper sound than the violin and can be extremely melancholy. The **sonnet**—a poem in fourteen lines with a specific rhyme scheme (the pattern varies)—is best compared to the violin itself, the most basic instrument for any ensemble or orchestra. Throughout the history of English poetry, the sonnet has been the poet's favorite instrument. Shakespeare, for instance, wrote a famous sequence of 154 sonnets that has never been equaled for intellectual depth or emotional range. Milton, Wordsworth, and Keats all excelled at the sonnet form, as have many of our best modern and contemporary poets, such as Robert Frost, Robert Lowell, and Seamus Heaney. We will examine next a number of sonnets from different periods to see how poets have used this flexible form. We'll look, too, at some other well known forms, such as the villanelle and the sestina, and at some examples of free verse, the most common (yet various) form that poems take today.

Roughly speaking, a sonnet is any fourteen-line poem written in rhyming iambic pentameter, though some contemporary poets have even dropped the metrical requirement, calling any fourteen-line poem a sonnet. One of the most popular rhyme schemes for the sonnet is the **Italian** or **Petrarchan** form, named after Petrarch, an Italian poet of the Middle Ages who specialized in this kind of sonnet. Its rhyme scheme goes as follows:

Lines:	1	2	3	4	5	6	7	8		1	2	3	4	5	6
	a	b	b	a	a	b	b	a		c	d	c	d	c	d
OR:	a	b	b	a	a	b	b	a		c	d	e	c	d	e

In this Italian form, the sonnet divides into two sections: the **octave** (eight lines) and the **sestet** (six lines). A good poet will exploit this division, and allow an emphatic shift or change of tone from octave to sestet. The following poem illustrates this technique.

WILLIAM WORDSWORTH   (1770–1850)

The World Is Too Much With Us

The world is too much with us; late and soon,
Getting and spending, we lay waste our powers:

Little we see in Nature that is ours;
We have given our hearts away, a sordid boon!
This Sea that bares her bosom to the moon,   5
The winds that will be howling at all hours,
And are up-gathered now like sleeping flowers,
For this, for everything, we are out of tune;
It moves us not.—Great God! I'd rather be
A Pagan suckled in a creed outworn;   10
So might I, standing on this pleasant lea,
Have glimpses that would make me less forlorn;
Have sight of Proteus rising from the sea;
Or hear old Triton° blow his wreathéd horn.   *a sea god*

The sonnet form itself helps to facilitate logical thought because of its restrictions: a paradox that poets all understand. If a poet has no limitations or given structure, anything is possible, which can be daunting. The human imagination seems to operate at its best within set limits, such as the sonnet. Indeed, the sonnet has proven to be an almost ideal form because of its relatively short length and provocative structure. Let's examine Wordsworth's poem as an exemplary sonnet. Throughout the octave, the first eight lines, the poet laments the sorry condition of life in a world in which so much time is spent "getting and spending"— the consumer society. The rhyme scheme enforces a certain economy of thought, as the notion that "we lay waste our powers" is followed, quickly, by the idea that so little we see around us in nature is really "ours." The need to find a rhyming word has often led poets into realms of thought they might not have otherwise discovered. In Wordsworth's sonnet, the octave extends into the ninth line, which is dramatically broken by an exclamation: "Great God!" The poet, meditating on the quality of life in the present world of England, wishes himself back in ancient times: "A Pagan suckled in a creed outworn." He probably refers to Roman Britain, when one could stand in the same place and view the world differently, in more imaginative terms, with the god Proteus "rising from the sea" and "old Triton" blowing his horn. The sonnet form perfectly embodies this simple, yet powerful, contrast of present with past.

The **English** or **Shakespearean** sonnet divides its fourteen lines into three quatrains (stanzas with four lines) and a final couplet. Its rhyme scheme goes like this:

		QUATRAINS										COUPLET	
Lines:	1	2	3	4	1	2	3	4	1	2	3	4	1	2
	a	b	a	b	c	d	c	d	e	f	e	f	g	g

Shakespeare was a master of this form, which he pioneered. Look carefully at the following sonnet to see how he uses the stanza divisions and final couplet to control the shape of his argument.

WILLIAM SHAKESPEARE (1564–1616)

Sonnet 29
When in Disgrace with Fortune and Men's Eyes

When in disgrace with fortune and men's eyes
   I all alone beweep my outcast state,
And trouble deaf heaven with my bootless cries,
   And look upon myself, and curse my fate,
Wishing me like to one more rich in hope,   5
   Featured like him, like him with friends possessed,
Desiring this man's art, and that man's scope,
   With what I most enjoy contented least;
Yet in these thoughts myself almost despising,
   Haply I think on thee, and then my state,   10
Like to the lark at break of day arising
   From sullen earth, sings hymns at heaven's gate;
     For thy sweet love remembered such wealth brings
     That then I scorn to change my state with kings.

QUESTIONS

1. What shift of emphasis takes place in line 5 (which starts the second quatrain)? How does Shakespeare signal the shift grammatically?
2. How does the beginning of the third quatrain (line 9) mark a further development in the chain of argument?
3. How would you characterize the final couplet? What is its relation to the main body of the poem?
4. What does the required rhyme do to the normal word order and what effect does this have on the meter and sound?

EXERCISE

Modern poets have worked in versions of the Italian or English sonnet with interesting and provocative results. Read the next four poems. Then write a short paper discussing the use the poets have made of the sonnet form. What seem to be the successes or failures of the form in these instances?

SEAMUS HEANEY   (1939–   )

The Forge

All I know is a door into the dark.
Outside, old axles and iron hoops rusting;
Inside, the hammered anvil's short-pitched ring,
The unpredictable fantail of sparks
Or hiss when a new shoe toughens in water.   5
The anvil must be somewhere in the centre,
Horned as a unicorn, at one end square,
Set there immoveable: an altar
Where he expends himself in shape and music.
Sometimes, leather-aproned, hairs in his nose,   10
He leans out on the jamb, recalls a clatter
Of hoofs where traffic is flashing in rows;
Then grunts and goes in, with a slam and flick
To beat real iron out, to work the bellows.

ROBERT FROST   (1874–1963)

Design°

I found a dimpled spider, fat and white,
On a white heal-all,° holding up a moth   *a common weed with white or blue flowers*
Like a white piece of rigid satin cloth—
Assorted characters of death and blight
Mixed ready to begin the morning right,   5
Like the ingredients of witches' broth—
A snow-drop spider, a flower like a froth,
And dead wings carried like a paper kite.

What had that flower to do with being white,
The wayside blue and innocent heal-all?   10
What brought the kindred spider to that height,
Then steered the white moth thither in the night?
What but design of darkness to appall?—
If design govern in a thing so small.

°The "argument from design" is a famous philosophical proof of the existence of God,
which uses as evidence the design underlying all of nature.

ROBERT LOWELL   (1917–1978)

History

History has to live with what was here,
clutching and close to fumbling all we had—

it is so dull and gruesome how we die,
unlike writing, life never finishes.
Abel was finished; death is not remote,   5
a flash-in-the-pan electrifies the skeptic,
his cows crowding like skulls against high-voltage wire,
his baby crying all night like a new machine.
As in our Bibles, white-faced, predatory,
the beautiful, mist-drunken hunter's moon ascends—   10
a child could give it a face: two holes, two holes,
my eyes, my mouth, between them a skull's no-nose—
O there's a terrifying innocence in my face
drenched with the silver salvage of the mornfrost.

RICHARD KENNEY (1948–   )

Witness

I've done my best; a fresh eye on the mystery
is what's required—like unblown planetary
rings the sandstorms pinwheeling over Mars mist
our eyes and drift our sleep down steep
inkwells where gravities collapse a sky to *blink,*   5
blink—and who on earth can scry the plan?
A notary is what's required, a star
witness: now you're new as lilypads, bones
good as gold spectacle rims—still half immersed,
what can you see? Where have you been? Justin   10
Huw, whisper me what breath has been
a blue falsework bracing up the stars?
The only grownups who have eyes like yours
can't, or won't, talk; old pipers; born astronomers.

The Villanelle and Sestina

     The villanelle and the sestina are two of many exotic forms of poetry
imported from France and Italy into England by poets who wanted the
opportunities of discovery that intricate forms afford. In a sense, a poet
"discovers" meaning through exploration, and takes on the challenge of
a complex form in order to see where the imagination might be led. As
we have already seen with the sonnet form, the restraints imposed on
the poet by intricate forms can be liberating instead of confining. Just
as the rules of basketball make it possible for a great player to excel
within the context of that specific game, so the sonnet, the villanelle, the
sestina, and other forms give certain poets a chance to display their wit
or explore the hidden intricacies of their own voice. To go back to the

analogy between poetic forms and musical instruments: Where would a great violinist be without a violin? The instrument itself provides the opportunity for the violinist to exploit a hitherto unknown and otherwise unknowable talent for making lovely music.

The **villanelle**, like many French and Italian forms, makes much of ingenious repetitions. It is nineteen lines long, and is divided into six stanzas: five triplets (three-line stanzas) and one final quatrain (a four-line stanza). The stanzas themselves must follow a strict rhyme scheme: ABA ABA ABA ABA ABA ABAA. In addition, the first and last lines of the first stanza become, alternately, the last lines of the second, third, fourth, and fifth stanzas. These same two repeating lines also form the last two lines of the poem. The trick is for the poet to write two lines rich enough in implications to convey deeper and deeper meanings throughout the changing context. Here is a fine modern example of the villanelle, by Dylan Thomas.

DYLAN THOMAS (1914–1953)

Do Not Go Gentle into That Good Night

Do not go gentle into that good night,
Old age should burn and rave at close of day;
Rage, rage against the dying of the light.

Though wise men at their end know dark is right,
Because their words had forked no lightning they   5
Do not go gentle into that good night.

Good men, the last wave by, crying how bright
Their frail deeds might have danced in a green bay,
Rage, rage against the dying of the light.

Wild men who caught and sang the sun in flight,   10
And learn, too late, they grieved it on its way,
Do not go gentle into that good night.

Grave men, near death, who see with blinding sight
Blind eyes could blaze like meteors and be gay,
Rage, rage against the dying of the light.   15

And you, my father, there on the sad height,
Curse, bless, me now with your fierce tears, I pray.
Do not go gentle into that good night.
Rage, rage against the dying of the light.

Notice how strong and memorable the first and third lines are: "Do not go gentle into that good night" and "Rage, rage against the dying of the light." Thomas has cleverly altered the grammar of the first line to jar us, slightly: Think how less interesting the line would be if he had written: "Do not go *gently* into that good night." In the second stanza, that first line is given a new shock of meaning: The dying man becomes "men," wise men who, "Because their words had forked no lightning" (that is, made no real impact on the world), are unable to die peaceably. The poet begins a succession of hypothetical "men," following up wise men with good, wild, and grave men, who respond differently to the challenge of death, depending on their limitations. The final stanza brings the poem back to the occasion of the death of the poet's father, who is addressed in the same terms as in the first stanza; these terms, however, have been made infinitely richer by the previous four stanzas. The poem ends with great resolve and fiercely controlled emotion. The two refrain lines have been elevated and subtly complicated by their progress through the form.

The **sestina** is another import from France that has been popular for centuries. It is even more intricate than the villanelle, because it consists of thirty-nine lines divided into six sestets (six-line stanzas) and one final triplet (a three-line stanza). Instead of being rhymed, the stanzas all use the same six end words, which are repeated according to a particular scheme: ABCDEF FAEBDC CFDABE ECBFAD DEACFB BDFECA BDF (ECA). Note that the final triplet must use all six end words, three of them embedded within the lines. Obviously, the sestina demands immense patience and skill from the poet. Here is a recent example of the form by Robert Pack.

ROBERT PACK (1929–   )

The Thrasher in the Willow by the Lake

Now I can tell you. Hearing the shrill leaves
Swishing with your hair, I can recall
Just how it happened: the air was thick and still,
Like now, and I could see the lake reflect
The thrasher in the willow tree. I paused,   5
Knowing that I could never make her change.

I told her that I thought no simple change
Could help—it was too late for help—but still
The thrasher in the willow tree had paused
As if it were an omen to reflect   10
What the lake desired so that I could recall
Myself in the stirred wind and fish-like leaves.

I stared at her among the willow leaves;
If she looked young or old or if some change
Showed rippling in her face, I can't recall.   *15*
I know the thrasher saw her when he paused
Over the lake as if he could reflect
Upon his past, stop it and keep it still.

Like this I held her—she would not stay still.
I watched, just like the thrasher, as the leaves   *20*
Stirred in the willow tree, and then I paused,
Groping for breath, to see the lake reflect
The blurring wind. Her face refused to change
Enough because she knew I would recall

That moment always, that I would recall   *25*
When her eye met the thrasher's eye—and paused,
And might have, but never did, let me change.
Her lake sounds gurgled with the fish-like leaves,
And if you listen, you can hear them still.
Listen, they call in the willow, they reflect   *30*

The crying of the lake, and they reflect
The words she might have said to make me change.
Maybe she said them, but I can't recall
Ever hearing them in the willow leaves
When the thrasher blinked and her eye went still.   *35*
You know now why I brought you here and paused,

And since I could not change when the sun paused
To reflect the thrasher's eye among the leaves,
The willow will recall your face when the lake goes still.

In this poem, the sestina form makes an eerie tale of murder even eerier.
The repetition seems to magnify the speaker's madness as he recounts
the murder scene to another person, lingering over and returning to a
succession of images. Even the name of the bird, the "thrasher," is ominous. The repeating words—*leaves, recall, still, reflect, paused, change*—
become an index of the narrator's insanity as he rehashes the story in
slow motion. The story culminates in the last stanza, which recapitulates
the main elements in compact form. Robert Pack could hardly have
found a form more appropriate to his story.

Free Verse—the Effects of Shape

In our discussion of free verse in Chapter 11, we emphasized that
no verse is really "free" if it's any good. Poets writing in free verse often
depend on echoing sounds, or rhyme, for effects. These effects are

simply unpredictable or irregular. The *shape* of a free verse poem, too, is important. All poems present a picture on the page; the eye responds to a poem well before the ear. Poets can do certain things with a "fat" or wide poem that they can't do with a long, thin one. Long lines create sweeping gestures that can't be attained by very short lines, for instance; short lines, with their staccato effects on the eye as well as the ear, are perfect for certain other kinds of images. In Walt Whitman's poem, "To a Locomotive in Winter," for example, the long lines seem appropriate for describing a hulking, powerful machine. The "canvas" is wide enough.

WALT WHITMAN   (1819–1892)

To a Locomotive in Winter

Thee for my recitative,
Thee in the driving storm even as now, the snow, the winter-day declining,
Thee in thy panoply, thy measur'd dual throbbing and thy beat convulsive,
Thy black cylindric body, golden brass and silvery steel,
Thy ponderous side-bars, parallel and connecting rods, gyrating, shut-   5
    tling at thy sides,
Thy metrical, now swelling pant and roar, now tapering in the distance,
Thy great protruding head-light fix'd in front,
Thy long, pale, floating vapor-pennants, tinged with delicate purple,
The dense and murky clouds out-belching from thy smoke-stack,
Thy knitted frame, thy springs and valves, the tremulous twinkle of   10
    thy wheels,
Thy train of cars behind, obedient, merrily following,
Through gale or calm, now swift, now slack, yet steadily careering;
Type of the modern—emblem of motion and power—pulse of the continent,
For once come serve the Muse and merge in verse, even as here I see thee,
With storm and buffeting gusts of wind and falling snow,   15
By day thy warning ringing bell to sound its notes,
By night thy silent signal lamps to swing.

Fierce-throated beauty!
Roll through my chant with all thy lawless music, thy swinging lamps
    at night,
Thy madly-whistled laughter, echoing, rumbling like an earthquake,   20
    rousing all,
Law of thyself complete, thine own track firmly holding,
(No sweetness debonair of tearful harp or glib piano thine,)
Thy trills of shrieks by rocks and hills return'd,
Launch'd o're the prairies wide, across the lakes,
To the free skies unpent and glad and strong.   25

Notice how lines in this poem gather weight by their very length, by the way they seem to spill over, much as an engine spills over in real life, barely able to contain its incredible power within the limits of its physical shape. If you read the poem aloud, you'll notice how the long lines contribute to the poem's majesty, which reflects the majesty of the machine and the imagination that invented and controls it.

The "thin" poem, a poem made up of short lines, also has its uses. "A Work of Artifice" by Marge Piercy focuses on a bonsai tree, a long thin tree, which, by the end of the poem, becomes a symbol for all "pruned" things. The poem, with its own "pruning," is deeply ironic. It argues *against* pruning, which stifles the growth of naturally blooming things in nature: trees, poems, or people. Notice how the short lines contribute to the poem's total effect.

MARGE PIERCY   (1936—   )

A Work of Artifice

The bonsai tree
in the attractive pot
could have grown eighty feet tall
on the side of a mountain
till split by lightning.   5
But a gardener
carefully pruned it.
It is nine inches high.
Every day as he
whittles back the branches   10
the gardener croons,
It is your nature
to be small and cozy,
domestic and weak;
how lucky, little tree,   15
to have a pot to grow in.
With living creatures
one must begin very early
to dwarf their growth:
the bound feet,   20
the crippled brain,
the hair in curlers,
the hands you
love to touch.

POEMS FOR FURTHER READING

Read each poem and answer the questions that follow.

RICHARD TILLINGHAST (1940–   )

Shooting Ducks in South Louisiana

For David Tillinghast

The cold moon led us coldly
  —three men in a motorboat—
down foggy canals before dawn
    past cut sugarcane in December.
    Mud-banks came alive by flashlight.   *5*
Black cottonmouth moccasins
  —the length of a man in the bayou—
slid into black water, head high,
  cocky as you might feel
stepping out on Canal Street   *10*
  going for coffee at 4 A.M.
    at the *Café du Monde.*

An Indian trapper called to us
  from his motorized pirogue,
    Cajun French on his radio,—   *15*
taking muskrat, swamp rat, weasel,
  "anything with fur."

Marsh life waking in the dark:
gurgling, sneaking, murdering, whooping—
  a muskrat breast-stroking through weeds toward food,   *20*
    his sleek coat parted smooth by black satin water—
frogs bellowing, bulbous waterlilies adrift
  cypresses digging their roots into water-borne ooze
dark juices collapsing cell-walls,
    oil rigs flaring thinly at daybreak.   *25*

Light dawned in our hunting-nerves.
We called to the ducks in their language.
They circled, set wing, glided into range.
  Our eyes saw keener.
Our blood leaped. We stood up and fired—   *30*
  And we didn't miss many that day,
    piling the boat between us with mallards.

The whole town of Cutoff ate ducks that Sunday.
　　I sat in the boat,
　　　　bloody swamp-juice sloshing my boots,　　　　　　　　*35*
　　　　　　ears dulled by the sound of my gun,—
and looked at a drake I had killed:
　　　sleek neck hanging limp,
　　　　　green head bloodied,
　　　　　　raucous energy stopped.　　　　　　　　　　　*40*
I plucked a purple feather from his dead wing,
and wore the life of that bird in my hat.

QUESTIONS

1. Count out the number of poetic feet in each line. (Remember: One strong beat equals one foot. There can be any number of extra, unstressed syllables.) Does any pattern seem to emerge?
2. Why does the poet break this poem into separate stanzas?
3. Notice that some lines are indented. Why do you think the poet chose to indent certain lines and not others?
4. What is the poet's tone in the last two lines? How does the relative formality of those lines (they are pentameters) affect their meaning?

MARILYN WANIEK　(1946–　　)

Old Bibles

I throw things away
usually, but there's
this whole shelf
of Bibles in my house.
Old Bibles, with pages missing　　　　　　　　　　　　*5*
or scribbled by children
and black covers chewed by puppies.
I believe in euthanasia,
but I can't get rid of them.
It's a sin,　　　　　　　　　　　　　　　　　　　　*10*
like stepping on a crack
or not crossing your fingers
or dropping the flag.

I did that once,
and for weeks　　　　　　　　　　　　　　　　　　　*15*
a gaunt bearded stranger
in tricolored clothes
came to get me,

moaning,
Give me my flag.   *20*
And Bibles are worse,
they maybe have souls
like little birds fluttering
over the dump
when the wind blows their pages.   *25*
Bibles are holy, blessed,
they're like
kosher.

So I keep them,
a row of solemn apostles   *30*
doomed to life.
and I wait for the great collection
and conflagration,
when they'll all burn together
with a sound like the wings   *35*
of a flock of doves:
little ash ascensions
of the Word.

QUESTIONS

1. How do the line breaks in this poem contribute to what the poet wants to say?
2. How does the poem's subject, including the title, exercise a unifying force on the poem?
3. What use does this poet make of stanza breaks?
4. A central image in this poem is the bird. Follow the image through the poem until its final incarnation in the flock of doves (or the mythical phoenix, said to rise up from its own ashes, to which the poet alludes in the last two lines). For what reasons might the poet have chosen to end the poem with this image? How does it relate to the flag image that arises earlier in the poem?

LUCILLE CLIFTON   (1936–   )

Homage to My Hips

these hips are big hips.
they need space to
move around in.
they don't fit into little
petty places. these hips   *5*
are free hips.
they don't like to be held back.

these hips have never been enslaved,
they go where they want to go
they do what they want to do.   *10*
these hips are mighty hips.
these hips are magic hips.
i have known them
to put a spell on a man and
spin him like a top!   *15*

QUESTIONS

1. "Homage to My Hips" is, of course, a funny poem. What are the sources of this humor? Cite specific lines and describe effects that may be called comic.

2. What "picture" does this poem make on the page and how is this appropriate?

3. Even though this poem is written in free verse, can you find any controlling factors?

4. This poem has an unusual tone. How would you describe it? (Begin by considering the word "petty" in the fifth line.)

5. Puns play a large role in the success of this poem (a pun is a word or phrase that contains more than one meaning). Find several puns and show how they enlarge the poem's sphere of meaning. ("these hips are free hips," for instance, is a punning line. You can begin there.)

JUDGING QUALITY
IN POETRY

In our age there is no such thing as "keeping out of politics." All issues are political issues, and politics itself is a mass of lies, evasions, folly, hatred and schizophrenia. When the general atmosphere is bad, language must suffer.

—*GEORGE ORWELL*

Evaluation: From the Inside Out

The place to begin an evaluation of a poem is on the inside. Read the poem carefully and judge it, word by word, line by line, then as a whole. Once you understand more completely the elements of poetry—things like metrics and rhyme, metaphors and symbols—you'll eventually be able to discern their proper use. As with any craft or discipline, the more you know about it, the easier it becomes to recognize quality.

Poetry, like all the arts and even some sciences, depends on subjective opinions, but this doesn't mean that "anything goes." Far from it: When you're sick, the doctor considers your symptoms, and then makes an educated guess about what illness might be producing these symptoms. So an experienced reader makes an estimate of a poem's value based on knowledge of what works and what doesn't in a good poem. Most of the poems included in this book have withstood decades, even centuries, of close reading—which says something about their quality. Bad poems tend, in time, to evaporate. There seems little doubt that the best poems of Shakespeare, Milton, Donne, Wordsworth, Eliot, and Frost are "good." Yet even the best poets write poems of differing quality. Most critics, for instance, now believe that the bulk of Wordsworth's poetry written after 1815 is quite awful, though Wordsworth lived and wrote until 1850! Perhaps we can learn something by comparing an early and widely praised poem of his with one written later. "Upon Westminster Bridge," dated September 3, 1802, is commonly thought of as one of Wordsworth's finest poems.

WILLIAM WORDSWORTH (1770–1850)

Composed upon Westminster Bridge, September 3, 1802

Earth has not anything to show more fair:
Dull would he be of soul who could pass by
A sight so touching in its majesty:
This city now doth, like a garment, wear
The beauty of the morning; silent, bare,   *5*
Ships, towers, domes, theaters, and temples lie
Open unto the fields, and to the sky;
All bright and glittering in the smokeless air.
Never did sun more beautifully steep
In his first spendor, valley, rock, or hill;   *10*
Ne'er saw I, never felt, a calm so deep!
The river glideth at his own sweet will:
Dear God! the very houses seem asleep;
And all that mighty heart is lying still!

Let's compare this poem to another Wordsworth sonnet on a similar theme, written twenty years later:

Patriotic Sympathies

Last night, without a voice, that Vision spake
Fear to my Soul, and sadness which might seem
Wholly dissevered from our present theme;
Yet, my beloved country! I partake
Of kindred agitations for thy sake;   *5*
Thou, too, dost visit oft my midnight dream;
Thy glory meets me with the earliest beam
Of light, which tells that Morning is awake.
If aught impair thy beauty or destroy,
Or but forbode destruction, I deplore   *10*
With filial love the sad vicissitude;
If thou hast fallen, and righteous Heaven restore
The prostrate, then my spring-time is renewed,
And sorrow bartered for exceeding joy.

A quick reading of both poems should confirm the judgment of the ages: The first poem is fresher, more vivid, more interesting in every way. It holds our attention. Reading the second poem seems too much like hard work! It is easy to keep losing one's place. Readers tend to forget this kind of poem as soon as they turn the page. Why should this be so?

Notice that in the first poem Wordsworth writes from a specific viewpoint, looking at the sleeping city at dawn from Westminster Bridge. The second, later poem has no viewpoint to speak of. It might as well take place in outer space! Simply comparing the two titles, in fact, illustrates that one poem takes place in a specific location, while the other lacks a foothold in the real world. As a title, "Patriotic Sympathies" calls up a tangle of **stock responses**—a set of ready-made emotions that go with a particular subject, such as patriotism. In "Upon Westminster Bridge," Wordsworth takes pains to present a sharp image in the form of a metaphor early in the poem: "This city now doth, like a garment, wear / the beauty of morning." By contrast, we find in the later sonnet almost no concrete imagery or arresting metaphors. The poet relies instead on sentimental phrases, such as "My beloved country!" He takes us by the elbow and screams, "Look, I adore my country. We should all adore our country!" In the earlier poem, he quietly makes us *feel* the majesty of London at dawn, with its domes and temples all "bright and glittering in the smokeless air." One clear difference between the poems emerges that could serve as a general rule: Strong poetry tends to present a situation directly, in fresh terms, using sharp imagery that calls up complex or original sentiments. Weaker poetry often relies on sentimentality and stock responses, on reactions that accompany the subject in general and are not necessarily specific to the poem at hand.

Let's focus briefly on some common aspects of weak poetry; remember, though, that poems can be weak in so many different ways that it would take volumes to explore the topic thoroughly. As we have seen, **sentimentality**, which may be defined as "unearned emotion," plagues many amateurish poems. If you write a poem about the death of a puppy dog, it will probably be sentimental, because this subject in itself is fraught with obvious emotions. When a poet doesn't have to work very hard to jerk a tear, he or she probably won't. Birthday cards and high school alma maters also tend to be sentimental, because they rely on situations that are emotional (such as one's nostalgia for high school days gone by) rather than seeking out original feelings. Here is a stanza from an actual high school anthem:

> As long as suns shall rise or set,
> As long as eagles fly so high,
> As long as ocean waves are wet,
> We'll cling to you, dear senior high.

EXERCISE

The poem that follows is full of sentimentality. Point out sentimental phrases or words and explain why the situation and the language used to descibe it are unequal to each other.

GENEVIEVE SMITH WHITFORD

Gray September Day

(published 1982)

On a gray September day
we drive away
from our last child,
standing uncertainly
on a strange college campus,   5
waving good-bye
to his childhood
and his family.
There is a wrench
and a rush of tears   ı   10
as this last cord is cut,
another one of life's connections
broken,
leaving us weakened
and detached.   15

Now we move in new directions,
following our interests,
developing our talents,
remembering what we were
before we had children,   20
for now we are all of that
and more.

Another common fault of weaker poems is their use of **clichés**, which are words or phrases that have become trite or hackneyed through overuse. Metaphors, especially, seem to attract clichés. "Quick as a flash," for instance, is a metaphor destined to kill any poem about speed. The mind turns off when it hears a clichéd metaphor; it doesn't picture something flashing and think how quickly flashes flash. Clichés are the enemy of real thought, because they give the readers the impression of having thought without making them actually visualize things. A related problem is the use of an inexact or inappropriate word, phrase, or metaphor. A famous stanza from "A Psalm of Life" by Henry Wadsworth Longfellow (1807–1882) features a misfired metaphor:

> Lives of great men all remind us
>   We can make our lives sublime,
> And, departing leave behind us
>   Footprints on the sands of time.

Apart from the commonplace cliché "the sands of time," how appropriate is this metaphor for the idea of permanence? Footprints on a beach last for only a few hours, at best, before the tide sweeps them away. One hopes that the lives of great men make a deeper impression on the memory of the world than this! Longfellow probably didn't stop to reflect on the inappropriateness of his metaphor. Inappropriateness is a major problem that plagues bad poetry, as we see in the following well-known lines from a poem on the death of Queen Victoria, written by one of her subjects from India:

> Dust to dust, and ashes to ashes,
> Into the tomb the Great Queen dashes.

How can a dead queen "dash"? The word "dashes" is absurd here, and its effect is unintentionally comic.

Lack of subtlety, clashing consonants, poor logic, fuzzy imagery, confused or "mixed" metaphors—these are more problems that occur frequently in weaker poems. Trained readers, those who have learned to read with their eyes and ears open and with their minds critically alert, will learn to spot these problems. Unquestioning readers are inevitably poor readers. So, as you read, keep asking yourself questions: Is this fresh? Have I read this kind of thing before? Does this make sense?

EXERCISE

The following poems vary in quality. Write a brief paragraph on each one, pointing out things that strike you as positive or negative aspects. Feel free to make comparisons.

LAURENCE BINYON   (1869–1943)

For the Fallen

With proud thanksgiving, a mother for her children,
England mourns for her dead across the sea.

Flesh of her flesh they were, spirit of her spirit,
Fallen in the cause of the free.

Solemn the drums thrill: Death august and royal   *5*
Sings sorrow up into immortal spheres.
There is music in the midst of desolation
And a glory that shines upon our tears.

They went with songs to the battle, they were young,
Straight of limb, true of eye, steady and aglow.   *10*
They were staunch to the end against odds uncounted,
They fell with their faces to the foe.

They shall grow not old, as we that are left grow old:
Age shall not weary them, nor the years condemn.
At the going down of the sun and in the morning   *15*
We will remember them.

They mingle not with their laughing comrades again;
They sit no more at familiar tables of home;
They have no lot in our labour of the day-time;
They sleep beyond England's foam.   *20*

But where our desires are and our hopes profound,
Felt as a well-spring that is bidden from sight,
To the innermost heart of their own land they are known
As the stars are known to the Night;

As the stars that shall be bright when we are dust,   *25*
Moving in marches upon the heavenly plain,
As the stars that are starry in the time of our darkness,
To the end, to the end, they remain.

RICHARD EBERHART (1904–   )

The Fury of Aerial Bombardment

You would think the fury of aerial bombardment
Would rouse God to relent; the infinite spaces
Are still silent. He looks on shock-pried faces.
History, even, does not know what is meant.

You would feel that after so many centuries
God would give man to repent; yet he can kill   *5*
As Cain could, but with multitudinous will,
No farther advanced than in his ancient furies.

Was man made stupid to see his own stupidity?
Is God by definition indifferent, beyond us all?   *10*

Is the eternal truth man's fighting soul
Wherein the Beast ravens in its own avidity?

Of Van Wettering I speak, and Averill,
Names on a list, whose faces I do not recall
But they are gone to early death, who late in school   *15*
Distinguished the belt feed lever from the belt holding pawl.

GENEVIEVE SMITH WHITFORD

To My Daughters

(published 1982)

Thank you, my daughters
for being feminine,
for wanting children,
for nursing babies,
(and spreading the word),   *5*
for being relaxed and loving
with your families,
but losing patience sometimes,
relieving me of the guilt I felt
when I couldn't cope with you.   *10*
Thank you for caring about your homes,
and for teaching me to use bright colors
and natural foods.
Thank you for being resourceful
and creative,   *15*
and for honing your intuitive minds
with an enlightened intelligence.
Thank you for being concerned
about the world,
but willing to stay home   *20*
while your children are young.
Thank you for giving
to family and friends,
but reserving some energy
for growing.   *25*
You are doing better than I
with your children
and your lives,
which makes me think
that I did something right,   *30*
after all.

PHILIP LEVINE   (1928–   )

My Son and I

In a coffee house at 3 a.m.
and he believes
I'm dying. Outside the wind
moves along the streets
of New York City picking up   5
abandoned scraps of newspapers
and tiny messages of hope
no one hears. He's dressed
in worn corduroy pants
and shirts over shirts,   10
and his hands are stained
as mine once were
with glue, ink, paint.
A brown stocking cap
hides the thick blond hair   15
so unlike mine. For forty
minutes he's tried not
to cry. How are his brothers?
I tell him I don't know,
they have grown away   20
from me. We are Americans
and never touch on this
stunned earth where a boy
sees his life fly past
through a car window. His mother?   25
She is deaf and works
in the earth for days, hearing
the dirt pray and guiding
the worm to its feasts. Why
do I have to die? Why   30
do I have to sit before him
no longer his father, only
a man? Because the given
must be taken, because
we hunger before we eat,   35
because each small spark
must turn to darkness.
As we said when we were kids
and knew the names of everything
. . . just because. I reach   40
across the table and take
his left hand in mine.
I have no blessing. I can

tell him how I found
the plum blossom before   *45*
I was thirty, how once
in a rooming house in Alicante
a man younger than I,
an Argentine I barely understood,
sat by me through the night   *50*
while my boy Teddy cried out
for help, and how when he slept
at last, my friend wept
with thanks in the cold light.
I can tell him that his hand   *55*
sweating in mine can raise
the Lord God of Stones,
bring down the Republic of Lies,
and hold a spoon. Instead
I say it's late, and he pays   *60*
and leads me back
through the empty streets
to the Earl Hotel, where
the room sours with the mould
of old Bibles dumped down   *65*
the air-shaft. In my coat
I stand alone in the dark
waiting for something,
a flash of light, a song,
a remembered sweetness   *70*
from all the lives I've lost.
Next door the TV babbles
on and on, and I give up
and sway toward the bed
in a last chant before dawn.   *75*

Difficulty in Poetry

Students often assume that poetry is "difficult," and it can be. Poems written a long time ago may refer to events and circumstances no longer familiar, and the language of these poems can present difficulties. Language is constantly in evolution, and words and expressions change their meanings over time. Words did not mean the same thing in Shakespeare's time that they mean now. That is why, without footnotes, even the dirty jokes in a Shakespearen play may be lost on the contemporary reader. Reading the literature of the past can thus seem like an act of exhumation—a digging up of old bones. It takes patience to read the footnotes or look up unfamiliar words or phrases in a dictionary. But the effort is rewarding. Great literature is the repository of human wisdom. It is, as Ezra Pound once said, "news that stays news." Few readers who persist in the study of literature find themselves disappointed in the end, because literature offers a kind of knowledge unavailable from any other source.

Poets themselves occasionally cultivate an element of difficulty. A beginning reader of poems, for example, can't expect to understand some of the more complex, visionary poems of William Blake (1757–1827), which depend on a private mythology developed by the poet himself. Likewise, some of the best poems by Keats, Shelley, and Hopkins—to name a few obvious examples—rely on allusions to ancient literature and mythology that go beyond the knowledge of the average modern reader. This can be discouraging. But no one ever said that learning was easy, nor has anyone ever denied that the effort pays off. Students have to begin with easier poems and work up to the more difficult ones, just as in mathematics they begin with arithmetic and proceed, via algebra and geometry, to the more difficult branches of that discipline, such as linear algebra or probability theory.

In modern poetry, difficulty frequently comes from the subject matter itself. In "The Waste Land" (1922), T. S. Eliot tried to incorporate the sense of dislocation and confusion that beset Europe in the wake of World War I. It seemed, to those who were aware of what was happening, that the great traditions of European thought and feeling had broken down, that "meaning" itself was impossible to find. Eliot's poem, which contains obscure fragments and dislocating quotations from other languages, including ancient Greek and Sanscrit, recreates the sense of cultural confusion that the poet believed was typical of the times. The ideal reader should bring a considerable knowledge of world literature and history to Eliot's poem, though even a reader without this knowledge can appreciate the poem's haunting tone and memorable cadences.

Many twentieth-century poets, moreover, have been influenced by modern painters, such as Picasso, who tried to subvert our "normal" ways of looking at objects in order to freshen our responses. Picasso once described his method of looking as "a dance around the object," a phrase that helps to explain the methods of many modern poets, who often confront their subjects from many different angles. Wallace Stevens was among those who tried to look at ordinary objects in unusual ways, as in "Anecdote of the Jar."

WALLACE STEVENS (1879–1955)

Anecdote of the Jar

I placed a jar in Tennessee,
And round it was, upon a hill.

It made the slovenly wilderness
Surround that hill.

The wilderness rose up to it,   5
And sprawled around, no longer wild.
The jar was round upon the ground
And tall and of a port in air.

QUESTIONS

1. How can the jar *make* the wilderness surround the hill? Was the wilderness "slovenly" before the jar was there?
2. Could the first line of this poem, which presents its premise, be called unusual? Why?
3. Why is the wilderness suddenly "no longer wild" in the second stanza?
4. What does Stevens mean when he says the jar "was of a port in air"?
5. In the final stanza, is Stevens *for* or *against* the effects produced by the placement of the jar? What does the jar represent?
6. How would you characterize the theme of this poem?

Difficulty in poetry can also stem from a particular poet's originality of phrasing, the unique way he or she addresses the world. Gerard Manley Hopkins, for example, was an extremely idiosyncratic stylist. The use of thickly clotted lines and heavy alliteration separate his poems from those of his Victorian contemporaries. There is real difficulty in his work, but it lies on the surface: The "meaning" of the poems is never far beyond the reader's immediate grasp. "God's Grandeur," which follows, is quite simple in meaning. The poet is saying that God is everywhere in nature, exhibiting His power. The difficulty exists in the poet's unusual metaphors and odd **diction** (for choice of words).

GERARD MANLEY HOPKINS   (1844–1889)

God's Grandeur

The world is charged with the grandeur of God.
    It will flame out, like shining from shook foil:
    It gathers to a greatness, like the ooze of oil
Crushed. Why do men then now not reck his rod?
Generations have trod, have trod, have trod;   5
    And all is seared with trade; bleared, smeared with toil;
    And wears man's smudge and shares man's smell: the soil
Is bare now, nor can foot feel, being shod.

And for all this, nature is never spent;
    There lives the dearest freshness deep down things;   10

And though the last lights off the black West went
   Oh, morning, at the brown brink eastward, springs—
Because the Holy Ghost over the bent
   World broods with warm breast and with ah! bright wings.

     Why has Hopkins chosen to write this way? Partly because he was
in search of a language adequate for the emotions he described. In a
letter to a friend, Hopkins once defined poetry as "the common language
heightened." He heightened what he took to be the common language
by using alliteration and assonance in a way peculiar to himself. Hopkins's idiosyncratic texture reflects his deeply original thought process,
and his language mirrors this process. The words explode on the page,
much as the images exploded in the poet's mind as he wrote them.

QUESTIONS

1. What does Hopkins mean when he says that God's greatness will flame out "like shining from shook foil"?
2. How does oil gather "to a greatness"? Examine the oil image in detail. Why does the word "Crushed" appear where it does?
3. The word "reck" means "heed." Paraphrase the question in which this word appears.
4. What effect does Hopkins achieve by repeating "have trod"?
5. Why can't feet feel anything, "being shod"?
6. Note that "God's Grandeur" is an Italian sonnet. How does the concluding sestet (the last six lines) differ from the octave (the first eight lines)?
7. Describe the impact of the final image in the last line. Is it appropriate for this poem? Why?

     Sometimes a poet's actual thought process is complex or in some
way disguised. Robert Frost is difficult in many respects because his
poems *seem* so easy (see "The Road Not Taken," which we analyzed in
Chapter 2). The surfaces of Frost's poems, unlike those of Hopkins, are
pellucid: They run brisk and clear as a mountain brook. But the depths
are often terribly murky. In the following interesting poem, Frost describes the kind of difficulty he encounters in his work.

ROBERT FROST (1874–1963)

For Once, Then, Something

Others taunt me with having knelt at well-curbs
Always wrong to the light, so never seeing

Deeper down in the well than where the water
Gives me back in a shining surface picture
Me myself in the summer heaven, godlike,   *5*
Looking out of a wreath of fern and cloud puffs.
Once, when trying with chin against a well-curb,
I discerned, as I thought, beyond the picture,
Through the picture, a something white, uncertain,
Something more of the depths—and then I lost it.   *10*
Water came to rebuke the too clear water.
One drop fell from a fern, and lo, a ripple
Shook whatever it was lay there at bottom,
Blurred it, blotted it out. What was that whiteness?
Truth? A pebble of quartz? For once, then, something.   *15*

QUESTIONS

1. How does Frost characterize the way other people see his way of looking at the world?
2. Where does the "story" in this poem begin?
3. What does Frost see in the depths?
4. "Water came to rebuke the too clear water," says Frost. How would you paraphrase this line? (Think of it as a subtle metaphor.)
5. Exactly what is it that the poet sees? How does he choose to interpret this? What is his tone at the end, when he says, "For once, then, something"?

It would be misleading, of course, to suggest that difficulty in poetry always springs from subtlety of thought or genuine complexity of subject matter. Especially in this century, poets have been allowed (by publishers and critics) to get away with obscurity that is inexcusable. Countless poems, lifted from the pages of most leading magazines that publish poetry, could be cited as examples. It's no wonder that most people, taking a new book of poems from the poetry section of a bookstore, find themselves overwhelmed or disgusted by what they read. The only positive side of this situation is that the best poets have rarely been indecipherable. Indeed, quite the opposite seems true: The best poets have always struggled to achieve great lucidity, and they always will.

Evaluation: From the Outside In

The place to begin reading poems is "up close," by looking at the words themselves to see how they fit together, by estimating tonal and thematic aspects of the poem—in short, by trying to understand the poem as a verbal object, a machine with multiple parts all in action together. Thus far, we have examined poems largely from the inside out, as if there were no world outside of these poems, almost as if they existed in a cultural vacuum. If this were the only level where poetry occurred, poems would still be worth reading, in themselves, for all sorts of personal reasons. Yet they would lack the extra dimension, the cultural dimension, that makes them especially valuable. Fortunately, poems exist as part of a living culture, and this culture is invariably replete with life assumptions that bear on one's reading of them. One way to get to know a particular time and place is to study its poetry. Through poetry you'll come to understand exactly what it felt like to be alive in that country, in that period. You'll discover what different people assumed was true about the nature of human relationships, their attitudes toward God and spiritual matters, their assumptions about what makes life worth living.

Innumerable ways of reading poems "from the outside in" have been developed through the centuries. There are Freudian critics and Marxian critics, for instance. The former bring psychological insights to bear on the poems, looking for instances of cultural neuroses, fixations, and so forth. The latter examine poems with an eye to the economic conditions that might lead poets to write in particular ways. These various approaches are valid. The important thing to remember is that any "outside" way of reading a poem has to be based on a firm grasp of what the poet has written, the actual words on the page. You can't just bring your own prejudices or wild theories to a poem and expect to read it well. Begin, as ever, with the poem itself. Find out what the poet meant to say. Then ask yourself what other critical tools or approaches might be helpful in understanding the assumptions that lie behind the poem, the social factors that led to its particular point of view.

Let's examine a famous poem "from the outside in," trying to ascertain the cultural assumptions that underpin the language. William Wordsworth wrote an important book-length poem called *The Prelude*, which tracks, in the poet's own words, the "growth of a poet mind." It is an autobiographical poem that traces the boy-hero, young Wordsworth, from childhood to young manhood, focusing on key moments when the poet was instructed by nature in the workings of the imagination. The poem follows the poet's spiritual growth, which is synonymous with his artistic growth. One often-read scene from *The Prelude*, written sometime between 1798 and 1800, concerns an episode in which the young boy steals a rowboat. The "her" referred to in the first line is Nature.

WILLIAM WORDSWORTH   (1770–1850)

From *The Prelude*

One summer evening (led by her) I found
A little boat tied to a willow tree
Within a rocky cave, its usual home.
Straight I unloosed her chain, and stepping in

Pushed from the shore. It was an act of stealth   *5*
And troubled pleasure, nor without the voice
Of mountain echoes did my boat move on;
Leaving behind her still, on either side,
Small circles glittering idly in the moon,
Until they melted all into one track   *10*
Of sparkling light. But now, like one who rows,
Proud of his skill, to reach a chosen point
With an unswerving line, I fixed my view
Upon the summit of a craggy ridge,
The horizon's utmost boundary; for above   *15*
Was nothing but the stars and the gray sky.
She was an elfin pinnace; lustily
I dipped my oars into the silent lake,
And, as I rose upon the stroke, my boat
Went heaving through the water like a swan;   *20*
When, from behind that craggy steep till then
The horizon's bound, a huge peak, black and huge,
As if with voluntary power instinct,
Upreared its head. I struck and struck again,
And growing still in stature the grim shape   *25*
Towered up between me and the stars, and still,
For so it seemed, with purpose of its own
And measured motion like a living thing,
Strode after me. With trembling oars I turned,
And through the silent water stole my way   *30*
Back to the covert of the willow tree;
There in her mooring place I left my bark,
And through the meadows homeward went, in grave
And serious mood; but after I had seen
That spectacle, for many days, my brain   *35*
Worked with a dim and undetermined sense
Of unknown modes of being; o'er my thoughts
There hung a darkness, call it solitude
Or blank desertion. No familiar shapes
Remained, no pleasant images of trees,   *40*
Of sea or sky, no colors of green fields;
But huge and mighty forms, that do not live
Like living men, moved slowly through the mind
By day, and were a trouble to my dreams.

   On the most obvious level, we can read this sequence of events like
this: One summer evening an impressionable, highly sensitive boy is
mysteriously led to pursue an adventure. He has a special relationship
with Nature, who calls him out. The boy steals a small boat and rows
himself out into the middle of a lake amidst a dramatic natural scene,

with moonlight and stars overhead and a huge craggy peak in the distance. The boy rows out until, suddenly, the presence of the craggy peak threatens him. He is overwhelmed by guilt and fear and dashes, rowing frantically, back to the safe moorings. The poet reflects that this little scene was instructive. He learned something about the power of the human conscience, embodied in the craggy peak. One could elaborate, of course, but this is essentially the literal level detected by most readers.

To read beyond this, however, involves looking more closely at the imagery and questioning the hidden cultural assumptions at work in the poem. That nature is feminine, for instance, is a common assumption. Look at the imagery, with its feminine terminology: the womblike "rocky cave" that offers the boat to the boy as a temptation, the mothering spirit that leads him on. The boat itself is "her," a traditional gender identity for boats, which "cradle" those who venture forth on water. The boy "lustily" rows, says Wordsworth, who unabashedly portrays the activity of rowing in an erotic way, the small boat "heaving through the water like a swan." The huge black peak that rears up its head contrasts with the silken femininity of the rowboat and "rocky cave." It represents the poet's conscience, which is masculine—another fairly traditional association. The child has "stolen" the boat and "trembles" as he rows back to the cove. That Wordsworth sees the peak (and the human conscience) in masculine terms is finally made explicit as he contemplates the incident; the feminine forms of nature seem erased from his memory, and what remains are "huge and mighty forms, that do not live / Like living men." They are supernatural, but masculine. Wordsworth goes on, throughout the poem, to argue that the young man is nurtured by the feminine spirit of nature, and he celebrates this instruction and the nurturing process; he seems grateful for the opportunity to "mate" with the feminine aspects of the world. But the male conscience in the end presides, however much it has been wedded to femininity. Men, Wordsworth argues later in the poem, must combine masculine and feminine sides; they must progress *through* nature to a more intellectual or mental state that is somehow "above" nature. In the final part of *The Prelude*, the poet ascends Mount Snowdon in Wales; the poet clearly identifies this ascent with a final stage of imaginative growth. In other words, men identify with feminine aspects of the world or nature, and they learn a good deal in the process. Their feelings are instructed by nature. But thought and feeling are viewed separately, and the former is associated with masculinity. The conscience is male, and men rise up to it, having been well taught by nature. The progress from feminine to masculine ideals is seen as heroic.

Wordsworth's view represents a fairly standard and important mythology of the imagination, one that pretty much forms a basis for modern views of creativity and people's relationship to the natural world.

Nevertheless, it pays to read beyond this view, to uncover implicit assumptions. The most obvious one is that nature is Mother Nature. Traditionally, the nurturing figure has been seen as a mother. For many reasons—women's lack of education and their consequent exclusion from the world of writing being the primary one—most poets have been men. As a result, the mother-son relationship evolved as a primary metaphor of men's relationship to nature. Wordsworth, like so many poets, assumes that the ideal man makes a necessary progression from his mother's arms to his wife's. He will, nevertheless, rise above the need for nurturing and become "a man." This involves rising above the feminine, much as the cliff in Wordsworth's boating scene rises above the small boy. In many poems, it is assumed that a man will incorporate feminine traits and grow beyond them, nevertheless benefiting from them. It is thought to be a good thing, for instance, for a man also to have nurturing instincts.

But what about women? The twentieth century is the first in which women have had equal access to the educational system, and the number of poets who are women has subsequently grown. Yet because the poetic tradition, with its myths and symbols, is in many ways male-biased, it has been difficult for women to graft onto this mythology. How does a woman, for instance, relate to Mother Nature? Nature is not, of course, really feminine. That's part of a mythology, one of thousands of cultural assumptions that we take for granted with every line we read. Reading "from the outside in" involves getting behind these crucial assumptions about life and understanding them for what they are. The mature reader, having understood a poem from the inside, can go further, can read for hidden biases, disguised assumptions, and unconscious meanings—*all of which are contained in the language itself.* He or she can learn more from a poem than what lies on the surface. This, of course, makes the act of reading much more challenging and, more importantly, much more rewarding.

Reading the World

Not many students who study poetry in college will go on, after they graduate, to read poems in any systematic way. One hopes, of course, that an interest will have been aroused, and that students who take poetry courses in college *will* occasionally read or reread poems. But something more is at stake than merely reading poems. Learning to read poems carefully, to understand the subtle nuances, the hidden metaphors, and the buried assumptions they contain, is one good way of learning to read or interpret the world.

The educated person, capable of reading *behind* the words when confronted with a political speech, a TV ad, a film or newspaper article, stands much less chance of being duped than the person untrained in close reading. As George Orwell points out in an important essay, "Politics and the English Language," language is too often used by unscrupulous or unconscious people as an instrument for obscuring or obstructing thought. The person trained in close reading, for instance, is not likely to let a politician off the hook who calls a concentration camp a "pacification center." One shudders to reread the newspapers of Hitler's Germany, which were crammed with signals that, to a trained eye, should have sounded an alarm. The close reader is a citizen on alert, ready to examine tone objectively, to expose sentimentality when it is used to disguise facts, to identify hidden and misused metaphors that may mislead an unwitting public. Failures of language often betray failures of intelligent thought or compassionate feeling. Viewed in this way, close reading becomes more than an aesthetic exercise. It becomes a political act that takes us well beyond the classroom or library. We learn to read mechanically in school; with perseverance, we can learn to read closely as well. But we must take this ability into the world, where language and symbols confront us at every turn, and where close reading can become, quite literally, a matter of life or death.

15

POETS IN DIALOGUE

No poet, no artist of any art, has his complete meaning alone. His significance, his appreciation is the appreciation of his relation to the dead poets and artists.

—T. S. ELIOT

Eliot's remark remains the classic formulation about poetic influence and the importance of tradition. No poet exists in isolation. Poets write in a public language, and they inherit from their predecessors a wealth of ideas, forms, linguistic tricks and turns, even phrases. Poems often grow out of poems, and there is nothing wrong with this. A heart surgeon would never imagine performing an operation without having a thorough knowledge of the kind of heart operations that have been done in the past. A variety of techniques and theories will have been passed down from doctor to doctor. Innovative heart surgeons don't invent operations from scratch; they improve upon already-existing types of operations, working within certain conventions of heart surgery. In this sense the art of poetry has much in common with surgery.

The aim of this concluding chapter is to show how poets work with an awareness of a continuous tradition—often by responding to earlier poems directly. The direct response of poet to poet, out present focus, is easy to track, but we should remember that poets more often respond indirectly, even unconsciously, to previous poems and poets. The library teems with critical studies of the influence of this or that poet on some later poet or group of poets; in fact, an entire theory of poetry has been erected on "the anxiety of influence," which suggests that poets often develop neurotic relationships to the poets who influence them most strongly. Except in rare cases, literary influence is rarely pathological. The best poets have always been grateful for the work that has gone before them, and they have modified it in their own individual ways. Let's examine a famous case of direct influence, a poem and a poem-in-response, written in Shakespeare's time.

CHRISTOPHER MARLOWE (1564–1593)

The Passionate Shepherd to His Love

Come live with me and be my love,
And we will all the pleasures prove
That hills and valleys, dale and field,
And all the craggy mountains yield!

There we will sit upon the rocks   5
And see the shepherds feed their flocks,
By shallow rivers, to whose falls
Melodious birds sing madrigals.

There will I make thee beds of roses
With a thousand fragrant posies;   10
A cap of flowers, and a kirtle
Embroider'd all with leaves of myrtle;

A gown made of the finest wool
Which from our pretty lambs we pull;
Fair lined slippers for the cold,   15
With buckles of the purest gold;

A belt of straw and ivy buds,
With coral clasps and amber studs:
And if these pleasures may thee move,
Come live with me and be my love!   20

Thy silver dishes, for thy meat
As precious as the gods do eat,
Shall on an ivory table be
Prepared each day for thee and me.

The shepherd swains shall dance and sing   25
For thy delight each May morning,
If these delights thy mind may move,
Then live with me and be my love!

SIR WALTER RALEIGH (1552?–1618)

The Nymph's Reply to the Shepherd

If all the world and love were young,
And truth in every shepherd's tongue,

These pretty pleasures might me move
To live with thee and be thy love.

Time drives the flocks from field to fold   5
When rivers rage and rocks grow cold,
And Philomel° becometh dumb;   *the nightingale*
The rest complains of cares to come.

The flowers do fade, and wanton fields
To wayward winter reckoning yields;   10
A honey tongue, a heart of gall,
Is fancy's spring, but sorrow's fall.

Thy gowns, thy shoes, thy beds of roses,
Thy cap, thy kirtle°, and thy posies   *dress*
Soon break, soon wither, soon forgotten—   15
In folly ripe, in reason rotten.

Thy belt of straw and ivy buds,
Thy coral clasps and amber studs,
All these in me no means can move
To come to thee and be thy love.   20

But could youth last and love still breed,
Had joys no date° nor age no need,   *conclusion*
Then these delights my mind might move
To live with thee and be thy love.

This poem-in-response by one poet to another represents the simplest
and most uncomplicated form of literary influence. Marlowe wrote his
poem without any knowledge that a famous response would be forth-
coming from his fellow poet, Sir Walter Raleigh. Raleigh apparently felt
that Marlowe's poem required this kind of response, in the voice of the
nymph. His "Nymph's Reply to the Shepherd" undercuts much of what
the naive shepherd in Marlowe's poem says to *his* nymph. Read the poems
again and answer these questions.

QUESTIONS

1. How does Raleigh's poem undercut or criticize Marlowe's?
2. In what ways does Raleigh's reply imitate in form and manner Marlowe's
   poem, and what tonal effects occur as a result of the imitation?
3. Are the last two lines of Raleigh's poem ironic? If so, why?
4. Can you identify irony in other parts of the Raleigh's poem? How does this
   irony depend on the earlier poem for its effects?
5. Consider Raleigh's poem from "the outside in," looking for cultural biases
   that underpin the poet's attitude toward male/female relations.

EXERCISE

Choose a poem from the Anthology that follows this chapter and write an ironic reply of your own. Imitate both the manner and form of the original.

An obvious form of imitation is **parody,** a literary work (poem, play, or story) that makes fun of another literary work, usually by imitating its style and form in a comic way. Here is the classic poem "Dover Beach" by Matthew Arnold, followed by a parody of it from the pen of a contemporary poet, Anthony Hecht.

MATTHEW ARNOLD   (1822–1888)

Dover Beach

The sea is calm to-night.
The tide is full, the moon lies fair
Upon the straits;—on the French coast the light
Gleams and is gone; the cliffs of England stand,
Glimmering and vast, out in the tranquil bay,   *5*
Come to the window, sweet is the night-air!
Only, from the long line of spray
Where the sea meets the moon-blanched land,
Listen! you hear the grating roar
Of pebbles which the waves draw back, and fling,   *10*
At their return, up the high strand,
Begin, and cease, and then again begin,
With tremulous cadence slow, and bring
The eternal note of sadness in.

Sophocles long ago   *15*
Heard it on the Ægæan, and it brought
Into his mind the turbid ebb and flow
Of human misery; we
Find also in the sound a thought,
Hearing it by this distant northern sea.   *20*

The Sea of Faith
Was once, too, at the full, and round earth's shore
Lay like the folds of a bright girdle furled.
But now I only hear
Its melancholy, long, withdrawing roar,   *25*
Retreating, to the breath
Of the night-wind, down the vast edges drear
And naked shingles of the world.

Ah, love, let us be true
To one another! for the world, which seems   *30*
To lie before us like a land of dreams,
So various, so beautiful, so new,
Hath really neither joy, nor love, nor light,
Nor certitude, nor peace, nor help for pain;
And we are here as on a darkling plain   *35*
Swept with confused alarms of struggle and flight,
Where ignorant armies clash by night.

ANTHONY HECHT (1923–   )

The Dover Bitch, A Criticism of Life

For Andrews Wanning

So there stood Matthew Arnold and this girl
With the cliffs of England crumbling away behind them,
And he said to her, "Try to be true to me,
And I'll do the same for you, for things are bad
All over, etc., etc."   *5*
Well now, I knew this girl. It's true she had read
Sophocles in a fairly good translation
And caught that bitter allusion to the sea,
But all the time he was talking she had in mind
The notion of what his whiskers would feel like   *10*
On the back of her neck. She told me later on
That after a while she got to looking out
At the lights across the channel, and really felt sad,
Thinking of all the wine and enormous beds
And blandishments in French and the perfumes.   *15*
And then she got really angry. To have been brought
All the way down from London, and then be addressed
As a sort of mournful cosmic last resort
Is really tough on a girl, and she was pretty.
Anyway, she watched him pace the room   *20*
And finger his watch-chain and seem to sweat a bit,
And then she said one or two unprintable things.
But you mustn't judge her by that. What I mean to say is,
She's really all right. I still see her once in a while
And she always treats me right. We have a drink   *25*
And I give her a good time, and perhaps it's a year
Before I see her again, but there she is,
Running to fat, but dependable as they come.
And sometimes I bring her a bottle of Nuit d'Amour.°   *a perfume*

Anthony Hecht's poem pokes fun at "Dover Beach" by referring directly to the circumstances and subject matter of Arnold's famous poem. Many parodies don't refer directly to the poems being mocked but merely imitate the manner of the poems and expect the readers to draw the associations. Most often, as in the preceding example, one poet takes another poet to task for his or her seriousness and turns a straight poem into a comic one. In "The Dover Bitch," Hecht has stolen his characters from Arnold and added a third, the speaker, who claims to have know the woman in the poem. Hecht lays bare a number of Arnold's hidden assumptions. In many ways, the Hecht poem proceeds in much the same way as the Raleigh poem, turning the same ideas on their heads.

QUESTIONS

1. What is the tone of Hecht's line, "With the cliffs of England crumbling behind them"?
2. How does Hecht's use of "etc., etc." affect the tone of his poem?
3. "It's true she had read/Sophocles in a fairly good translation," says the speaker in Hecht's poem. Discuss the effect of these lines on the reader. How are we to regard her? Does our attitude toward Arnold's heroine change as a result?
4. Has Hecht exposed any cultural biases implicit in Arnold's poem? Be specific.
4. Find some comic moments in the Hecht poem and show how they make fun of the Arnold poem. Relate specific passage to specific passage.
5. Compare the two endings. How does Hecht's poem differ in tone and manner?

Poets sometimes rely on a similar tradition or make use of a traditional subject, such as the Ulysses theme, which has its origin in Homer's epic poem, *The Odyssey*—a narrative in verse that tells the story of Odysseus, the Greek hero of the Trojan War. After the war, Odysseus set off by ship for his native island of Ithaca, where Penelope, his faithful wife, was waiting. Unfortunately, incident after incident prevented Odysseus from getting home quickly. He sailed for years, from disaster to disaster, while Penelope desperately fought off suitors. The story of Odysseus' homecoming remains a centerpiece of Western European Literature. Let's first see how a Victorian poet, Alfred, Lord Tennyson, approached the subject from a different angle, one stressing Ulysses restlessness *after* his arrival and settling in.

ALFRED, LORD TENNYSON   (1809–1892)

Ulysses

It little profits that an idle king,
By this still hearth, among these barren crags,
Matched with an agèd wife, I mete and dole°   *administer*
Unequal laws unto a savage race,
That hoard, and sleep, and feed, and know not me.   *5*
I cannot rest from travel: I will drink
Life to the lees: all times I have enjoyed
Greatly, have suffered greatly, both with those
That loved me, and alone; on shore, and when
Through scudding drifts the rainy Hyades°   *stars that were said to cause rain*   *10*
Vexed the dim sea. I am become a name;
For always roaming with a hungry heart
Much have I seen and known—cities of men
And manners, climates, councils, governments,
Myself not least, but honored of them all—   *15*
And drunk delight of battle with my peers,
Far on the ringing plains of windy Troy.
I am a part of all that I have met;
Yet all experience is an arch wherethrough
Gleams that untraveled world whose margin fades   *20*
Forever and forever when I move.
How dull it is to pause, to make an end,
To rust unburnished, not to shine in use!
As though to breathe were life! Life piled on life
Were all too little, and of one to me   *25*
Little remains; but every hour is saved
From that eternal silence, something more,
A bringer of new things; and vile it were
For some three suns to store and hoard myself,
And this grey spirit yearning in desire   *30*
To follow knowledge like a sinking star,
Beyond the utmost bound of human thought.
   This is my son, mine own Telemachus,
To whom I leave the scepter and the isle—
Well-loved of me, discerning to fulfill   *35*
This labor, by slow prudence to make mild
A rugged people, and through soft degrees
Subdue them to the useful and the good.
Most blameless is he, centered in the sphere
Of common duties, decent not to fail   *40*
In offices of tenderness, and pay
Meet adoration to my household gods,
When I am gone. He works his work, I mine.

There lies the port; the vessel puffs her sail;
There gloom the dark, broad seas. My mariners,   *45*
Souls that have toiled, and wrought, and thought with me—
That ever with a frolic welcome took
The thunder and the sunshine, and opposed
Free hearts, free foreheads—you and I are old;
Old age hath yet his honor and his toil.   *50*
Death closes all; but something ere the end,
Some work of noble note, may yet be done,
Not unbecoming men that strove with Gods.
The lights begin to twinkle from the rocks;
The long day wanes; the slow moon climbs; the deep   *55*
Moans round with many voices. Come, my friends,
'Tis not too late to seek a newer world.
Push off, and sitting well in order smite
The sounding furrows; for my purpose holds
To sail beyond the sunset, and the baths   *60*
Of all the western stars, until I die.
It may be that the gulfs will wash us down;
It may be we shall touch the Happy Isles,
And see the great Achilles, whom we knew.
Though much is taken, much abides; and though   *65*
We are not now that strength which in old days
Moved earth and heaven, that which we are, we are—
One equal temper of heroic hearts,
Made weak by time and fate, but strong in will
To strive, to seek, to find, and not to yield.   *70*

This poem, with its emphasis on Ulysses' urge to leave home in search of new adventures once again, has been popular since it appeared. It was certainly known to Robert Graves and Wallace Stevens, two recent poets who have chosen to write poems on the same subject. See how differently each approaches the original story.

ROBERT GRAVES (1895–1985)

Ulysses

To the much-tossed Ulysses, never done
   With woman whether gowned as wife or whore,
Penelope and Circe° seemed as one:
She like a whore made his lewd fancies run,
   And wifely she a hero to him bore.   5

³*Circe:* mythical sorceress who held Ulysses captive for a year.

Their counter-changings terrified his way;
    They were the clashing rocks, Symplegades,
Scylla and Charybdis° too were they;
Now they were storms frosting the sea with spray
    And now the lotus island's drunken ease.   10

They multiplied into the Sirens' throng,
    Forewarned by fear of whom he stood bound fast
Hand and foot helpless to the vessel's mast,
Yet would not stop his ears: daring their song
    He groaned and sweated till that shore was past.°   15

One, two and many: flesh had made him blind,
    Flesh had one pleasure only in the act,
Flesh set one purpose only in the mind—
Triumph of flesh and afterwards to find
    Still those same terrors wherewith flesh was racked.   20

His wiles were witty and his fame far known,
Every king's daughter sought him for her own,
    Yet he was nothing to be won or lost.
    All lands to him were Ithaca: love-tossed
He loathed the fraud, yet would not bed alone.   25

[8]*Scylla and Charybdis:* female monsters personifying twin perils in the Straits of
Messina—a dangerous rock and a whirlpool. If a ship evaded one, it was doomed by
the other.

[15]Ulysses' ship had to pass the land where the Sirens' irresistible song lured men onto
the rocks. He insisted on listening as he passed.

WALLACE STEVENS (1879–1955)

The World as Meditation

Is it Ulysses that approaches from the east,
The interminable adventurer? The trees are mended.
The winter is washed away. Someone is moving

On the horizon and lifting himself up above it.
A form of fire approaches the cretonnes of Penelope,   5
Whose mere savage presence awakens the world in which she dwells.

She has composed, so long, a self with which to welcome him,
Companion to his self for her, which she imagined,
Two in a deep-founded sheltering, friend and dear friend.

The trees had been mended, as an essential exercise   10
In an inhuman meditation, larger than her own.
No winds like dogs watched over her at night.

She wanted nothing he could not bring her by coming alone.
She wanted no fetchings. His arms would be her necklace
And her belt, the final fortune of their desire.   *15*

But was it Ulysses? Or was it only the warmth of the sun
On her pillow? The thought kept beating in her like her heart.
The two kept beating together. It was only day.

It was Ulysses and it was not. Yet they had met,
Friend and dear friend and a planet's encouragement.   *20*
The barbarous strength within her would never fail.

She would talk a little to herself as she combed her hair,
Repeating his name with its patient syllables,
Never forgetting him that kept coming constantly so near.

All three poets—Tennyson, Graves, and Stevens—write in some kind of
dialogue with their great predecessor, Homer. Yet each poet reinvents
the Ulysses myth in a unique way. Read all three poems again and then
answer the following questions.

QUESTIONS

1. In Homer's *Odyssey*, Ulysses is overjoyed to make it back to his native island
   and his wife's side. Tennyson, however, has drastically altered Ulysses' feelings
   to conform to certain Romantic notions of the hero that were popular in his
   day. What are Tennyson's hero's feelings about being home? What aspects
   of his own character does he recognize and value?
2. In the Greek myth, Ulysses has a son, Telemachus, who appears in Tennyson's
   poem. What views does Tennyson give his Ulysses with regard to his son?
   How do their assumptions about life differ?
3. In what ways is Graves's Ulysses different from Tennyson's?
4. Circe was the mythical temptress who waylaid Ulysses for a year and changed
   his shipmates into swine. Graves says, "Penelope and Circe seemed as one."
   He ends the poem with the idea that "All lands to him were Ithaca." What
   does this suggest about his Ulysses' perception of women and his attitude
   toward the home he has lost? Do you find this view objectionable?
5. Stevens looks at the story from Penelope's viewpoint. How would you characterize her state of mind as she awaits the homecoming of her long-lost
   husband?
6. What does Stevens mean when he says, "The trees had been mended, as an
   essential exercise/In an inhuman meditation, larger than her own"?
7. Stevens doesn't say whether or not Ulysses and Penelope were really reunited.
   "It was Ulysses and it was not," he writes. What does this poem suggest about
   the way Penelope viewed her marriage?
8. Can you learn anything about time-specific cultural biases, especially where
   sex roles are concerned, in these poems? Discuss the poems in turn.

EXERCISE

In the next two poems the speakers address their would-be lovers, and present various arguments in favor of closer, indeed sexual, involvement. The Parini poem consciously imitates Marvell in many respects. Compare the two poems, discussing the nature of the influence. How are these poems alike? How are they different?

ANDREW MARVELL   (1621–1678)

To His Coy Mistress

Had we but world enough, and time,
This coyness, Lady, were no crime.
We would sit down and think which way
To walk and pass our long love's day.
Thou by the Indian Ganges' side   5
Shouldst rubies find: I by the tide
Of Humber would complain. I would
Love you ten years before the Flood,
And you should, if you please, refuse
Till the conversion of the Jews.   10
My vegetable love should grow
Vaster than empires, and more slow;
An hundred years should go to praise
Thine eyes and on thy forehead gaze;
Two hundred to adore each breast;   15
But thirty thousand to the rest;
An age at least to every part,
And the last age should show your heart;
For, Lady, you deserve this state,
Nor would I love at lower rate.   20
   But at my back I always hear
Time's wingèd chariot hurrying near;
And yonder all before us lie
Deserts of vast eternity.
Thy beauty shall no more be found,   25
Nor, in thy marble vault, shall sound
My echoing song: then worms shall try
That long preserved virginity,
And your quaint honour turn to dust,
And into ashes all my lust: 30
The grave's a fine and private place,
But none, I think, do there embrace.
   Now therefore, while the youthful hue
Sits on thy skin like morning dew,

And while thy willing soul transpires   *35*
At every pore with instant fires,
Now let us sport us while we may,
And now, like amorous birds of prey,
Rather at once our time devour
Than languish in his slow-chapt power.   *40*
Let us roll all our strength and all
Our sweetness up into one ball,
And tear our pleasures with rough strife
Thorough the iron gates of life:
Thus, though we cannot make our sun   *45*
Stand still, yet we will make him run.

JAY PARINI   (1948–   )

To His Dear Friend, Bones

The arguments against restraint
in love, in retrospect, seem quaint;
I would have thought this obvious
to you, at least, whose serious
pursuit of intellectual grace   *5*
is not less equal to your taste
for all things richly formed. No good
will come of what we force. I should
be hesitant to say how long
this shy devotion has gone on,   *10*
how days beyond account have turned
to seasons as we've slowly learned
to speak a common tongue, to find
the world's erratic text defined
and stabilized. I should be vexed   *15*
to mention time at all, except
that, even as I write, a blear
October dampness feels like fear
externalized; I number days
in lots of thirty—all the ways   *20*
we have for counting breaths, so brief,
beside the measures of our grief
and joy. So let me obviate
this cold chronology and state
more simply what I mean: it's sure   *25*
enough, the grave will make obscure
whatever fierce, light moments love
affords. I should not have to prove
by metaphysical displays

of wit how numerous are the ways   *30*
in which it matters that we touch,
not merely with our hearts; so much
depends upon the skin, dear bones,
with all its various, humid tones,
the only barrier which contrives   *35*
to keep us in separate lives.

ANTHOLOGY I
Matters of Life and Death

ROBERT FROST (1874–1963)

"Out, Out—"

The buzz-saw snarled and rattled in the yard
And made dust and dropped stove-length sticks of wood,
Sweet-scented stuff when the breeze drew across it.
And from there those that lifted eyes could count
Five mountain ranges one behind the other   5
Under the sunset far into Vermont.
And the saw snarled and rattled, snarled and rattled,
As it ran light, or had to bear a load.
And nothing happened: day was all but done.
Call it a day, I wish they might have said   10
To please the boy by giving him the half hour
That a boy counts so much when saved from work.
His sister stood beside them in her apron
To tell them "Supper." At the word, the saw,
As if to prove saws knew what supper meant,   15
Leaped out at the boy's hand, or seemed to leap—
He must have given the hand. However it was,
Neither refused the meeting. But the hand!
The boy's first outcry was a rueful laugh,
As he swung toward them holding up the hand   20
Half in appeal, but half as if to keep
The life from spilling. Then the boy saw all—
Since he was old enough to know, big boy
Doing a man's work, though a child at heart—
He saw all spoiled. "Don't let him cut my hand off—   25
The doctor, when he comes. Don't let him, sister!"

So. But the hand was gone already.
The doctor put him in the dark of ether.
He lay and puffed his lips out with his breath.
And then—the watcher at his pulse too fright.   *30*
No one believed. They listened at his heart.
Little—less—nothing!—and that ended it.
No more to build on there. And they, since they
Were not the one dead, turned to their affairs.

WILLIAM SHAKESPEARE   (1564–1616)

That Time of Year Thou Mayst in Me Behold

That time of year thou mayst in me behold
When yellow leaves, or none, or few, do hang
Upon those boughs which shake against the cold,
Bare ruined choirs, where late the sweet birds sang.
In me thou see'st the twilight of such day   *5*
As after sunset fadeth in the west,
Which by and by black night doth take away,
Death's second self that seals up all in rest.
In me thou see'st the glowing of such fire,
That on the ashes of his youth doth lie,   *10*
As the deathbed whereon it must expire,
Consumed with that which it was nourished by.
This thou perceiv'st, which makes thy love more strong,
To love that well which thou must leave ere long.

WENDELL BERRY   (1934–   )

The Old Elm Tree by the River

Shrugging in the flight of its leaves,
it is dying. Death is slowly
standing up in its trunk and branches
like a camouflaged hunter. In the night
I am wakened by one of its branches   *5*
crashing down, heavy as a wall, and then
lie sleepless, the world changed.
That is a life I know the country by.
Mine is a life I know the country by.
Willing to live and die, we stand here,   *10*
timely and at home, neighborly as two men.
Our place is changing in us as we stand,
and we hold up the weight that will bring us down.
In us the land enacts its history.

When we stood it was beneath us, and was   *15*
the strength by which we held to it
and stood, the daylight over it
a mighty blessing we cannot bear for long.

JOHN KEATS (1795–1821)

Last Sonnet

Bright star, would I were steadfast as thou art—
    Not in lone splendour hung aloft the night,
And watching, with eternal lids apart,
    Like Nature's patient sleepless Eremite,
The moving waters at their priest-like task   *5*
    Of pure ablution round earth's human shores,
Or gazing on the new soft-fallen mask
    Of snow upon the mountains and the moors—
No—yet still steadfast, still unchangeable,
    Pillowed upon my fair love's ripening breast,   *10*
To feel for ever its soft fall and swell,
    Awake for ever in a sweet unrest,
        Still, still to hear her tender-taken breath,
        And so live ever—or else swoon to death.

PETER DAVISON (1928–   )

Cross Cut

Slumped on a pallet of winter-withered grass
you lie dead at my feet, in age not quite
a century, perhaps, but twice as old as I am,
in a pose your twisted trunk and dwindling leaves
had never hinted, even at your sickest.   *5*
How many stubs your gangrened upper branches
had turned into sockets and armpits
for squirrel, coon and starling
to burrow in! You thrust erect as stiff
as the memory of my oldest neighbor who watches   *10*
each new spring for your fluttering bloom
and every August for a pride of pears—
green to the eye, woody to the tooth,
taut and cidery to the fumbling tongue.
For years we've watched you dying from the top,   *15*
a peril to climbing children and seekers of shade,
but knew that, pear-like, you could stand for years,
heart eaten out, just fingering your life.

Perhaps I could have helped you out of the air
with some shreds of your stature left intact,   *20*
but now I've failed you. You lie invisible
behind the wall, your most disgraceful branches
lopped and hauled for firewood, resting scarred,
beyond your element, crushed by your own weight,
shapeless and pitiful as a beachbound whale.   *25*
Only inches above the nourishing ground
a cross-cut stump, stark white, reveals at bottom
you're still as lively as the day you bloomed.
The hearts of your leaves shone out in valentines
and your windborne, lilting, sinewy boughs   *30*
heaped proudly up toward the waning sun
those glowing, softly tinted, bumper bushels.

JOHN DRYDEN   (1631–1700)

To the Memory of Mr. Oldham°

Farewell, too little and too lately known,
Whom I began to think and call my own;
For sure our souls were near allied, and thine
Cast in the same poetic mould with mine.
One common note on either lyre did strike,   *5*
And knaves and fools we both abhorred alike.
To the same goal did both our studies drive,
The last set out the soonest did arrive.
Thus Nisus fell upon the slippery place,°
Whilst his young friend performed and won the race.   *10*
Oh, early ripe! to thy abundant store
What could advancing age have added more?
It might (what Nature never gives the young)
Have taught the numbers of thy native tongue.
But satire needs not those, and wit will shine   *15*
Through the harsh cadence of a rugged line.
A noble error, and but seldom made,
When poets are by too much force betrayed.
Thy generous fruits, though gathered ere their prime,
Still showed a quickness; and maturing time   *20*
But mellows what we write to the dull sweets of rhyme.
Once more, hail and farewell! farewell, thou young,
But ah! too short, Marcellus° of our tongue!

°John Oldham (1653–1683), a satiric poet.
⁹Nisus slipped in a pool of blood as he was about to win a race.
²³*Marcellus:* nephew of the Roman Emperor Augustus, who died young.

Thy brow's with ivy and with laurels bound;
But fate and gloomy night encompass thee around.   *25*

THEODORE ROETHKE   (1908–1963)

Wish for a Young Wife

My lizard, my lively writher,
May your limbs never wither,
May the eyes in your face
Survive the green ice
Of envy's mean gaze;   *5*
May you live out your life
Without hate, without grief,
May your hair ever blaze,
In the sun, in the sun,
When I am undone,   *10*
When I am no one.

HENRY VAUGHAN   (1621?–1695)

Peace

My soul, there is a country
  Far beyond the stars,
Where stands a wingèd sentry
  All skillful in the wars;
There, above noise and danger,   *5*
  Sweet peace sits crowned with smiles,
And one born in a manger
  Commands the beauteous files.
He is thy gracious friend,
  And (O my soul, awake!)   *10*
Did in pure love descend
  To die here for thy sake.
If thou canst get but thither,
  There grows the flower of peace,
The rose that cannot wither,   *15*
  Thy fortress, and thy ease.
Leave then thy foolish ranges;
  For none can thee secure,
But one who never changes,
  Thy God, thy life, thy cure.   *20*

JONATHAN SWIFT (1667–1745)

A Description of the Morning

Now hardly here and there an hackney-coach,
Appearing, showed the ruddy morn's approach.
Now Betty from her master's bed had flown,
And softly stole to discompose her own.
The slipshod prentice from his master's door   5
Had pared the dirt, and sprinkled round the floor.
Now Moll had whirled her mop with dextrous airs,
Prepared to scrub the entry and the stairs.
The youth with broomy stumps° began to trace   *worn-out brooms*
The kennel-edge,° where wheels had worn the place,   *sewer edge   10*
The small-coal man was heard with cadence deep,
Till drowned in shriller notes of chimney-sweep,
Duns° at his lordship's gate began to meet,   *creditors*
And Brickdust° Moll had screamed through half the street.   *used for cleaning*
The turnkey° now his flock returning sees,   *jailor*
Duly let out a-nights to steal for fees;
The watchful bailiffs take their silent stands;
And schoolboys lag with satchels in their hands.

THOMAS NASHE (1567–1601)

Spring, the Sweet Spring

Spring, the sweet spring, is the year's pleasant king,
Then blooms each thing, then maids dance in a ring,
Cold doth not sting, the pretty birds do sing:
Cuckoo, jug-jug, pu-we, to-witta-woo!

The palm and may make country houses gay,   5
Lambs frisk and play, the shepherds pipe all day,
And we hear aye birds tune this merry lay:
Cuckoo, jug-jug, pu-we, to-witta-woo!

The fields breathe sweet, the daisies kiss our feet,
Young lovers meet, old wives a-sunning sit,   10
In every street these tunes our ears do greet:
Cuckoo, jug-jug, pu-we, to-witta-woo!
Spring, the sweet spring!

WALT WHITMAN (1819–1892)

When I Heard the Learn'd Astronomer

When I heard the learn'd astronomer,
When the proofs, the figures, were ranged in columns before me,

When I was shown the charts and diagrams, to add, divide, and measure
        them,
When I sitting heard the astronomer where he lectured with much   5
        applause in the lecture-room,
How soon unaccountable I became tired and sick,
Till rising and gliding out I wander'd off by myself,
In the mystical moist night-air, and from time to time,
Look'd up in perfect silence at the stars.   10

JOHN CROWE RANSOM   (1888–1974)

Bells for John Whiteside's Daughter

There was such speed in her little body,
And such lightness in her footfall,
It is no wonder that her brown study
Astonishes us all.

Her wars were bruited in our high window.   5
We looked among orchard trees and beyond,
Where she took arms against her shadow,
Or harried unto the pond

The lazy geese, like a snow cloud
Dripping their snow on the green grass,   10
Tricking and stopping, sleepy and proud,
Who cried in goose, Alas,

For the tireless heart within the little
Lady with rod that made them rise
From their noon apple dreams, and scuttle   15
Goose-fashion under the skies!

But now go the bells, and we are ready;
In one house we are sternly stopped
To say we are vexed at her brown study,
Lying so primly propped.   20

E. A. ROBINSON   (1869–1935)

Richard Cory

Whenever Richard Cory went down town,
We people on the pavement looked at him:
He was a gentleman from sole to crown,
Clean favored, and imperially slim.
And he was always quietly arrayed,   5
And he was always human when he talked;

But still he fluttered pulses when he said,
"Good-morning," and he glittered when he walked.

And he was rich—yes, richer than a king—
And admirably schooled in every grace: 10
In fine, we thought that he was everything
To make us wish that we were in his place.

So on we worked, and waited for the light,
And went without the meat, and cursed the bread;
And Richard Cory, one calm summer night,   15
Went home and put a bullet through his head.

GREGORY ORR   (1947–   )

We Must Make a Kingdom of It

So that a colony will breed here,
love rubs together two words:
"I" and "she." How the long bone
of the personal pronoun
warms its cold length against her fur.   5

She plants the word "desire"
that makes the very air
amorous, that causes the light,
from its tall stalk, to bend down
until it almost kisses the ground.   10

It was green, I saw it—tendril
flickering from dry soil
like a grass snake's tongue;
call it "flame"—light
become life, what the word   15
wants, what the earth
in its turning
yearns for: to writhe and rise up,
even to fly briefly
like the shovelful over   20
the gravedigger's shoulder.

WALLACE STEVENS   (1879–1955)

The Emperor of Ice-Cream

Call the roller of big cigars,
The muscular one, and bid him whip
In kitchen cups concupiscent curds.

Let the wenches dawdle in such dress
As they are used to wear, and let the boys   5
Bring flowers in last month's newspapers.
Let be be finale of seem.
The only emperor is the emperor of ice-cream.

Take from the dresser of deal,
Lacking the three glass knobs, that sheet   10
On which she embroidered fantails once
And spread it so as to cover her face.
If her horny feet protrude, they come
To show how cold she is, and dumb.
Let the lamp affix its beam.
The only emperor is the emperor of ice-cream.   15

ANN SEXTON   (1928–1974)

Wanting to Die

Since you ask, most days I cannot remember.
I walk in my clothing, unmarked by that voyage.
Then the almost unnameable lust returns.

Even though I have nothing against life.
I know well the grass blades you mention,   5
the furniture you have placed under the sun.

But suicides have a special language.
Like carpenters they want to know *which tools*.
They never ask *why build*.

Twice I have so simply declared myself,   10
have possessed the enemy, eaten the enemy,
have taken on his craft, his magic

In this way, heavy and thoughtful,
warmer than oil or water,
I have rested, drooling at the mouth-hole.   15

I did not think of my body at needle point.
Even the cornea and the leftover urine were gone.
Suicides have already betrayed the body.

Still-born, they don't always die,
but dazzled, they can't forget a drug so sweet   20
that even children would look on and smile.

To thrust all that life under your tongue!—
that, all by itself, becomes a passion.
Death's a sad bone; bruised, you'd say,

and yet she waits for me, year after year,   *25*
to so delicately undo an old wound,
to empty my breath from its bad prison.

Balanced there, suicides sometimes meet,
raging at the fruit, a pumped-up moon,
leaving the bread they mistook for a kiss,   *30*

leaving the page of the book carelessly open,
something unsaid, the phone off the hook
and the love, whatever it was, an infection.

SYLVIA PLATH   (1932–1963)

Death & Co.

Two, of course there are two.
It seems perfectly natural now—
The one who never looks up, whose eyes are lidded
And balled, like Blake's,
Who exhibits   *5*

The birthmarks that are his trademark—
The scald scar of water,
The nude
Verdigris of the condor.
I am red meat. His beak   *10*

Claps sidewise: I am not his yet.
He tells me how badly I photograph.
He tells me how sweet
The babies look in their hospital
Icebox, a simple   *15*

Frill at the neck,
Then the flutings of their Ionian
Death-gowns,
Then two little feet.
He does not smile or smoke.   *20*

The other does that,
His hair long and plausive.
Bastard
Masturbating a glitter,
He wants to be loved.   *25*

I do not stir.
The frost makes a flower,
The dew makes a star,

The dead bell,
The dead bell.   *30*

Somebody's done for.

ROBERT PENN WARREN   (1905–   )

Blow, West Wind

I know, I know—though the evidence
Is lost, and the last who might speak are dead.
Blow, west wind, blow, and the evidence, O,

Is lost, and wind shakes the cedar, and O,
I know how the kestrel hung over Wyoming,   *5*
Breast reddened in sunset, and O, the cedar

Shakes, and I know how cold
Was the sweat on my father's mouth, dead.
Blow, west wind, blow, shake the cedar, I know

How once I, a boy, crouching at creekside,   *10*
Watched, in the sunlight, a handful of water
Drip, drip, from my hand. The drops—they were bright!

But you believe nothing, with the evidence lost.

JAY PARINI   (1948–   )

Skater in Blue

The lid broke, and suddenly the child
in all her innocence was underneath
the ice in zero water, growing wild
with numbness and with fear. The child fell
so gently through the ice that none could tell   *5*
at first that she was gone. They skated on
without the backward looks that might have saved
her when she slipped, feet first, beneath the glaze.
She saw the sun distorted by the haze
of river ice, a splay of light, a lost   *10*
imperfect kingdom. Fallen out of sight,
she found a blue and simple, solid night.
It never came to her that no one knew
how far from them she'd fallen or how blue
her world had grown so quickly, at such cost.   *15*

DYLAN THOMAS   (1914–1953)

Fern Hill

Now as I was young and easy under the apple boughs
About the lilting house and happy as the grass was green,
   The night above the dingle starry,
    Time let me hail and climb
   Golden in the heydays of his eyes,   *5*
And honoured among wagons I was prince of the apple towns
And once below a time I lordly had the trees and leaves
    Trail with daisies and barley
   Down the rivers of the windfall light.

And as I was green and carefree, famous among the barns   *10*
About the happy yard and singing as the farm was home;
   In the sun that is young once only,
    Time let me play and be
   Golden in the mercy of his means,
And green and golden I was huntsman and herdsman, the calves   *15*
Sang to my horn, the foxes on the hills barked clear and cold,
    And the sabbath rang slowly
   In the pebbles of the holy streams.

All the sun long it was running, it was lovely, the hay
Fields high as the house, the tunes from the chimneys, it was air   *20*
   And playing, lovely and watery
    And fire green as grass.
   And nightly under the simple stars
As I rode to sleep the owls were bearing the farm away,
All the moon long I heard, blessed among stables, the nightjars   *25*
   Flying with the ricks, and the horses
    Flashing into the dark.

And then to awake, and the farm, like a wanderer white
With the dew, come back, the cock on his shoulder: it was all
   Shining, it was Adam and maiden,   *30*
    The sky gathered again
   And the sun grew round that very day.
So it must have been after the birth of the simple light
In the first, spinning place, the spellbound horses walking warm
   Out of the whinnying green stable   *35*
    On to the fields of praise.

And honoured among foxes and pheasants by the gay house
Under the new made clouds and happy as the heart was long,
   In the sun born over and over,
    I ran my heedless ways,   *40*
   My wishes raced through the house high hay

And nothing I cared, at my sky blue trades, that time allows
In all his tuneful turning so few and such morning songs
  Before the children green and golden
    Follow him out of grace,   45

Nothing I cared, in the lamb white days, that time would take me
Up to the swallow thronged loft by the shadow of my hand,
  In the moon that is always rising,
    Nor that riding to sleep
  I should hear him fly with the high fields   50
And wake to the farm forever fled from the childless land.
Oh as I was young and easy in the mercy of his means,
    Time held me green and dying
  Though I sang in my chains like the sea.

DYLAN THOMAS   (1914–1953)

The Force that Through the Green Fuse Drives the Flower

The force that through the green fuse drives the flower
Drives my green age; that blasts the roots of trees
Is my destroyer.
And I am dumb to tell the crooked rose
My youth is bent by the same wintry fever.   5

The force that drives the water through the rocks
Drives my red blood; that dries the mouthing streams
Turns mine to wax.
And I am dumb to mouth unto my veins
How at the mountain spring the same mouth sucks.   10

The hand that whirls the water in the pool
Stirs the quicksand; that ropes the blowing wind
Hauls my shroud sail.
And I am dumb to tell the hanging man
How of my clay is made the hangman's lime.   15
The lips of time leech to the fountain head;
Love drips and gathers, but the fallen blood
Shall calm her sores.
And I am dumb to tell a weather's wind
How time has ticked a heaven round the stars.   20

And I am dumb to tell the lover's tomb
How at my sheet goes the same crooked worm.

STEVIE SMITH   (1902–1971)

Not Waving but Drowning

Nobody heard him, the dead man,
But still he lay moaning:
I was much further out than you thought
And not waving but drowning.
Poor chap, he always loved larking   5
And now he's dead
It must have been too cold for him his heart gave way.
They said.

Oh, no no no, it was too cold always
(Still the dead one lay moaning)   10
I was much too far out all my life
And not waving but drowning.

A. E. HOUSMAN   (1859–1936)

To an Athlete Dying Young

The time you won your town the race
We chaired you through the market-place;
Man and boy stood cheering by,
And home we brought you shoulder-high.

To-day, the road all runners come,   5
Shoulder-higher we bring you home,
And set you at your threshold down,
Townsman of a stiller town.

Smart lad, to slip betimes away
From fields where glory does not stay   10
And early though the laurel grows
It withers quicker than the rose.

Eyes the shady night has shut
Cannot see the record cut,
And silence sounds no worse than cheers   15
After earth has stopped the ears:

Now you will not swell the rout
Of lads that wore their honours out,
Runners whom renown outran
And the name died before the man.   20

So set, before its echoes fade,
The fleet foot on the sill of shade,

And hold to the low lintel up
The still-defended challenge-cup.

And round that early-laurelled head   *25*
Will flock to gaze the strengthless dead
And find unwithered on its curls
The garland briefer than a girl's.

EMILY BRONTË   (1818–1848)

Last Lines

'The following are the last lines my sister Emily ever wrote.'—*Charlotte Brontë*

No coward soul is mine,
No trembler in the world's storm-troubled sphere:
I see Heaven's glories shine,
And faith shines equal, arming me from fear.

O God within my breast,   *5*
Almighty, ever-present Deity!
Life—that in me has rest,
As I—undying Life—have power in thee!

Vain are the thousand creeds
That move men's hearts: unutterably vain;   *10*
Worthless as withered weeds,
Or idlest froth amid the boundless main,

To waken doubt in one
Holding so fast by thine infinity;
So surely anchored on   *15*
The steadfast rock of immortality.

With wide-embracing love
Thy spirit animates eternal years,
Pervades and broods above,
Changes, sustains, dissolves, creates, and rears.   *20*

Though earth and man were gone,
And suns and universes cease to be,
And thou were left alone,
Every existence would exist in thee.

There is not room for Death,   *25*
Nor atom that his might could render void:
Thou—thou art Being and Breath,
And what thou art may never be destroyed.

JOHN DONNE   (1572–1631)

Death Be Not Proud

Death, be not proud, though some have callèd thee
Mighty and dreadful, for thou art not so;
For those whom thou think'st thou dost overthrow
Die not, poor Death, nor yet canst thou kill me.
From rest and sleep, which but thy pictures be,   5
Much pleasure, then from thee much more must flow,
And soonest our best men with thee do go,
Rest of their bones, and soul's delivery.
Thou art slave to fate, chance, kings, and desperate men,
And dost with poison, war, and sickness dwell,   10
And poppy° or charms can make up sleep as well   *opium*
And better than thy stroke; why swell'st thou then?
One short sleep past, we wake eternally
And death shall be no more; Death, thou shalt die.

WILLIAM STAFFORD   (1914–   )

Travelling Through the Dark

Travelling through the dark I found a deer
dead on the edge of the Wilson River road.
It is usually best to roll them into the canyon:
that road is narrow; to swerve might make more dead.

By glow of the tail-light I stumbled back of the car   5
and stood by the heap, a doe, a recent killing;
she had stiffened already, almost cold.
I dragged her off; she was large in the belly.

My fingers touching her side brought me the reason—
her side was warm; her fawn lay there waiting,   10
alive, still, never to be born.
Beside that mountain road I hesitated.

The car aimed ahead its lowered parking lights;
under the hood purred the steady engine.
I stood in the glare of the warm exhaust turning red;   15
around our group I could hear the wilderness listen.

I thought hard for us all—my only swerving—,
then pushed her over the edge into the river.

ANNE STEVENSON   (1933–   )

Dreaming of Immortality in a Thatched Hut

(After the painting by Chin Ch'ang-t'ang)

Drowsing over his verses or drifting
lazily through the sutras,
he blinked in the hazy August silence
through which a blind stream bore on
and the locusts endlessly sawed, performing mistakes   5
and catching themselves up again like nervous musicians.

The soft rain dropped on the dust at nightfall,
dawns poured revelations over the peaks
until, as he slept, he could see it all—
the graceful ascent from the shelving eaves of the hut.   10
The ease of detachment. The flowing out of his sleeves.
The slow half sorrowful movement of regret
as he rose with the steadying mists about his knees,
away from the rocks and the stunted, gripping pine
and the books stacked neatly out of the way of the rain.   15

ANTHOLOGY II
A Time for Joy, a Time for Grief

ANONYMOUS   (early thirteenth century)

Sumer Is Icumen in°

Sumer is icumen in,
Loudeè sing cuccu!
Groweth sed and bloweth med
And springth the wudè nu.
Sing cuccu!   *5*

Ewè bleteth after lomb,
Loweth after calvè cu;
Bullock sterteth, buckè verteth,
Murie sing cuccu!
Cuccu, cuccu,   *10*
Wel singest thu, cuccu;
Ne swik thu nave nu.

Sing cuccu nu! Sing cuccu!
Sing cuccu! Sing cuccu nu!

°This poem translates into modern English as follows: Sumer (spring) is coming in,
Loud sing the cuckoo! Seeds grow and meadows bloom, and woods spring out anew.
Sing, cuckoo! The ewe bleats for the lamb; the cow lows for the calf; the bullock leaps,
the buck farts; sing merrily, cuckoo! Cuckoo, cuckoo, well do you sing, cuckoo; never
stop now. Sing cuckoo, etc.

RICHARD KENNEY   (1948–   )

Harvest

Bounty, bounty,
silver corn husks cracked down by fat raccoons,
pumpkins squat amidst the sift and fall of seeds,
racks of acorn squash collapsed,
tomatoes split and leaking in the boggy tangle of their vines,   *5*
apples bruising in their bins,
the half-Harvest Moon itself
a tipped snifter—
I incline my chin.

WILLIAM WORDSWORTH   (1770–1850)

It Is a Beauteous Evening

It is a beauteous evening, calm and free,
The holy time is quiet as a nun
Breathless with adoration; the broad sun
Is sinking down in its tranquillity;
The gentleness of heaven broods o'er the sea: *5*
Listen! the mighty being is awake,
And doth with his eternal motion make
A sound like thunder—everlastingly.
Dear Child! dear Girl! that walkest with me here,
If you appear untouched by solemn thought,   *10*
Thy nature is not therefore less divine:
Thou liest in Abraham's bosom all the year;
And worship'st at the temple's inner shrine,
God being with thee when we know it not.

W. H. AUDEN   (1907–1973)

Musée des Beaux Arts

About suffering they were never wrong,
The Old Masters: how well they understood
Its human position; how it takes place
While someone else is eating or opening a window
   or just walking dully along;
How, when the aged are reverently, passionately waiting   *5*
For the miraculous birth, there always must be
Children who did not specially want it to happen, skating

On a pond at the edge of the wood:
They never forgot
That even the dreadful martyrdom must run its course   *10*
Anyhow in a corner, some untidy spot
Where the dogs go on with their doggy life and the torturer's horse
Scratches its innocent behind on a tree.

In Brueghel's *Icarus,* for instance: how everything turns away
Quite leisurely from the disaster; the ploughman may   *15*
Have heard the splash, the forsaken cry,
But for him it was not an important failure; the sun shone
As it had to on the white legs disappearing into the green
Water; and the expensive delicate ship that must have seen
Something amazing, a boy falling out of the sky,   *20*
Had somewhere to get to and sailed calmly on.

WILLIAM SHAKESPEARE   (1564–1616)

When Icicles Hang by the Wall

When icicles hang by the wall,
    And Dick the shepherd blows his nail,°   *breathes on his fingernails to warm them*
And Tom bears logs into the hall,
    And milk comes frozen home in pail,
When blood is nipped and ways° be foul,   *roads*   *5*
    Then nightly sings the staring owl:
      "Tu-whit, to-who!"
      A merry note,
While greasy Joan doth keel° the pot.   *cool, by skimming*

When all aloud the wind doth blow   *10*
    And coughing drowns the parson's saw,°   *wise saying*
And birds sit brooding in the snow,
    And Marian's nose looks red and raw,
When roasted crabs° hiss in the bowl,   *crab apples*
    Then nightly sings the staring owl: *15*
      "Tu-whit, to-who!"
      A merry note,
While greasy Joan doth keel the pot.

ROBERT BROWNING   (1812–1889)

Home Thoughts from Abroad

Oh, to be in England
Now that April's there,
And whoever wakes in England

Sees, some morning, unaware,
That the lowest boughs and the brushwood sheaf   5
Round the elm-tree bole are in tiny leaf,
While the chaffinch sings on the orchard bough
In England—now!

JOHN CLARE   (1793–1864)

Farewell

Farewell to the bushy clump close to the river
And the flags where the butter-bump° hides in forever;   *bittern*
Farewell to the weedy nook, hemmed in by waters;
Farewell to the miller's brook and his three bonny daughters;
Farewell to them all while in prison I lie—   5
In the prison a thrall sees naught but the sky.

Shut out are the green fields and birds in the bushes;
In the prison yard nothing builds, blackbirds or thrushes.
Farewell to the old mill and dash of the waters,
To the miller and, dearer still, to his three bonny daughters.   10

In the nook, the larger burdock grows near the green willow;
In the flood, round the moor-cock dashes under the billow;
To the old mill farewell, to the lock, pens, and waters,
To the miller himsel', and his three bonny daughters.

EMILY DICKINSON   (1830–1886)

After Great Pain, a Formal Feeling Comes

After great pain, a formal feeling comes—
The Nerves sit ceremonious, like Tombs—
The stiff Heart questions was it He, that bore,
And Yesterday, or Centuries before?

The Feet, mechanical, go round—   5
Of Ground, or Air, or Ought—
A Wooden way
Regardless grown,
A Quartz contentment, like a stone—

This is the Hour of Lead—   10
Remembered, if outlived,
As Freezing persons, recollect the Snow—
First—Chill—then Stupor—then the letting go—

GERARD MANLEY HOPKINS (1844–1889)

I Wake and Feel the Fell of Dark

I wake and feel the fell of dark, not day.
What hours, O what black hours we have spent
This night! what sights you, heart, saw; ways you went!
And more must, in yet longer light's delay.

With witness I speak this. But where I say   5
Hours I mean years, mean life. And my lament
Is cries countless, cries like dead letters sent
To dearest him that lives alas! away.

I am gall, I am heartburn. God's most deep decree
Bitter would have me taste: my taste was me;   10
Bones built in me, flesh filled, blood brimmed the curse.

Selfyeast of spirit a dull dough sours. I see
The lost are like this, and their scourge to be
As I am mine, their sweating selves; but worse.

ALFRED, LORD TENNYSON (1809–1892)

Tears, Idle Tears

Tears, idle tears, I know not what they mean,
Tears from the depth of some divine despair
Rise in the heart, and gather to the eyes,
In looking on the happy Autumn-fields,
And thinking of the days that are no more.   5

Fresh as the first beam glittering on a sail,
That brings our friends up from the underworld,
Sad as the last which reddens over one
That sinks with all we love below the verge;
So sad, so fresh, the days that are no more.   10

Ah, sad and strange as in dark summer dawns
The earliest pipe of half-awakened birds
To dying ears, when unto dying eyes
The casement slowly grows a glimmering square;
So sad, so strange, the days that are no more.   15

Dear as remembered kisses after death,
And sweet as those by hopeless fancy feigned
On lips that are for others; deep as love,
Deep as first love, and wild with all regret;
O Death in Life, the days that are no more.   20

ROBERT BURNS   (1759–1796)

The Banks o' Doon

Ye banks and braes o' bonnie Doon,
   How can ye bloom sae fresh and fair?
How can ye chant, ye little birds,
   And I sae weary fu' o' care?
Thou'lt break my heart, thou warbling bird,   *5*
   That wantons thro' the flowering thorn:
Thou minds me o' departed joys,
   Departed never to return.

Aft hae I roved by bonnie Doon,
   To see the rose and woodbine twine;   *10*
And ilka bird sang o' its love,
   And fondly sae did I o' mine.
Wi' lightsome heart I pu'd a rose,
   Fu' sweet upon its thorny tree;
And my fause lover stole my rose,   *15*
   But ah! he left the thorn wi' me.

ANNE STEVENSON   (1933–   )

In March

The snow melts
exposing what was
buried there all winter—
tricycles and
fire-engines and   *5*
all sizes of children
waiting in boots and
yellow mackintoshes
for the mud.

D. H. LAWRENCE   (1885–1930)

Piano

Softly, in the dusk, a woman is singing to me;
Taking me back down the vista of years, till I see
A child sitting under the piano, in the boom of the tingling strings
And pressing the small, poised feet of a mother who smiles as she sings.

In spite of myself, the insidious mastery of song   5
Betrays me back, till the heart of me weeps to belong
To the old Sunday evenings at home, with winter outside
And hymns in the cozy parlor, the tinkling piano our guide.

So now it is vain for the singer to burst into clamor
With the great black piano appassionato. The glamour   10
Of childish days is upon me, my manhood is cast
Down in the flood of remembrance, I weep like a child for the past.

HENRY VAUGHAN   (1622–1695)

The Retreat

Happy those early days when I
Shined in my angel-infancy:
Before I understood this place
Appointed for my second race,
Or taught my soul to fancy aught   5
But a white, celestial thought;
When yet I had not walked above
A mile or two from my first love,
And looking back, at the short space,
Could see a glimpse of His bright face;   10
When on some gilded cloud or flower
My gazing soul would dwell an hour,
And in those weaker glories spy
Some shadows of eternity;
Before I taught my tongue to wound   15
My conscience with a sinful sound,
Or had the black art to dispense°   *serve out*
A several° sin to every sense,   *separate*
But felt through all this fleshly dress
Bright shoots of everlastingness.   20
   O how I long to travel back
And tread again that ancient track!
That I might once more reach that plain
Where first I left my glorious train,°   *angels who followed*
From whence th' enlightened spirit sees   25
That shady city of palm tress.°   *in heaven*
But, ah, my soul with too much stay°   *too much remaining flesh*
Is drunk, and staggers in the way.
Some men a forward motion love,
But I by backward steps would move;   30

And when this dust falls to the urn,°   *burial urn*
In that state I came, return.

JOHN KEATS   (1795–1821)

To Autumn

I

   Season of mists and mellow fruitfulness,
    Close bosom-friend of the maturing sun;
Conspiring with him how to load and bless
    With fruit the vines that round the thatch-eaves run;
To bend with apples the mossed cottage-trees,   5
    And fill all fruit with ripeness to the core;
      To swell the gourd, and plump the hazel shells
With a sweet kernel; to set budding more,
    And still more, later flowers for the bees,
    Until they think warm days will never cease,   10
      For summer has o'er-brimmed their clammy cells.

II

   Who hath not seen thee oft amid thy store?
    Sometimes who ever seeks abroad may find
Thee sitting careless on a granary floor,
    Thy hair soft-lifted by the winnowing wind;   15
Or on a half-reaped furrow sound asleep,
    Drowsed with the fume of poppies, while thy hook
      Spares the next swath and all its twinèd flowers:
And sometimes like a gleaner thou dost keep
    Steady thy laden head across a brook;   20
    Or by a cider-press, with patient look,
      Thou watchest the last oozings hours by hours.

III

   Where are the songs of spring? Aye, where are they?
    Think not of them, thou hast thy music too,—
While barrèd clouds bloom the soft-dying day,   25
    And touch the stubble-plains with rosy hue;
Then in a wailful choir the small gnats mourn
    Among the river sallows, borne aloft
      Or sinking as the light wind lives or dies;
And full-grown lambs loud bleat from hilly bourn;   30
    Hedge-crickets sing; and now with treble soft

The redbreast whistles from a garden-croft;
   And gathering swallows twitter in the skies.

THOMAS HARDY   (1840–1928)

Neutral Tones

We stood by a pond that winter day,
And the sun was white, as though chidden of God,
And a few leaves lay on the starving sod;
   —They had fallen from an ash, and were gray.

Your eyes on me were as eyes that rove   5
Over tedious riddles of years ago;
And some words played between us to and fro
   On which lost the more by our love.

The smile on your mouth was the deadest thing
Alive enough to have strength to die;   10
And a grin of bitterness swept thereby
   Like an ominous bird a-wing. . . .

Since then, keen lessons that love deceives,
And wrings with wrong, have shaped to me
Your face, and the God-curst sun, and a tree,   15
   And a pond edged with grayish leaves.

PHILIP LEVINE   (1928–   )

Belle Isle, 1949

We stripped in the first warm spring night
and ran down into the Detroit River
to baptize ourselves in the brine
of car parts, dead fish, stolen bicycles,
melted snow. I remember going under   5
hand in hand with a Polish highschool girl
I'd never seen before, and the cries
our breath made caught at the same time
on the cold, and rising through the layers
of darkness into the final moonless atmosphere   10
that was this world, the girl breaking
the surface after me and swimming out
on the starless waters towards the lights
of Jefferson Ave. and the stacks
of the old stove factory unwinking.   15

Turning at last to see no island at all
but a perfect calm dark as far
as there was sight, and then a light
and another riding low out ahead
to bring us home, ore boats maybe, or smokers   20
walking alone. Back panting
to the gray coarse beach we didn't dare
fall on, the damp piles of clothes,
and dressing side by side in silence
to go back where we came from.   25

CHARLES WRIGHT (1935–   )

Sitting at Night on the Front Porch

I'm here, on the dark porch, restyled in my mother's chair.
10:45 and no moon.
Below the house, car lights
Swing down, on the canyon floor, to the sea.

In this they resemble us,   5
Dropping like match flames through the great void
Under our feet.
In this they resemble her, burning and disappearing.

Everyone's gone
And I'm here, sizing the dark, saving my mother's seat. 10

SEAMUS HEANEY (1939–   )

Sunlight

There was a sunlit absence.
The helmeted pump in the yard
heated its iron,
water honeyed

in the slung bucket   5
and the sun stood
like a griddle cooling
against the wall

of each long afternoon.
So, her hands scuffled   10
over the bakeboard,
the reddening stove

sent its plaque of heat
against her where she stood
in a floury apron   *15*
by the window.

Now she dusts the board
with a goose's wing,
now sits, broad-lapped,
with whitened nails   *20*

and measling shins:
here is a space
again, the scone rising
to the tick of two clocks.

And here is love   *25*
like a tinsmith's scoop
sunk past its gleam
in the meal-bin.

ANTHOLOGY III
War, and Rumors of War

A. E. HOUSMAN (1859–1936)

With Rue My Heart Is laden

With rue my heart is laden
  For golden friends I had,
For many a rose-lipt maiden
  And many a lightfoot lad.

By brooks too broad for leaping   5
  The lightfoot boys are laid;
The rose-lipt girls are sleeping
  In fields where roses fade.

JOHN MILTON (1608–1674)

On the Late Massacre in Piemont°

Avenge, O Lord, thy slaughtered saints, whose bones
  Lie scattered on the Alpine mountains cold;
  Even them who kept thy truth so pure of old
  When all our fathers worshipped stocks and stones,°   *graven images*

°In 1655 the Waldenses, a Protestant sect living in the Piedmont valley (northern Italy
and southern France), were denounced as heretics and brutally slaughtered by the
Roman Catholic Church. Protestants in England and Europe raised their voices in
outrage against the Waldensian massacre.

Forget not: in Thy book record their groans   *5*
    Who were Thy sheep and in their ancient fold
    Slain by the bloody Piemontese, that rolled
    Mother with infant down the rocks. Their moans
The vales redoubled to the hills, and they
    To Heaven. Their martyred blood and ashes sow   *10*
    O'er all th' Italian fields where still doth sway
The triple tyrant:° that from these may grow
    A hundred-fold, who having learnt Thy way
    Early may fly the Babylonian woe.°

¹²*triple tyrant:* the Pope, who wore a triple crown.
¹⁴In Milton's day, Protestants associated Catholics with the infamous "whore of
Babylon" mentioned in Revelations: xvii, xviii.

WALT WHITMAN   (1819–1892)

Vigil Strange I Kept on the Field One Night

Vigil strange I kept on the field one night;
When you, my son and my comrade, dropt at my side that day,
One look I but gave which your dear eyes return'd with a look
        I shall never forget,
One touch of your hand to mine, O boy, reach'd up as you lay
        on the ground,
Then onward I sped in the battle, the even-contested battle,   *5*
Till late in the night reliev'd to the place at last again I made my way,
Found you in death so cold, dear comrade, found your body,
        son of responding kisses (never again on earth responding),
Bared your face in the starlight, curious the scene, cool blew
        the moderate nightwind,
Long there and then in vigil I stood, dimly around me the battle-field
        spreading,
Vigil wondrous and vigil sweet there in the fragrant silent night,   *10*
But not a tear fell, not even a long-drawn sigh, long, long I gazed,
Then on the earth partially reclining sat by your side leaning
        my chin in my hands,
Passing sweet hours, immortal and mystic hours with you,
        dearest comrade—not a tear, not a word,
Vigil of silence, love and death, vigil for you, my son and my soldier,
As onward silently stars aloft, eastward new ones upward stole,   *15*
Vigil final for you, brave boy (I could not save you, swift was your death,
I faithfully loved you and cared for you living, I think we shall surely
        meet again),
Till at latest lingering of the night, indeed just as the dawn appear'd,
My comrade I wrapt in his blanket, envelop'd well his form,

Folded the blanket well, tucking it carefully over head and carefully
    under feet, *20*
And there and then and bathed by the rising sun, my son in his grave,
    in his rudedug grave I deposited,
Ending my vigil strange with that, vigil of night and battlefield dim,
Vigil for boy of responding kisses (never again on earth responding),
Vigil for comrade swiftly slain, vigil I never forget, how as day brighten'd,
I rose from the chill ground and folded my soldier well in his blanket, *25*
And buried him where he fell.

WALT WHITMAN (1819–1892)

Cavalry Crossing a Ford

A line in long array where they wind betwixt green islands,
They take a serpentine course, their arms flash in the sun—hark to the
    musical clank,
Behold the silvery river, in it the splashing horses loitering stop to drink,
Behold the brown-faced men, each group, each person a picture,
    the negligent rest on the saddles,
Some emerge on the opposite bank, others are just entering the ford—
    while, *5*
Scarlet and blue and snowy white,
The guidon flags flutter gayly in the wind.

RUPERT BROOKE (1887–1915)

The Soldier

If I should die, think only this of me:
  That there's some corner of a foreign field
That is for ever England. There shall be
  In that rich earth a richer dust concealed;
A dust whom England bore, shaped, made aware, *5*
  Gave, once, her flowers to love, her ways to roam,
A body of England's, breathing English air,
  Washed by the rivers, blest by suns of home.

And think, this heart, all evil shed away,
  A pulse in the eternal mind, no less *10*
    Gives somewhere back the thoughts by England given;
Her sights and sounds; dreams happy as her day;
  And laughter, learnt of friends; and gentleness,
    In hearts at peace, under an English heaven.

SIEGFRIED SASSOON   (1886–1967)

Attack

At dawn the ridge emerges massed and dun
In the wild purple of the glow'ring sun,
Smouldering through spouts of drifting smoke that shroud
The menacing scarred slope; and, one by one,
Tanks creep and topple forward to the wire.   5
The barrage roars and lifts. Then, clumsily bowed
With bombs and guns and shovels and battle-gear,
Men jostle and climb to meet the bristling fire.
Lines of grey, muttering faces, masked with fear,
They leave their trenches, going over the top,   10
While time ticks blank and busy on their wrists,
And hope, with furtive eyes and grappling fists,
Flounders in mud. O Jesus, make it stop!

ISAAC ROSENBERG   (1890–1918)

August 1914

What in our lives is burnt
In the fire of this?
The heart's dear granary?
The much we shall miss?

Three lives hath one life—   5
Iron, honey, gold.
The gold, the honey gone—
Left is the hard and cold.

Iron are our lives
Molten right through our youth.   10
A burnt space through ripe fields
A fair mouth's broken tooth.

WILFRED OWEN   (1893–1918)

Anthem for Doomed Youth

What passing-bells for these who die as cattle?
   Only the monstrous anger of the guns.
Only the stuttering rifles' rapid rattle
   Can patter out their hasty orisons.

No mockeries now for them; no prayers nor bells,   *5*
   Nor any voice of mourning save the choirs, —
The shrill, demented choirs of wailing shells;
   And bugles calling for them from sad shires.

What candles may be held to speed them all?
   Not in the hands of boys, but in their eyes   *10*
   Shall shine the holy glimmers of good-byes.
The pallor of girls' brows shall be their pall;
   Their flowers the tenderness of patient minds,
   And each slow dusk a drawing-down of blinds.

WILFRED OWEN   (1893–1918)

Strange Meeting

It seemed that out of battle I escaped
Down some profound dull tunnel, long since scooped
Through granites which titanic wars had groined.
Yet also there encumbered sleepers groaned,
Too fast in thought or death to be bestirred.   *5*
Then, as I probed them, one sprang up, and stared
With piteous recognition in fixed eyes,
Lifting distressful hands as if to bless.
And by his smile I knew that sullen hall,
By his dead smile I knew we stood in Hell.   *10*
With a thousand pains that vision's face was grained;
Yet no blood reached there from the upper ground,
And no guns thumped, or down the flues made moan.
'Strange friend,' I said, 'here is no cause to mourn.'
'None,' said the other, 'save the undone years,   *15*
The hopelessness. Whatever hope is yours,
Was my life also; I went hunting wild
After the wildest beauty in the world,
Which lies not calm in eyes, or braided hair,
But mocks the steady running of the hour,   *20*
And if it grieves, grieves richlier than here.
For by my glee might many men have laughed,
And of my weeping something had been left,
Which must die now. I mean the truth untold,
The pity of war, the pity war distilled.   *25*
Now men will go content with what we spoiled.
Or, discontent, boil bloody, and be spilled.
They will be swift with swiftness of the tigress,
None will break ranks, though nations trek from progress.

Courage was mine, and I had mystery,   *30*
Wisdom was mine, and I had mastery;
To miss the march of this retreating world
Into vain citadels that are not walled.
Then, when much blood had clogged their chariot-wheels
I would go up and wash them from sweet wells,   *35*
Even with truths that lie too deep for taint.
I would have poured my spirit without stint
But not through wounds; not on the cess of war.
Foreheads of men have bled where no wounds were.
I am the enemy you killed, my friend.   *40*
I knew you in this dark; for so you frowned
Yesterday through me as you jabbed and killed.
I parried; but my hands were loath and cold.
Let us sleep now . . .'

KEITH DOUGLAS   (1920–1944)

How to Kill

Under the parabola of a ball,
a child turning into a man,
I looked into the air too long.
The ball fell in my hand, it sang
in the closed fist: *Open Open*   *5*
Behold a gift designed to kill.

Now in my dial of glass appears
the soldier who is going to die.
He smiles, and moves about in ways
his mother knows, habits of his.   *10*
The wires touch his face: I cry
Now. Death, like a familiar, hears

and look, has made a man of dust
of a man of flesh. This sorcery
I do. Being damned, I am amused   *15*
to see the centre of love diffused
and the waves of love travel into vacancy.
How easy it is to make a ghost.

The weightless mosquito touches
her tiny shadow on the stone,   *20*
and with how like, how infinite
a lightness, man and shadow meet.
They fuse. A shadow is a man
when the mosquito death approaches.

RANDALL JARRELL   (1914–1965)

The Death of the Ball Turret Gunner

From my mother's sleep I fell into the State,
And I hunched in its belly till my wet fur froze.
Six miles from earth, loosed from its dream of life,
I woke to black flak and the nightmare fighters.
When I died they washed me out of the turret with a hose.   5

EZRA POUND   (1885–1972)

From *Hugh Selwyn Mauberley*

I

The tea-rose tea-gown, etc.
Supplants the mousseline of Cos,
The pianola 'replaces'
Sappho's barbitos.

Christ follows Dionysus,   5
Phallic and ambrosial
Made way for macerations;
Caliban casts out Ariel.

All things are a flowing,
Sage Heracleitus says;   10
But a tawdry cheapness
Shall outlast our days.

Even the Christian beauty
Defects—after Samothrace;
We see τὸ καλὸν°   *(tŏ kalon) beauty*   15
Decreed in the market place.

Faun's flesh is not to us,
Nor the saint's vision.
We have the Press for wafer;
Franchise for circumcision.   20

All men, in law, are equals.
Free of Pisistratus,
We choose a knave or an eunuch
To rule over us.

O bright Apollo,
τίν' ἄνδρα, τίν' ἥρωα, τίνα θεον,°   *(tin'andra, tin' hērōa, tina theon) what man,*   25
                                    what hero, what god

What god, man, or hero
Shall I place a tin wreath upon!

II
These fought in any case,
and some believing,
                    pro domo, in any case . . .   *30*

Some quick to arm,
some for adventure,
some from fear of weakness,
some from fear of censure,
some for love of slaughter, in imagination,   *35*
learning later . . .
some in fear, learning love of slaughter;

Died some, pro partia,
                    non 'dulce' non 'et decor'. . .
walked eye-deep in hell   *40*
believing in old men's lies, then unbelieving
came home, home to a lie,
home to many deceits,
home to old lies and new infamy;
usury age-old and age-thick   *45*
and liars in public places.

WILLIAM BUTLER YEATS   (1865–1939)

An Irish Airman Foresees His Death

I know that I shall meet my fate
Somewhere among the clouds above;
Those that I fight I do not hate,
Those that I guard I do not love;
My country is Kiltartan Cross,   *5*
My countrymen Kiltartan's poor,
No likely end could bring them loss
Or leave them happier than before.
Nor law, nor duty bade me fight,
Nor public men, nor cheering crowds,   *10*
A lonely impulse of delight
Drove to this tumult in the clouds;
I balanced all, brought all to mind,
The years to come seemed waste of breath,
A waste of breath the years behind   *15*
In balance with this life, this death.

HENRY REED   (1914–   )

Naming of Parts

Today we have naming of parts. Yesterday,
We had daily cleaning. And tomorrow morning,
We shall have what to do after firing. But today,
Today we have naming of parts. Japonica
Glistens like coral in all of the neighboring gardens,   *5*
    And today we have naming of parts.

This is the lower sling swivel. And this
Is the upper sling swivel, whose use you will see,
When you are given your slings. And this is the piling swivel,
Which in your case you have not got. The branches   *10*
Hold in the gardens their silent, eloquent gestures,
    Which in our case we have not got.

This is the safety-catch, which is always released
With an easy flick of the thumb. And please do not let me
See anyone using his finger. You can do it quite easy   *15*
If you have any strength in your thumb. The blossoms
Are fragile and motionless, never letting anyone see
    Any of them using their finger.

And this you can see is the bolt. The purpose of this
Is to open the breech, as you see. We can slide it   *20*
Rapidly backwards and forwards: we call this
Easing the spring. And rapidly backwards and forwards
The early bees are assaulting and fumbling the flowers:
    They call it easing the Spring.

They call it easing the Spring: it is perfectly easy   *25*
If you have any strength in your thumb: like the bolt,
And the breech, and the cocking-piece, and the point of balance,
Which in our case we have not got; and the almond-blossom
Silent in all of the gardens and the bees going backwards and forwards,
For to-day we have naming parts.   *30*

W. H. AUDEN   (1907–1973)

O What Is That Sound

O what is that sound which so thrills the ear
    Down in the valley drumming, drumming?
Only the scarlet soldiers, dear,
    The soldiers coming.

O what is that light I see flashing so clear   *5*
  Over the distance brightly, brightly?
Only the sun on their weapons, dear,
  As they step lightly.

O what are they doing with all that gear,
  What are they doing this morning, this morning?   *10*
Only their usual manoeuvres, dear,
  Or perhaps a warning.

O why have they left the road down there,
  Why are they suddenly wheeling, wheeling?
Perhaps a change in their orders, dear.   *15*
  Why are you kneeling?

O haven't they stopped for the doctor's care,
  Haven't they reined their horses, their horses?
Why, they are none of them wounded, dear,
  None of these forces.   *20*

O is it the parson they want, with white hair,
  Is it the parson, is it, is it?
No, they are passing his gateway, dear,
  Without a visit.

O it must be the farmer who lives so near.   *25*
  It must be the farmer so cunning, so cunning?
They have passed the farmyard already, dear,
  And now they are running.

O where are you going? Stay with me here!
  Were the vows you swore deceiving, deceiving?   *30*
No, I promised to love you, dear,
  But I must be leaving.

O it's broken the lock and splintered the door,
  O it's the gate where they're turning, turning;
Their boots are heavy on the floor   *35*
  And their eyes are burning.

ALUN LEWIS (1915–1944)

All Day It Has Rained . . .

All day it has rained, and we on the edge of the moors
Have sprawled in our bell-tents, moody and dull as boors,
Groundsheets and blankets spread on the muddy ground
And from the first grey wakening we have found
No refuge from the skirmishing fine rain   *5*
And the wind that made the canvas heave and flap

And the taut wet guy-ropes ravel out and snap.
All day the rain has glided, wave and mist and dream,
Drenching the gorse and heather, a gossamer stream
Too light to stir the acorns that suddenly   *10*
Snatched from their cups by the wild south-westerly
Pattered against the tent and our upturned dreaming faces.
And we stretched out, unbuttoning our braces,
Smoking a Woodbine, darning dirty socks,
Reading the Sunday papers—I saw a fox   *15*
And mentioned it in the note I scribbled home;—
And we talked of girls, and dropping bombs on Rome,
And thought of the quiet dead and the loud celebrities
Exhorting us to slaughter, and the herded refugees;
—Yet thought softly, morosely of them, and as indifferently   *20*
As of ourselves or those whom we
For years have loved, and will again
Tomorrow maybe love; but not it is the rain
Possesses us entirely, the twilight and the rain.

And I can remember nothing dearer or more to my heart   *25*
Than the children I watched in the woods on Saturday
Shaking down burning chestnuts for the schoolyard's merry play,
Or the shaggy patient dog who followed me
By Sheet and Steep and up the wooded scree
To the Sholder o' Mutton where Edward Thomas° brooded long   *30*
On death and beauty—till a bullet stopped his song.

³⁰poet, killed in World War I

E. E. CUMMINGS   (1894–1962)

I Sing of Olaf

i sing of Olaf glad and big
whose warmest heart recoiled at war:
a conscientious object-or

his wellbelovéd colonel (trig°   *trim, stylish*
wcspointer most succintly bred)   *5*
took erring Olaf soon in hand;
but—though an host of overjoyed
noncoms (first knocking of the head
him) do through icy waters roll
that helplessness which others stoke   *10*
with brushes recently employed
ancnt° this muddy toiletbowl,   *concerning*
while kindred intellects evoke
allegiance per blunt instruments—

Olaf (being to all intents   *15*
a corpse and wanting any rag
upon what God unto him gave)
responds, without getting annoyed
"I will not kiss your f.ing flag"

straightway the silver bird looked grave   *20*
(departing hurriedly to shave)

but—though all kinds of officers
(a yearning nation's blueeyed pride)
their passive prey did kick and curse
until for wear their clarion   *25*
voices and boots were much the worse,
and egged the firstclassprivates on
his rectum wickedly to tease
by means of skillfully applied
bayonets roasted hot with heat—   *30*
Olaf (upon what were once knees)
does almost ceaselessly repeat
"there is some s. I will not eat"

our president, being of which
assertions duly notified
threw the yellowsonofabitch
into a dungeon, where he died

Christ (of His mercy infinite)
i pray to see; and Olaf, too

preponderatingly because   *40*
unless statistics lie he was
more brave than me: more blond than you.

SEAMUS HEANEY   (1939–   )

A Constable Calls°

His bicycle stood at the window-sill,
The rubber cowl of a mud-spasher
Skirting the front mudguard,
Its fat black handlegrips

Heating in sunlight, the 'spud'   *5*
Of the dynamo gleaming and cocked back,
The pedal treads hanging relieved
Of the boot of the law.

°A constable is a government officer or policeman. The poem is set in Northern Ireland
and concerns a Protestant constable's visit to a Catholic family.

His cap was upside down
On the floor, next his chair.   *10*
The line of its pressure ran like a bevel
In his slightly sweating hair.

He had unstrapped
The heavy ledger, and my father
Was making tillage returns   *15*
In acres, roods, and perches.°

Arithmetic and fear.
I sat staring at the polished holster
With its buttoned flap, the braid cord
Looped into the revolver butt.   *20*

'Any other root crops?
Mangolds? Marrowstems? Anything like that?'
'No.' But was there not a line
Of turnips where the seed ran out

In the potato field? I assumed   *25*
Small guilts and sat
Imagining the black hole in the barracks.
He stood up, shifted the baton-case

Further round on his belt,
Closed the domesday book,   *30*
Fitted his cap back with two hands,
And looked at me as he said goodbye.

A shadow bobbed in the window.
He was snapping the carrier spring
Over the ledger. His boot pushed off   *35*
And the bicycle ticked, ticked, ticked.

[16]*acres, roods, perches,* ways to measure crop yields.

LUCIEN STRYK   (1924–   )

Watching War Movies

Always the same: watching
World War II movies on TV,
landing barges bursting onto

islands, my skin crawls—
heat, dust—the scorpion   *5*
bites again. How I deceived

myself. Certain my role would
not make me killer, my unarmed
body called down fire from

scarred hills. As life took
life, blood coursed into   *10*
one stream. I knew one day,

the madness stopped, I'd make
my pilgrimage to temples,
gardens, serene masters of

a Way which pain was bonding.   *15*
Atoms fuse, a mushroom cloud,
the movie ends. But I still

stumble under camouflage, near
books of tranquil Buddhas by the
screen. The war goes on and on.   *20*

PHILIP LEVINE   (1928–   )

On the Murder of Lieutenant José del Castillo by the Falangist
Bravo Martinez, July 12, 1936

When the Lieutenant of the Guardia de Asalto
heard the automatic go off, he turned
and took the second shot just above
the sternum, the third tore away
the right shoulder of his uniform,   *5*
the fourth perforated his cheek. As he
slid out of his comrade's hold
toward the gray cement of the Ramblas
he lost count and knew only
that he would not die and that the blue sky   *10*
smudged with clouds was not heaven
for heaven was nowhere and in his eyes
slowly filling with their own light.
The pigeons that spotted the cold floor
of Barcelona rose as he sank below   *15*
the waves of silence crashing
on the far shores of his legs, growing
faint and watery. His hands opened
a last time to receive the benedictions
of automobile exhaust and rain   *20*
and the rain of soot. His mouth,
that would never again say "I am afraid,"
closed on nothing. The old grandfather

hawking daisies at his stand pressed
a handkerchief against his lips   25
and turned his eyes away before they held
the eyes of a gunman. The shepherd dogs
on sale howled in their cages
and turned in circles. There is more
to be said, but by someone who has suffered   30
and died for his sister the earth
and his brothers the beasts and the trees.
The Lieutenant can hear it, the prayer
that comes on the voices of water, today
or yesterday, from Chicago or Valladolid,   35
and hangs like smoke above this street
he won't walk as a man ever again.

ROBERT PINSKY (1940–   )

Serpent Knowledge

In something you have written in school, you say°
That snakes are born (or hatched) already knowing
Everything they will ever need to know—
Weazened and prematurely shrewd, like Merlin;
Something you read somewhere, I think, some textbook   5
Coy on the subject of the reptile brain.
(Perhaps the author half-remembered reading
About the Serpent of Experience
That changes manna to gall.) I don't believe it;
Even a snake's horizon must expand,   10
Inwardly, when an instinct is confirmed
By some new stage of life: to mate, kill, die.

Like angels, who have no genitals or place
Of national origin, however, snakes
Are not historical creatures; unlike chickens,   15
Who teach their chicks to scratch the dust for food—
Or people, who teach ours how to spell their names:
Not born already knowing all we need,
One generation differing from the next
In what it needs, and knows.   20
         So what I know,
What you know, what your sister knows (approaching
The age you were when I began this poem)
All differ, like different overlapping stretches

---

[1]The poet is addressing his daughter.

Of the same highway: with different lacks, and visions.   *25*
The words—*"Vietnam"*—that I can't use in poems
Without the one word threatening to gape
And swallow and enclose the poem, for you
May grow more finite; able to be touched.

The actual highway—snake's-back where it seems
That any strange thing may be happening, now,   *30*
Somewhere along its endless length—once twisted
And straightened, and took us past a vivid place:
Brave in the isolation of its profile,
"Ten miles from nowhere" on the rolling range,
A family graveyard on an Indian mound   *35*
Or little elevation above the grassland. . . .
Fenced in against the sky's huge vault at dusk
By a waist-high iron fence with spear-head tips,
The grass around and over the mound like surf.   *40*

A mile more down the flat fast road, the homestead:
Regretted, vertical, and unadorned
As its white gravestones on their lonely mound—
Abandoned now, the paneless windows breathing
Easily in the wind, and no more need   *45*
For courage to survive the open range
With just the graveyard for a nearest neighbor;
The sones of Limit—comforting and depriving.

Elsewhere along the highway, other limits—
Hanging in shades of neon from dusk to dusk,   *50*
The signs of people who know how to take
Pleasure in places where it seems unlikely:
New kinds of places, the "overdeveloped" strips
With their arousing, vacant-minded jumble;
Or garbegey lake-towns, and the tourist-pits   *55*
Where crimes unspeakably bizarre come true
To astonish countries older, or more savage . . .
As though the rapes and murders of the French
Or Indonesians were less inventive than ours,
Less goofy than those happenings that grow   *60*
Like air-plants—out of nothing, and alone.

They make us parents want to keep our children
Locked up, safe even from the daily papers
That keep the grisly record of that frontier
Where things unspeakable happen along the highways.   *65*

In today's paper, you see the teen-aged girl
From down the street; camping in Oregon
At the far point of a trip across the country,
Together with another girl her age,
They suffered and survived a random evil.   *70*

An unidentified, youngish man in jeans
Aimed his car off the highway, into the park
And at their tent (apparently at random)
And drove it over them once, and then again;
And then got out, and struck at them with a hatchet   75
Over and over, while they struggled; until
From fear, or for some other reason, or none,
He stopped; and got back into his car again
And drove off down the night-time highway. No rape,
No robbery, no "motive." Not even words,   80
Or any sound from him that they remember.
The girl still conscious, by crawling, reached the road
And even some way down it; where some people
Drove by and saw her, and brought them both to help,
So doctors could save them—barely marked.   85
                            You see
Our neighbor's picture in the paper: smiling,
A pretty child with a kerchief on her head
Covering where the surgeons had to shave it.
You read the story, and in a peculiar tone—   90
Factual, not unfeeling, like two policemen—
Discuss it with your sister. You seem to feel
Comforted that it happened far away,
As in a crazy place, in *Oregon:*
For me, a place of wholesome reputation;   95
For you, a highway where strangers go amok,
As in the universal provincial myth
That sees, in every stranger, a mad attacker . . .
(And in one's victims, it may be, a stranger).

Strangers: the Foreign who, coupling with their cousins   100
Or with their livestock, or even with wild beasts,
Spawn children with tails, or claws and spotted fur,
Ugly—and though their daughters are beautiful
seen dancing from the front, behind their backs
Or underneath their garments are the tails   105
Of reptiles, or teeth of bears.
                 So one might feel—
Thinking about the people who cross the mountains
And oceans of the earth with separate legends,
To die inside the squalor of sod huts,   110
Shanties, or tenements; and leave behind
Their legends, or the legend of themselves,
Broken and mended by the generations:
Their alien, orphaned, and disconsolate spooks,
Earth-trolls or Kallikaks or Snopes or golems,° *all subhuman types* 115
Descended of Hessians,° runaway slaves and Indians, *German mercenary soldiers*
Legends confused and loose on the roads at night . . .
The Alien or Creature of the movies.

As people die, their monsters grow more tame;
So that the people who survived Saguntum,°   *120*
Or in the towns that saw the Thirty Years' War,°
Must have felt that the wash of blood and horror
Changed something, inside. Perhaps they came to see
The state or empire as a kind of Whale
Or Serpent, in whose body they must live—   *125*
Not that mere suffering could make us wiser,
Or nobler, but only older, and more ourselves. . . .

On television, I used to see, each week,
Americans descending in machines
With wasted bravery and blood; to spread   *130*
Pain and vast fires amid a foreign place,
Among the strangers to whom we were new—
Americans: a spook or golem, there.
I think it made our country older, forever.
I don't mean better or not better, but merely   *135*
As though a person should come to a certain place
And have his hair turn gray, that very night.

Someday, the War in Southeast Asia, somewhere—
Perhaps for you and your people younger than you—
Will be the kind of history and pain   *140*
Saguntum is for me; but never tamed
Or "history" for me, I think. I think
That I may always feel as if I lived
In a time when the country aged itself:
More lonely together in our common strangeness . . .   *145*
As if we were a family, and some members
Had done an awful thing on a road at night,
And all of us had grown white hair, or tails:
And though the tails or white hair would afflict
Only that generation then alive   *150*
And of a certain age, regardless whether
They were the ones that did or planned the thing—
Or even heard about it—nevertheless
The members of that family ever after
Would bear some consequence or demarcation,   *155*
Forgotten maybe, taken for granted, a trait,
A new syllable buried in their name.

[120]Roman battle fought in 219.
[121]A series of wars fought in Germany, 1615–1648.

RICHARD TILLINGHAST (1940–   )

Hearing of the End of the War

1

Clouds dissolve into blueness.
  The Rockies float like clouds,
white ridge over blue,
  in the shimmery blue heat.

The moon floats there still
  like some round marble relic,   5
its classic face rubbed away by time.

A stranger arrives, all the way from Denver.
  We feed him.
He tells us that the war is over.   10

For years I have stopped to wonder
  what it would feel like now.
And now I only hear the slight noise
  the moment makes,
    like ice cracking,   15
as it flows behind me into the past.

2

I go to the well
  and draw up a bottle of homemade beer.
The coldness from thirty feet down
    beads out wet on the brown bottle.   20

Breathing dusty pine fragrance,
  I pop open the beer, and drink
till my skull aches from the coldness.

Rubbed white dust is on plum skins
    as they ripen,
      green wild blueberries   25
    growing from the rocks.

Wind blows in off the peaks,
    high in the dust-flecked sun-shafts
  that light up the dark trees.
Rustlings and murmured syllables from other days   30
    pass through and linger
      and leave their ponies
to roam among the trees and graze the coarse grass
    off the forest floor.   35

Treetop breezes, and voices
    returning home
from a fight somebody lost in these mountains
    a hundred and ten years ago—   *40*

A horse cries out,
    loose in the woods,
        running and free.
His unshod hooves thud
    on the hard-packed dirt.

And then each sound drops away   *45*
—like a dream you can't even remember—

deep behind the leaves of the forest.

3
From bark-covered rafters
  white sheets hang squarely down,
dividing the still afternoon into rooms   *50*
    where we sleep, or read,
    or play a slow game of hearts.

Everyone is unbuttoned and at their ease.

  The baby's clear syllables
    rise into space: *55*
milky like the half-moons
  on his tiny fingernails,

finer than fine paper.

A new life breathes in the world—
    fragile, radiant,   *60*
  unused to the ways of men.

From halfway down the valley
  bamboo flute notes rise float
    flutter
      and shatter   *65*
  against the Great Divide.

ANTHOLOGY IV
Aspects of Love

ROBERT HAYDEN (1913–1980)

Those Winter Sundays

Sundays too my father got up early
and put his clothes on in the blueblack cold,
then with cracked hands that ached
from labor in the weekday weather made
banked fires blaze. No one ever thanked him.   5

I'd wake and hear the cold splintering, breaking.
When the rooms were warm, he'd call,
and slowly I would rise and dress,
fearing the chronic angers of that house,

Speaking indifferently to him,   10
who had driven out the cold
and polished my good shoes as well.
What did I know, what did I know
of love's austere and lonely offices?

GEORGE HERBERT (1573–1633)

Love

Love bade me welcome; yet my soul drew back,
    Guilty of dust and sin.
But quick-eyed Love, observing me grow slack
    From my first entrance in,

Drew nearer to me, sweetly questioning   *5*
    If I lacked anything.

"A guest," I answered, "worthy to be here."
    Love said, "You shall be he."
"I, the unkind, ungrateful? Ah my dear,
    I cannot look on thee."   *10*
Love took my hand, and smiling did reply,
    "Who made the eyes but I?"

"Truth, Lord, but I have marred them; let my shame
    Go where it doth deserve."
"And know you not," says Love, "who bore the blame?"   *15*
    "My dear, then I will serve."
"You must sit down," says Love, "and taste my meat."
    So I did sit and eat.

SIR THOMAS WYATT   (1503–1542)

They Flee from Me

They flee from me, that sometime did me seek,
With naked foot stalking in my chamber.
I have seen them, gentle, tame, and meek,
That now are wild, and do not remember
That sometime they put themselves in danger   *5*
To take bread at my hand; and now they range,
Busily seeking with a continual change.

Thankéd be fortune it hath been otherwise.
Twenty times better; but once in special,
In thin array, after a pleasant guise,   *10*
What her loose gown from her shoulders did fall,
And she me caught in her arms long and small,°   *slender*
Therewithall sweetly did me kiss
And softly said, "Dear heart, how like you this?"

It was no dream, I lay broad waking.   *15*
But all is turned, thorough my gentleness,
Into a strange fashion of forsaking;
And I have leave to go, of her goodness,

And she also to use newfangleness°   *fickleness*
But since that I so kindely am servéd,   *20*
I fain would know what she hath deservéd.

ANONYMOUS

Madrigal

My love in her attire doth show her wit,
   It doth so well become her;
For every season she hath dressings fit,
   For winter, spring, and summer.
   No beauty she doth miss   5
   When all her robes are on;
   But beauty's self she is
   When all her robes are gone.

JOHN CLARE   (1793–1864)

First Love

I ne'er was struck before that hour
   With love so sudden and so sweet,
Her face it bloomed like a sweet flower
   And stole my heart away complete.
My face turned pale as deadly pale.   5
   My legs refused to walk away,
And when she looked, what could I ail?
   My life and all seemed turned to clay.

And then my blood rushed to my face
   And took my eyesight quite away,   10
The trees and bushes round the place
   Seemed midnight at noonday.
I could not see a single thing,
   Words from my eyes did start—
They spoke as chords do from the string,   15
   And blood burnt round my heart.

Are flowers the winter's choice?
   Is love's bed always snow?
She seemed to hear my silent voice,
   Not love's appeals to know.   20
I never saw so sweet a face
   As that I stood before.
My heart has left its dwelling-place
   And can return no more.

THOMAS STANLEY   (1625–1678)

The Magnet

Ask the Empress of the night
  How the hand which guides her sphere,
Constant in unconstant light,
  Taught the waves her yoke to bear,
And did thus by loving force   5
Curb or tame the rude sea's course.

Ask the female palm how she
  First did woo her husband's love;
And the magnet, ask how he
  Doth the obsequious iron move;   10
Waters, plants and stones know this,
That they love, not what love is.

Be not then less kind than these,
  Or from love exempt alone;
Let us twine like amorous trees,   15
  And like rivers melt in one;
Or, if thou more cruel prove
Learn of steel and stones to love.

SIDNEY GODOLPHIN   (1610–1643)

Why So Pale and Wan

Why so pale and wan, fond lover?
    Prithee, who so pale?
Will, when looking well can't move her,
    Looking ill prevail?
    Prithee, who so pale?   5

Why so dull and mute, young sinner?
    Prithee, why so mute?
Will, when speaking well can't win her,
    Saying nothing do 't?
    Prithee, who so mute?   10

Quit, quit for shame! This will not move;
    This cannot take her.
If of herself she will not love,
    Nothing can make her:
    The devil take her!   15

THOMAS CAMPION (1567–1620)

There Is a Garden in Her Face

There is a garden in her face
Where roses and white lilies grow;
  A heav'nly paradise is that place
Wherein all pleasant fruits do flow.
    There cherries grow which none may buy   *5*
    Till "Cherry-ripe" themselves do cry.°

Those cherries fairly do enclose
Of orient pearl a double row,
  Which when her lovely laughter shows,
They look like rose-buds filled with snow;   *10*
    Yet them nor peer nor prince can buy,
    Till "Cherry-ripe" themselves do cry.

Her eyes like angels watch them still;
Her brows like bended bows do stand,
  Threat'ning with piercing frowns to kill   *15*
All that attempt, with eye or hand
    Those sacred cherries to come nigh
    Till "Cherry-ripe" themselves do cry.

[6]"Cherry-ripe" is a familiar cry of London street vendors.

ROBERT HERRICK (1591–1674)

To the Virgins, to Make Much of Time

Gather ye rosebuds while ye may,
  Old Time is still a-flying:
And this same flower that smiles to-day
  To-morrow will be dying.

The glorious lamp of heaven, the sun,   *5*
  The higher he's a-getting,
The sooner will his race be run,
  And nearer he's to setting.

That age is best which is the first,
  When youth and blood are warmer;   *10*
But being spent, the worse, and worst
  Times still succeed the former.

Then be not coy, but use your time,
   And while ye may, go marry:
For having lost but once your prime,   *15*
   You may for ever tarry.

BEN JONSON   (1572–1637)

To Celia

Drink to me only with thine eyes,
   And I will pledge with mine;
Or leave a kiss but in the cup
   And I'll not look for wine.
The thirst that from the soil doth rise   *5*
   Doth ask a drink divine;
But might I of Jove's nectar sup,
   I would not change for thine.

I sent thee late a rosy wreath,
   Not so much honouring thee   *10*
As giving it a hope that there
   It could not withered be;
But thou thereon didst only breathe,
   And sent'st it back to me;
Since when it grows, and smells, I swear,   *15*
   Not of itself but thee!

JOHN DONNE   (1572–1631)

The Sun Rising

   Busy old fool, unruly Sun,
     Why dost thou thus
Through windows and through curtains call on us?
Must to thy motions lovers' seasons run?
     Saucy pedantic wretch, go chide   *5*
     Late schoolboys and sour prentices,
  Go tell court-huntsmen that the king will ride,
  Call country ants to harvest offices;
Love, all alike, no season knows, nor clime,
Nor hours, days, months, which are the rags of time.   *10*

   Thy beams so reverend and strong
     Why shouldst thou think?

I could eclipse and cloud them with a wink,
But that I would not lose her sight so long;
    If her eyes have not blinded thine,   *15*
    Look, and tomorrow late tell me,
   Whether both th' Indias of spice and mine
   Be where thou left'st them, or lie here with me.
Ask for those kings whom thou saw'st yesterday,
And thou shalt hear, "All here in one bed lay."   *20*

    She's all states, and all princes I;
    Nothing else is.
Princes do but play us; compared to this,
All honor's mimic, all wealth alchemy.
    Thou, Sun, art half as happy as we,   *25*
    In that the world's contracted thus;
   Thine age asks ease, and since thy duties be
   To warm the world, that's done in warming us.
Shine here to us, and thou art everywhere;
This bed thy center is, these walls thy sphere.   *30*

ROBERT PINSKY   (1940–   )

First Early Mornings Together

Waking up over the candy store together
We hear birds waking up below the sill
And slowly recognize ourselves, the weather,
The time, and the birds that rustle there until

Down to the street as fog and quiet lift   *5*
The pigeons from the wrinkled awning flutter
To reconnoiter, mutter, stare and shift
Pecking by ones or twos the rainbowed gutter.

GEORGE GORDON NOEL, LORD BYRON   (1788–1824)

She Walks in Beauty

She walks in beauty, like the night
   Of cloudless climes and starry skies;
And all that's best of dark and bright
   Meet in her aspect and her eyes:
Thus mellowed to that tender light   *5*
   Which heaven to gaudy day denies.

One shade the more, one ray the less,
　　Had half impaired the nameless grace
Which waves in every raven tress,
　　Or softly lightens o'er her face;　　　　　　　　　　　　　*10*
Where thoughts serenely sweet express
　　How pure, how dear their dwelling-place.

And on that cheek, and o'er that brow,
　　So soft, so calm, yet eloquent,
The smiles that win, the tints that glow,　　　　　　　　　*15*
　　But tell of days in goodness spent,
A mind at peace with all below,
　　A heart whose love is innocent.

ROBERT BURNS   (1759–1796)

John Anderson My Jo

John Anderson my jo,° John,　　　　　　　　　　　　*sweetheart*
　　When we were first acquent,
Your locks were like the raven,
　　Your bonnie brow was brent;°　　　　　　　　　　　*smooth*
But now your brow is beld, John,　　　　　　　　　　　*5*
　　Your locks are like the snaw,
But blessings on your frosty pow,°　　　　　　　　　　*head*
　　John Anderson my jo!

John Anderson my jo, John,
　　We clamb the hill thegither,　　　　　　　　　　　*10*
And monie a cantie° day, John　　　　　　　　　　　*happy*
　　We've had wi' ane anither:
Now we maun° totter down, John,　　　　　　　　　　*must*
　　And hand in hand we'll go,
And sleep thegither at the foot,　　　　　　　　　　*15*
　　John Anderson my jo!

ELIZABETH BARRETT BROWNING   (1809–1861)

How Do I Love Thee?

How do I love thee? Let me count the ways.
I love thee to the depth and breadth and height
My soul can reach, when feeling out of sight
For the ends of Being and ideal Grace.
I love thee to the level of everyday's　　　　　　　　　*5*
Most quiet need, by sun and candle-light.

I love thee freely, as men strive for Right;
I love thee purely, as they turn from Praise.
I love thee with the passion put to use
In my old griefs, and with my childhood's faith.   *10*
I love thee with a love I seemed to lose
With my lost saints,—I love thee with the breath,
Smiles, tears, of all my life!—and, if God choose,
I shall but love thee better after death.

ROBERT PENN WARREN   (1905–   )

Love Recognized

There are many things in the world and you
Are one of them. Many things keep happening and
You are one of them, and the happening that
Is you keeps falling like snow
On the landscape of not-you, hiding hideousness, until   *5*
The streets and the world of wrath are choked with snow.

How many things have become silent? Traffic
Is throttled. The mayor
Has been, clearly, remiss, and the city
Was totally unprepared for such a crisis. Nor   *10*
Was I—yes, why should this happen to me?
I have always been a law-abiding citizen.

But you, like snow, like love, keep falling,

And it is not certain that the world will not be
Covered in a glitter of crystalline whiteness.   *15*

Silence.

ROBERT GRAVES   (1895–1985)

She Tells Her Love While Half Asleep

She tells her love while half asleep
  In the dark hours,
    With half-words whispered low:
As Earth stirs in her winter sleep
  And puts out grass and flowers   *5*
    Despite the snow,
    Despite the falling snow.

THEODORE ROETHKE   (1908–1963)

I Knew a Woman

I knew a woman, lovely in her bones,
When small birds sighed, she would sigh back at them;
Ah, when she moved, she moved more ways than one:
The shapes a bright container can contain!
Of her choice virtues only gods should speak,   5
Or English poets who grew up on Greek
(I'd have them sing in chorus, cheek to cheek).

How well her wishes went! She stroked my chin,
She taught me Turn, and Counter-turn, and Stand;
She taught me Touch, that undulant white skin;   10
I nibbled meekly from her proffered hand;
She was the sickle; I, poor I, the rake,
Coming behind her for her pretty sake
(But what prodigious mowing we did make).

Love likes a gander, and adores a goose: 15
Her full lips pursed, the errant note to seize;
She played it quick, she played it light and loose;
My eyes, they dazzled at her flowing knees;
Her several parts could keep a pure repose,
Or one hip quiver with a mobile nose   20
(She moved in circles, and those circles moved).

Let seed be grass, and grass turn into hay:
I'm martyr to a motion not my own;
What's freedom for? To know eternity.
I swear she cast a shadow white as stone.   25
But who would count eternity in days?
These old bones live to learn her wanton ways:
(I measure time by how a body sways).

HENRY HOWARD, EARL OF SURREY   (1517–1547)

A Complaint by Night of the Lover Not Beloved

Alas, so all things now do hold their peace,
Heaven and earth disturbèd in nothing;
The beasts, the air, the birds their song do cease,
The nightë's chair the stars about doth bring;
Calm is the sea, the waves work less and less.   5
So am not I, whom love, alas, doth wring,

Bringing before my face the great increase
Of my desires, whereat I weep and sing
In joy and woe, as in a doubtful ease
For my sweet thoughts sometime do pleasure bring,   10
But by and by the cause of my disease
Gives me pang that inwardly doth sting,
When that I think what grief it is again
To live and lack the thing should rid my pain.

WILLIAM JOHNSON CORY   (1823–1892)

Amaturus

Somewhere beneath the sun,
    These quivering heart-strings prove it,
Somewhere there must be one
    Made for this soul, to move it;
Some one that hides her sweetness   5
    From neighbours whom she slights,
Nor can attain completeness,
    Nor give her heart its rights;
Some one whom I could court
    With no great change of manner,   10
Still holding reason's fort,
    Though waving fancy's banner;
A lady, not so queenly
    As to disdain my hand,
Yet born to smile serenely   15
    Like those that rule the land;
Noble, but not too proud;
    With soft hair simply folded,
And bright face crescent-browed,
    And throat by Muses moulded;   20
And eyelids lightly falling
    On little glistening seas,
Deep-calm, when gales are brawling,
    Though stirred by every breeze:
Swift voice, like flight of dove   25
    Through minster arches floating,
With sudden turns, when love
    Gets overnear to doting;
Keen lips, that shape soft sayings
    Like crystals of the snow,   30
With pretty half-betrayings
        Of things one may not know;

Fair hand, whose touches thrill,
    Like golden rod of wonder,
Which Hermes wields at will   *35*
    Spirit and flesh to sunder;
Light foot, to press the stirrup
    In fearlessness and glee,
Or dance, till finches chirrup,
    And stars sink to the sea.   *40*

Forth, Love, and find this maid,
    Wherever she be hidden:
Speak, Love, be not afraid,
    But plead as thou art bidden;
And say, that he who taught thee   *45*
    His yearning want and pain,
Too dearly, dearly bought thee
    To part with thee in vain.

W. H. AUDEN   (1907–1973)

Lay Your Sleeping Head, My Love

Lay your sleeping head, my love,
Human on my faithless arm;
Time and fevers burn away
Individual beauty from
Thoughtful children, and the grave   *5*
Proves the child ephemeral:
But in my arms till break of day
Let the living creature lie,
Mortal, guilty, but to me
The entirely beautiful.   *10*

Soul and body have no bounds:
To lovers as they lie upon
Her tolerant enchanted slope
In their ordinary swoon,
Grave the vision Venus° sends   *goddess of love* *15*
Of supernatural sympathy,
Universal love and hope;
While an abstract insight wakes
Among the glaciers and the rocks
The hermit's sensual ecstasy.   *20*

Certainty, fidelity
On the stroke of midnight pass
Like vibrations of a bell,
And fashionable madmen raise

Their pedantic boring cry: 25
Every farthing° of the cost,   *quarter of a penny*
All the dreaded cards foretell,
Shall be paid, but from this night
Not a whisper, not a thought,
Not a kiss nor look be lost.   30

Beauty, midnight, vision dies:
Let the winds of dawn that blow
Softly round your dreaming head
Such a day of sweetness show
Eye and knocking heart may bless,   35
Find the mortal world enough;
Noons of dryness see you fed
By the involuntary powers,
Nights of insult let you pass
Watched by every human love.   40

ROBERT LOWELL   (1917–1978)

Man and Wife

Tamed by *Miltown*,° we lie on Mother's bed;   *a tranquilizer*
the rising sun in war paint dyes us red;
in broad daylight her gilded bed-posts shine,
abandoned, almost Dionysian.
At last the trees are green on Marlborough Street,°   *in Boston*   5
blossoms on our magnolia ignite
the morning with their murderous five days' white.
All night I've held your hand,
as if you had
a fourth time faced the kingdom of the mad—   10
its hackneyed speech, its homicidal eye—
and dragged me home alive . . . . Oh my *Petite*,°   *my little one*
clearest of all God's creatures, still all air and nerve:
you were in your twenties, and I,
once hand on glass   15
and heart in mouth,
outdrank the Rahvs° in the heat   *friends of the poet*
of Greenwich Village, fainting at your feet—
too boiled and shy
and poker-faced to make a pass,   20
while the shrill verve
of your invective scorched the traditional South.

Now twelve years later, you turn your back.
Sleepless, you hold

your pillow to your hollows like a child;   *25*
your old-fashioned tirade—
loving, rapid, merciless—
breaks like the Atlantic Ocean on my head.

DENISE LEVERTOV   (1923–   )

The Ache of Marriage

The ache of marriage:

thigh and tongue, beloved,
are heavy with it,
it throbs in the teeth

We look for communion   *5*
and are turned away, beloved,
each and each

It is leviathan° and we   *a legendary monster*
in its belly
looking for joy, some joy   *10*
not to be known outside it

two by two in the ark of
the ache of it.

ANNE STEVENSON   (1933–   )

The Marriage

They will fit, she thinks,
but only if her backbone
cuts exactly into his rib cage,
and only if his knees
dock exactly under her knees   *5*
and all four
agree on a common angle.

All would be well
if only
they could face each other.   *10*

Even as it is
there are compensations
for having to meet
nose to neck
chest to scapula   *15*
groin to rump
when they sleep.

They look, at least,
as if they were going
in the same direction.   *20*

WENDELL BERRY   (1934–   )

The Country of Marriage

1
I dream of you walking at night along the streams
of the country of my birth, warm blooms and the
    nightsongs
of birds opening around you as you walk.
You are holding in your body the dark seed of my
    sleep.

2
This comes after silence. Was it something I said   *5*
that bound me to you, some mere promise
or, worse, the fear of loneliness and death?
A man lost in the woods in the dark, I stood
still and said nothing. And then there rose in me,
like the earth's empowering brew rising   *10*
in root and branch, the words of a dream of you
I did not know I had dreamed. I was a wanderer
who feels the solace of his native land
under his feet again and moving in his blood.
I went on, blind and faithful. Where I stepped   *15*
my track was there to steady me. It was no abyss
that lay before me, but only the level ground.

3
Sometimes our life reminds me
of a forest in which there is a graceful clearing
and in that opening a house,   *20*
an orchard and garden,
comfortable shades, and flowers
red and yellow in the sun, a pattern
made in the light for the light to return to.
The forest is mostly dark, its ways   *25*
to be made anew day after day, the dark
richer than the light and more blessed
provided we stay brave
enough to keep on going in.

4

How many times have I come into you out of my   *30*
   head
with joy, if ever a man was,
for to approach you I have given up the light
and all directions. I come to you
lost, wholly trusting, as a man who goes
into the forest unarmed. It is as though I descend   *35*
slowly earthward out of the air. I rest in peace
in you, when I arrive at last.

DAVE SMITH   (1942–   )

August, On the Rented Farm

For Jeddie

In this season, through the clear tears
of discovery, my son calls me
to an abandoned barn. Among
spiders' goldspinning and the small
eulogies of crickets, he has entered   *5*
the showering secret of our lives,
and the light fur of something
half-eaten mats his hands.
Later, on a rotting length
of pine, we sit   *10*
under the star-brilliance
of birds fretting
the hollow light.
Under them, dreamless,
we have come to cast   *15*
our lot with songs
of celebration.
All afternoon we sit and become
lovers, his hand in mine
like a bird's delicate wing.   *20*
Everywhere the sparrows go down
to the river for the sweet
tears of communion. Soon,
in the yellow last light,
we will begin again to speak   *25*
of that light in the house
that is not ours, that is only
what we come to out of the fields
in the slow-plunging knowledge
of words trying to find a way home.   *30*

PAUL MARIANI   (1940–   )

North/South

For Bob Pack

In the long run for both of us
it will be the willow darkening
in a northern twilight
as the dominant key of winter

reasserts itself. As even now   5
in late August outside this window
the small birds hesitate among
the branches before they arc

their bodies south for the three
days' flight above the darkening   10
waters. Angel-winged they turn,
before they lock on their own

essential homings. Or, to see it
from your perspective: flight
to a southernmost extreme. Robert,   15
for whom if not for you

could I feel this bond, your north
anchoring my still-vexed south?
Even these so-called free-verse
lines arc in a double *pas-de-deux*   20

pan-foot, goat-foot rocking back
and forth, playing counter
to that granite bass of yours.
You grin that flinty grin glistening

in the wintry air you call   25
your home now, made native
by the will itself. "You still
dance a little crazy," you say,

"but no cop could say you didn't
toe the line. What *you* have   30
is a case of free form hurtling
after form. Count yourself among

the blessèd ones who still have
something to go home to." Robert,
who was it warned us both to work   35
while there was still light enough

to work with, knowing the long night
must needs be coming on? The night:

when all hands must willy-nilly rest,
the last line edging into granite   *40*

or the upturn of the wind, the same wind
which turns the feathers of the small birds
up as they chatter in the branches.
They too must sense the great change

coming on and so begin again while there is   *45*
still time to test their wings, half shaped
by years of trial and half again by luck, before
they turn at last into the very air itself.

SYDNEY LEA   (1942–   )

Young Man Leaving Home

Over the dropped eggs and hash, his elders
poured unaccustomed benedictions.

The morning broke fair, but they
insisted on sensing rain.

That last spring, after so many,   *5*
the tree with the rope swing blossomed,

random plum blooms dropping groundward
where the playhouse leaned.

Later, the tracks with their switchbacks among
the shanties outside the station   *10*

had a somewhat surprising Protestant look
of a hopeless proposition.

Adieu: to the father who fobbed and fondled
his watch, at the end of his chain,

whose simple grief no halting final   *15*
declaration seemed to soften;

to the mother feigning impatience
with the lateness of the train.

They. Tree. House. Yard.
All had called for his valediction,   *20*

but now was already the hour prior
to greeting whatever it is that this is,

hour of assembly, of public instead
of certain longed-for private kisses,

hour of livered grandmothers, aunts,   25
whose cheeks the plain tears stained. . . .

It passed in the fashion of dreams, at once
chaotic and sluggish.

En route: in silence, he hailed The Future,
that unimaginable lode of riches,   30

this hero, composed of a dozen young rebels
out of thin novels, groaning with luggage.

MICHAEL S. HARPER   (1938–   )

New Season

My woman has picked
all the leaves,
rolled her hands into locks,
gone into the woods
where I have taught her   5
the language of these wood leaves,
and the red sand plum trees.
It is a digest
of my taking these leaves with hunger;
it is love she understands.   10
From my own wooden smell
she has shed her raisin skin
and come back
sweetened into brilliant music:
Her song is our new season.   15

ANTHOLOGY V
The Animals Are Coming

ALASTAIR REID (1926–   )

Curiosity

may have killed the cat. More likely,
the cat was just unlucky, or else curious
to see what death was like, having no cause
to go on licking paws, or fathering
litter on litter of kittens, predictably.   *5*

Nevertheless, to be curious
is dangerous enough. To distrust
what is always said, what seems,
to ask odd questions, interfere in dreams,
smell rats, leave home, have hunches,   *10*
does not endear cats to those doggy circles
where well-smelt baskets, suitable wives, good lunches
are the order of things, and where prevails
much wagging of incurious heads and tails.

Face it. Curiosity   *15*
will not cause us to die—
only lack of it will.
Never to want to see
the other side of the hill
or that improbable country   *20*
where living is an idyll
(although a probable hell)
would kill us all.
Only the curious

have if they live a tale   *25*
worth telling at all.

Dogs say cats love too much, are irresponsible,
are dangerous, marry too many wives,
desert their children, chill all dinner tables
with tales of their nine lives.   *30*

Well, they are lucky. Let them be
nine-lived and contradictory,
curious enough to change, prepared to pay
the cat-price, which is to die
and die again and again,   *35*
each time with no less pain.
A cat-minority of one
is all that can be counted on
to tell the truth; and what cats have to tell
on each return from hell   *40*
is this: that dying is what the living do,
that dying is what the loving do,
and that dead dogs are those who never know
that dying is what, to live, each has to do.

THOMAS GRAY   (1716–1771)

Ode: On the Death of a Favorite Cat, Drowned in a Tub of Goldfishes

'Twas on a lofty vase's side,
Where China's gayest art had dyed
    The azure flowers that blow;°   *bloom*
Demurest of the tabby kind,
The pensive Selima reclined,   *5*
    Gazed on the lake below.

Her conscious tail her joy declared;
The fair round face, the snowy beard,
    The velvet of her paws,
Her coat, that with the tortoise vies,   *10*
Her ears of jet, and emerald eyes,
    She saw; and purred applause.

Still had she gazed; but 'midst the tide
Two angel forms were seen to glide,
    The genii° of the stream: *spirits*   *15*
Their scaly armor's Tyrian hue°

---

[16]Purple hue of a dye made in ancient Tyre.

Through richest purple to the view
 Betrayed a golden gleam.

The hapless nymph with wonder saw:
A whisker first, and then a claw,   *20*
 With many an ardent wish
She stretched in vain to reach the prize.
What female heart can gold despise?
 What cat's averse to fish?

Presumptuous maid! with looks intent   *25*
Again she stretched, again she bent,
 Nor knew the gulf between.
(Malignant Fate sat by and smiled)
The slippery verge° her feet beguiled,   *edge*
 She tumbled headlong in.   *30*

Eight times° emerging from the flood
She mewed to every water god
 Some speedy aid to send:
No dolphin came, no Nereid° stirred;   *sea nymph*
Nor cruel Tom, nor Susan heard—   *35*
 A favorite has no friend!

From hence, ye beauties, undeceived,
Know, one false step is ne'er retrieved,
 And be with caution bold:
Not all that tempts your wandering eyes   *40*
And heedless hearts is lawful prize;
 Nor all that glistens, gold.

[31]Cats have nine lives, according to an old myth.

WILLIAM HENRY DAVIES   (1871–1940)

The Cat

Within that porch, across the way,
 I see two naked eyes this night;
Two eyes that neither shut nor blink,
 Searching my face with a green light.

But cats to me are strange, so strange—   5
 I cannot sleep if one is near;
And though I'm sure I see those eyes
 I'm not so sure a body's there!

WALT WHITMAN   (1819–1892)

A Noiseless Patient Spider

A noiseless patient spider,
I marked where on a little promontory it stood isolated,
Marked how to explore the vacant vast surrounding,
It launched forth filament, filament, filament, out of itself,
Ever unreeling them, ever tirelessly speeding them.   *5*

And you O my soul where you stand,
Surrounded, detached, in measureless oceans of space,
Ceaselessly musing, venturing, throwing, seeking the spheres to connect
    them,
Till the bridge you will need be formed, till the ductile anchor hold,
Till the gossamer threat you fling catch somewhere, O my soul.   *10*

EMILY DICKINSON   (1830–1886)

A Narrow Fellow in the Grass

A narrow Fellow in the Grass
Occasionally rides—
You may have met Him—did you not
His notice sudden is—

The Grass divides as with a Comb—   *5*
A spotted shaft is seen—
And then it closes at your feet
And opens further on—

He likes a Boggy Acre
A Floor too cool for Corn—   *10*
Yet when a Boy, and Barefoot—
I more than once at Noon
Have passed, I thought, a Whip lash
Unbraiding in the Sun
When stopping to secure it   *15*
It wrinkled, and was gone—

Several of Nature's People
I know, and they know me—
I feel for them a transport
Of cordiality—   *20*

But never met this Fellow
Attended, or alone
Without a tighter breathing
And Zero at the Bone—

WILLIAM CARLOS WILLIAMS   (1883–1963)

The Bull

It is in captivity—
ringed, haltered, chained
to a drag
the bull is godlike

Unlike the cows   5
he lives alone, nozzles
the sweet grass gingerly
to pass the time away

He kneels, lies down
and stretching out   10
a foreleg licks himself
about the hoof

then stays
with half-closed eyes,
Olympian commentary on   15
the bright passage of days.

—The round sun
smooth his lacquer
through
the glossy pinetrees   20

his substance hard
as ivory or glass—
through which the wind
yet plays—
        milkless   25

he nods
and the hair between his horns
and eyes matted
with hyacinthine curls

EDWIN MUIR   (1887–1959)

The Horses

Barely a twelvemonth after
The seven days war that put the world to sleep,
Late in the evening the strange horses came.
By then we had made our covenant with silence,
But in the first few days it was so still   5

We listened to our breathing and were afraid.
On the second day
The radios failed; we turned the knobs; no answer.
On the third day a warship passed us, heading north,
Dead bodies piled on the deck. On the sixth day   *10*
A plane plunged over us into the sea. Thereafter
Nothing. The radios dumb;
And still they stand in corners of our kitchens,
And stand, perhaps, turned on, in a million rooms
All over the world. But now if they should speak,   *15*
If on a sudden they should speak again,
If on the stroke of noon a voice should speak,
We would not listen, we would not let it bring
That old bad world that swallowed its children quick
At one great gulp. We would not have it again.   *20*
Sometimes we think of the nations lying asleep,
Curled blindly in impenetrable sorrow,
And then the thought confounds us with its strangeness.
The tractors lie about our fields; at evening
They look like dank sea-monsters couched and waiting.   *25*
We leave them where they are and let them rust:
'They'll moulder away and be like other loam'.
We make our oxen drag our rusty ploughs,
Long laid aside. We have gone back
Far past our fathers' land.   *30*
         And then, that evening
Late in the summer the strange horses came.
We heard a distant tapping on the road,
A deepening drumming; it stopped, went on again
And at the corner changed to hollow thunder.   *35*
We saw the heads
Like a wild wave charging and were afraid.
We had sold our horses in our fathers' time
To buy new tractors. Now they were strange to us
As fabulous steeds set on an ancient shield   *40*
Or illustrations in a book of knights.
We did not dare go near them. Yet they waited,
Stubborn and shy, as if they had been sent
By an old command to find our whereabouts
And that long-lost archaic companionship.   *45*
In the first moment we had never a thought
That they were creatures to be owned and used.
Among them were some half-a-dozen colts
Dropped in some wilderness of the broken world,
Yet new as if they had come from their own Eden.   *50*
Since then they have pulled our ploughs and borne our loads,
But that free servitude still can pierce our hearts.
Our life is changed; their coming our beginning.

PABLO NERUDA   (1904–1972)

Horses

From the window I saw the horses.

I was in Berlin, in winter. The light
was without light, the sky skyless.

The air white like a moistened loaf.

From my window, I could see a deserted arena,   5
a circle bitten out by the teeth of winter.

All at once, led out by a single man,
ten horses were stepping, stepping into the snow.

Scarcely had they rippled into existence
like flame, than they filled the whole world of my eyes,   10
empty till now. Faultless, flaming,
they stepped like ten gods on broad, clean hoofs,
their manes recalling a dream of salt spray.

Their rumps were globes, were oranges.

Their colour was amber and honey, was on fire.   15

Their necks were towers
carved from the stone of pride,
and in their furious eyes, sheer energy
showed itself, a prisoner inside them.

And there, in the silence, at the mid—   20
point of the day, in a dirty, disgruntled winter,
the horses' intense presence was blood,
was rhythm, was the beckoning light of all being.

I saw, I saw, and seeing, I came to life.
There was the unwitting fountain, the dance of gold, the sky,   25
the fire that sprang to life in beautiful things.

I have obliterated that gloomy Berlin winter.
I shall not forget the light from these horses.

—translated by Alastair Reid

JAMES DICKEY   (1923–   )

The Dusk of Horses

Right under their noses, the green
Of the field is paling away
Because of something fallen from the sky.

They see this, and put down
Their long heads deeper in grass   5
That only just escapes reflecting them

As the dream of a millpond would.
The color green flees over the grass
Like an insect, following the red sun over

The next hill. The grass is white.   10
There is no cloud so dark and white at once;
There is no pool at dawn that deepens

Their faces and thirsts as this does.
Now they are feeding on solid
Cloud, and, one by one,   15

With nails as silent as stars among the wood
Hewed down years ago and now rotten,
The stalls are put up around them.

Now if they lean, they come
On wood on any side. Not touching it, they sleep.   20
No beast ever lived who understood

What happened among the sun's fields,
Or cared why the color of grass
Fled over the hill while he stumbled,

Led by the halter to sleep   25
On his four taxed, worthy legs.
Each thinks he awakens where

The sun is black on the rooftop,
That the green is dancing in the next pasture,
And that the way to sleep   30

In a cloud, or in a risen lake,
Is to walk as though he were still
In the drained field standing, head down,

To pretend to sleep when led,   35
And thus to go under the ancient white
Of the meadow, as green goes

And whiteness comes up through his face
Holding stars and rotten rafters,
Quiet, fragrant, and relieved.

RICHARD EBERHART (1904–   )

The Groundhog

In June, amid the golden fields,
I saw a groundhog lying dead.

Dead lay he; my senses shook,
And mind outshot our naked frailty.
There lowly in the vigorous summer   5
His form began its senseless change,
And made my senses waver dim
Seeing nature ferocious in him.
Inspecting close his maggots' might
And seething cauldron of his being,   10
Half with loathing, half with a strange love,
I poked him with an angry stick.
The fever arose, became a flame
And Vigour circumscribed the skies,
Immense energy in the sun,   15
And through my frame a sunless trembling.
My stick had done nor good nor harm.
Then stood I silent in the day
Watching the object, as before;
And kept my reverence for knowledge   20
Trying for control, to be still,
To quell the passion of the blood;
Until I had bent down on my knees
Praying for joy in the sight of decay.
And so I left; and I returned   25
In Autumn strict of eye, to see
The sap gone out of the groundhog,
But the bony sodden hulk remained.
But the year had lost its meaning,
And in intellectual chains   30
I lost both love and loathing,
Mured up in the wall of wisdom.
Another summer took the fields again
Massive and burning, full of life,
But when I chanced upon the spot   35
There was only a little hair left,
And bones bleaching in the sunlight
Beautiful as architecture;
I watched them like a geometer,
And cut a walking stick from a birch.   40
It has been three years, now.
There is no sign of the groundhog.
I stood there in the whirling summer,
My hand capped a withered heart,
And thought of China and of Greece,   45
Of Alexander in his tent;°

---

[46]Alexander the Great, the Greek conqueror.

Of Montaigne in his tower,°
Of Saint Theresa in her wild lament.°

[47]The French essayist Montaigne wrote in a tower study.
[48]Saint Theresa was said to have strange raptures.

ELIZABETH BISHOP   (1911–1980)

The Fish

I caught a tremendous fish
and held him beside the boat
half out of water, with my hook
fast in a corner of his mouth.
He didn't fight.   5
He hadn't fought at all.
He hung a grunting weight,
battered and venerable
and homely. Here and there
his brown skin hung in strips   10
like ancient wallpaper,
and its pattern of darker brown
was like wallpaper:
shapes like full-blown roses
stained and lost through age.   15
He was speckled with barnacles,
fine rosettes of lime,
and infested
with tiny white sea-lice,
and underneath two or three   20
rags of green weed hung down.
While his gills were breathing in
the terrible oxygen
—the frightening gills,
fresh and crisp with blood,   25
that can cut so badly—
I thought of the coarse white flesh
packed in like feathers,
the big bones and the little bones,
the dramatic reds and blacks   30
of his shiny entrails,
and the pink swim-bladder
like a big peony.
I looked into his eyes
which were far larger than mine   35
but shallower, and yellowed,

the irises backed and packed
with tarnished tinfoil
seen through the lenses
of old scratched isinglass.   *40*
They shifted a little but not
to return my stare.
—It was more like the tipping
of an object toward the light.
I admired his sullen face,   *45*
the mechanism of his jaw,
and then I saw
that from his lower lip
—if you could call it a lip—
grim, wet, and weaponlike,   *50*
hung five old pieces of fish-line,
of four and a wire leader
with the swivel still attached,
with all their five big hooks
grown firmly in his mouth.   *55*
A green line, frayed at the end
where he broke it, two heavier lines,
and a fine black thread
still crimped from the strain and snap
when it broke and he got away.   *60*
Like medals with their ribbons
frayed and wavering,
a five-haired beard of wisdom
trailing from his aching jaw.
I stared and stared   *65*
and victory filled up
the little rented boat
from the pool of bilge
where oil had spread a rainbow
around the rusted engine   *70*
to the bailer rusted orange,
the sun-cracked thwarts,
the oarlocks on their strings,
the gunnels—until everything
was rainbow, rainbow, rainbow!   *75*
And I let the fish go.

ROBINSON JEFFERS   (1887–1962)

Hurt Hawks

I

The broken pillar of the wing jags from the clotted shoulder,
The wing trails like a banner in defeat,

No more to use the sky forever but live with famine
And pain a few days: cat nor coyote
Will shorten the week of waiting for death, there is game without talons.   *5*
He stands under the oak-bush and waits
The lame feet of salvation; at night he remembers freedom
And flies in a dream, the dawns ruin it.
He is strong and pain is worse to the strong, incapacity is worse.
The curs of the day come and torment him   *10*
At distance, no one but death the redeemer will humble that head,
The intrepid readiness, the terrible eyes.
The wild God of the world is sometimes merciful to those
That ask mercy, not often to the arrogant,
You do not know him, you communal people, or you have for-
    gotten him;   *15*
Intemperate and savage, the hawk remembers him;
Beautiful and wild, the hawks, and men that are dying,
    remember him.

II

I'd sooner, except the penalties, kill a man than a hawk; but the great
    redtail°   *red-tail hawk*
Had nothing left but unable misery
From the bone too shattered for mending, the wing that trailed under
    his talons when he moved.   *20*
We had fed him six weeks, I gave him freedom,
He wandered over the foreland hill and returned in the evening,
    asking for death,
Not like a beggar, still eyed with the old
Implacable arrogance. I gave him the lead gift in the twilight. What fell
    was relaxed,
Owl-downy, soft feminine feathers; but what   *25*
Soared: the fierce rush: the night-herons by the flooded river cried fear
    at its rising
Before it was quite unsheathed from reality.

ROBERT PENN WARREN   (1905–   )

Evening Hawk

From plane of light to plane, wings dipping through
Geometries and orchids that the sunset builds,
Out of the peak's black angularity of shadow, riding
The last tumultuous avalanche of
Light above pines and the guttural gorge,   *5*
The hawk comes.

    His wing
Scythes down another day, his motion
Is that of the honed steel-edge, we hear
The crashless fall of stalks of Time.   *10*

The head of each stalk is heavy with the gold of our error.

Look! look! he is climbing the last light
Who knows neither Time nor error, and under
Whose eye, unforgiving, the world, unforgiven, swings
Into shadow.   *15*

    Long now,
The last thrush is still, the last bat
Now cruises in his sharp heiroglyphics. His wisdom
Is ancient, too, and immense. The star
Is steady, like Plato, over the mountain.   *20*
If there were no wind we might, we thing, hear
The earth grind on its axis, or history
Drip in darkness like a leaking pipe in the cellar.

WILLIAM BUTLER YEATS   (1865–1939)

The Wild Swans at Coole

The trees are in their autumn beauty,
The woodland paths are dry,
Under the October twilight the water
Mirrors a still sky;
Upon the brimming water among the stones   *5*
Are nine-and-fifty swans.

The nineteenth autumn has come upon me
Since I first made my count;
I saw, before I had well finished,
All suddenly mount   *10*
And scatter wheeling in great broken rings
Upon their clamorous wings.

I have looked upon those brilliant creatures,
And now my heart is sore,
All's changed since I, hearing at twilight,   *15*
The first time on this shore,
The bell-beat of their wings above my head,
Trod with a lighter tread.

Unwearied still, lover by lover,
They paddle in the cold   *20*
Companionable streams or climb the air;

Their hearts have not grown old;
Passion or conquest, wander where they will,
Attend upon them still.

But now they drift on the still water,   25
Mysterious, beautiful;
Among what rushes will they build,
By what lake's edge or pool
Delight men's eyes when I awake some day
To find they have flown away?   30

ALFRED, LORD TENNYSON   (1809–1982)

The Eagle

He clasps the crag with crooked hands;
Close to the sun in lonely lands,
Ringed with the azure world, he stands.

The wrinkled sea beneath him crawls;
He watches from his mountain walls,   5
And like a thunderbolt he falls.

J. D. McCLATCHY   (1945–   )

Hummingbird

There is no hum, of course, nor is the bird
That shiver of stained glass iridescence
Through which the garden appears—itself
In flight not from but toward an intensity
Of outline, color, scent, each flower   5
An imperium—as in a paragraph of Proust.

Mine is a shade of that branch it rests on
Between rounds: bark-wing, lichen-breast,
The butternut's furthest, hollow twig.
How to make from sow thistle to purslane?   10
So, into this airy vault of jewelweed,
Slipped past the drowsing bee watch,

Deep into the half-inch, bloodgold
Petal curve, tongue of the still untold.
Deaf to tones so low, the bees never mind   15
The dull grinding, these rusted gears
Pushed to the limit of extracting
From so many its little myth of rarity.

D. H. LAWRENCE   (1885–1930)

Humming-Bird

I can imagine, in some other world
Primeval-dumb, far back
In that most awful stillness, that only gasped and hummed,
Humming-birds raced down the avenues.

Before anything had a soul,   5
While life was a heave of Matter, half inanimate,
This little bit chipped off in brilliance
And went whizzing through the slow, vast, succulent stems.

I believe there were no flowers then,
In the world where the humming-bird flashed ahead of creation.   10
I believe he pierced the slow vegetable veins with his long beak.

Probably he was big
As mosses, and little lizards, they say, were once big.
Probably he was a jabbing, terrifying monster.

We look at him through the wrong end of the telescope of Time,   15
Luckily for us.

MARY OLIVER   (1930–   )

The Truro Bear

There's a bear in the Truro woods.
People have seen it—three or four,
or two, or one. I think
of the thickness of the serious woods
around the dark bowls of the Truro ponds;   5
I think of the blueberry fields, the blackberry tangles,
the cranberry bogs. And the sky
with its new moon, its familiar star-trails,
burns down like a brand-new heaven,
while everywhere I look on the scratchy hillsides   10
shadows seem to grow shoulders. Surely
a beast might be clever, be lucky, move quietly
through the woods for years, learning to stay away
from roads and houses. Common sense mutters:
it can't be true, it must be somebody's   15
runaway dog. But the seed
has been planted, and when has happiness ever
required much evidence to begin
its leaf-green breathing?

TED HUGHES   (1930–   )

The Thought-Fox

I imagine this midnight moment's forest:
Something else is alive
Beside the clock's loneliness
And this blank page where my fingers move.

Through the window I see no star: 5
Something more near
Though deeper within darkness
Is entering the loneliness:

Cold, delicately as the dark snow,
A fox's nose touches twig, leaf;   10
Two eyes serve a movement, that now
And again now, and now, and now

Sets neat prints into the snow
Between trees, and warily a lame
Shadow lags by stump and in hollow   15
Of a body that is bold to come

Across clearings, an eye,
A widening deepening greenness,
Brilliantly, concentratedly,
Coming about its own business   20

Till, with a sudden sharp hot stink of fox
It enters the dark hole of the head.
The window is starless still; the clock ticks,
The page is printed.

GREGORY CORSO   (1930–   )

The Mad Yak

I am watching them churn the last milk
        they'll ever get from me.
They are waiting for me to die;
They want to make buttons out of my bones.
Where are my sisters and brothers?   5
The tall monk there, loading my uncle,
        he has a new cap.

And that idiot student of his—
    I never saw that muffler before.
Poor uncle, he lets them load him.   *10*
How sad he is, how tired!
I wonder what they'll do with his bones?
And that beautiful tail!
How many shoelaces will they make of that!

RICHARD WILBUR (1921–   )

Cigales°

You know those windless summer evenings, swollen to stasis
by too-substantial melodies, rich as a
running-down record, ground round
to full quiet. Even the leaves
have thick tongues.   *5*

And if the first crickets quicken then,
other inhabitants, at window or door
or rising from table, feel in the lungs
a slim false-freshness, by this
trick of the ear.   *10*

Chanters of miracles took for a simple sign
the Latin cigale, because of his long waiting
and sweet change in daylight, and his singing
all his life, pinched on the ash leaf,
heedless of ants.   *15*

Others made morals; all were puzzled and joyed
by this gratuitous song. Such a plain thing
morals could not surround, nor listening:
not "chirr" nor "cri-cri." There is no straight
way of approaching it.   *20*

This thin uncomprehended song it is
springs healing questions into binding air.
Fabre,° by firing all the municipal cannon
under a piping tree, found out
cigales cannot hear.   *25*

°*cigales:* French for grasshoppers.
²³J. F. Fabre (1823–1915), a French entomologist.

PETER DAVISON (1928–   )

The Ram Beneath the Barn

Deep in the dark beneath foundation walls
the thick ram lies, his bent forefeet tucked under.

The droppings of a winter foul his straw,
but I dare no longer venture to his level
with grain, hay, water. I lower them to him   5
as to a tribe closed off by mountain snows.

He walks out into the sun, looks up at me,
his eyes expressionless as agates. He waits
for the moment of revenge. One day he may
catch me in a corner! Meanwhile, to prime his aim,   10
he taps his head and horns against the granite.

Of course when autumn comes he will again
curl up his lips into the sneer of lust
and leap his docile ewes, rolling their stupid
eyes as he does them service—   15

but in this March we stare each other down,
two rams caught in a thicket by the horns.

ADRIENNE RICH (1929–   )

Aunt Jennifer's Tigers

Aunt Jennifer's tigers prance across a screen,
Bright topaz denizens of a world of green.
They do not fear the men beneath the tree;
They pace in sleek chivalric certainty.

Aunt Jennifer's fingers fluttering through her wool   5
Find even the ivory needle hard to pull.
The massive weight of Uncle's wedding band
Sits heavily upon Aunt Jennifer's hand.

When Aunt is dead, her terrified hands will lie
Still ringed with ordeals she was mastered by.   10
The tigers in the panel that she made
Will go on prancing, proud and unafraid.

CHRISTOPHER SMART   (1722–1771)

From *Jubilate Agno*°

For I will consider my Cat Jeoffry.
For he is the servant of the Living God, duly and daily serving him.
For at the first glance of the glory of God in the East he worships
    in his way.
For is this done by wreathing his body seven times round with elegant
    quickness.
For then he leaps up to catch the musk,° which is   *musky-scented plant*   5
    the blessing of God upon his prayer.
For he rolls upon prank to work it in.
For having done duty and received blessing he begins to consider himself.
For this he performs in ten degrees.
For first he looks upon his fore-paws to see if they are clean.
For secondly he kicks up behind to clear away there.   *10*
For thirdly he works it upon stretch with the fore-paws extended.
For fourthly he sharpens his paws by wood.
For fifthly he washes himself.
For sixthly he rolls upon wash.
For seventhly he fleas himself, that he may not be interrupted upon   *15*
    the beat.
For eighthly he rubs himself against a post.
For ninthly he looks up for his instructions.
For tenthly he goes in quest of food.
For having considered God and himself he will consider his neighbor.
For if he meets another cat he will kiss her in kindness.   *20*
For when he takes his prey he plays with it to give it chance.
For one mouse in seven escapes by his dallying.
For when his day's work is done his business more properly begins.
For when he keeps the Lord's watch in the night against the adversary.
For he counteracts the powers of darkness by his electrical skin and   *25*
    glaring eyes.
For he counteracts the Devil, who is death, by brisking about the life.
For in his morning orisons he loves the sun and the sun loves him.
For he is of the tribe of Tiger.
For the Cherub Cat is a term of the Angel Tiger.
For he has the subtlety and hissing of a serpent, which in goodness   *30*
    he suppresses.
For he will not do destruction if he is well-fed, neither will he spit
    without provocation.
For he purrs in thankfulness, when God tells him he's a good Cat.
For he is an instrument for the children to learn benevolence upon.

°*Jubilate agno:* (Latin), In Praise of the Lamb.

For every house is incomplete without him and a blessing is lacking in
    the spirit.
For the Lord commanded Moses concerning the cats at the departure
    of the Children of Israel from Egypt.   *35*
For every family had one cat at least in the bag.
For the English Cats are the best in Europe.

ERICA JONG (1941–   )

Jubilate Canis°

(With apologies to Christopher Smart)

For I will consider my dog Poochkin
(& his long-lost brothers, Chekarf & Dogstoyevsky).
For he is the reincarnation of a great canine poet.
For he barks in meter, & when I leave him alone
his yelps at the door are epic.   *5*
For he is white, furry, & resembles a bathmat.
For he sleeps at my feet as I write
& therefore is my greatest critic.
For he follows me into the bathroom
& faithfully pees on paper.   *10*
For his is *almost* housebroken.
For he eats the dogfood I give him
but also loves Jarlsburg and Swiss cheese.
For he disdains nothing that reeks—
whether feet or roses.   *15*
For to him, all smells are created equal by God—
both turds and perfumes.
For he loves toilet bowls no less than soup bowls.
For by watching him, I have understood democracy.
For by stroking him, I have understood joy.   *20*
For he turns his belly toward God
& raises his paws & penis in supplication.
For he hangs his pink tongue out of his mouth
like a festival banner for God.
For though he is male, he has pink nipples on his belly   *25*
like the female.
For though he is canine, he is more humane
than most humans.
For when he dreams he mutters in his sleep
like any poet.   *30*

°*Jubilate canis:* (Latin), In Praise of the Dog.

For when he wakes he yawns & stretches
& stands on his hind legs to greet me.
For, after he shits, he romps and frolics
with supreme abandon.
For, after he eats, he is more contented   *35*
than any human.
For in every room he will find the coolest corner,
& having found it, he has the sense to stay there.
For when I show him my poems,
he eats them.   *40*
For an old shoe makes him happier than a Rolls-Royce
makes a rock star.
For he has convinced me of the infinite wisdom
of dog-consciousness.
For, thanks to Poochkin, I praise the Lord   *45*
& no longer fear death.
For when my spirit flees my body through my nostrils,
may it sail into the pregnant belly
of a furry bitch,
and may I praise God always   *50*
as a dog.

EDWARD HIRSCH   (1950–   )

Wild Gratitude

Tonight when I knelt down next to our cat, Zooey,
And put my fingers into her clean cat's mouth,
And rubbed her swollen belly that will never know kittens,
And watched her wriggle onto her side, pawing the air,
And listen to her solemn little squeals of delight,   *5*
I was thinking about the poet Christopher Smart,
Who wanted to kneel down and pray without ceasing
In every one of the splintered London streets,

And was locked away in the madhouse at St. Luke's   *10*
With his sad religious mania, and his wild gratitude,
And his grave prayers for the other lunatics,
And his great love for his speckled cat, Jeoffry.
All day today—August 13, 1983—I remembered how
Christopher Smart blessed this same day in August, 1759,
For its calm bravery and ordinary good conscience.   *15*

This was the day that he blessed the Postmaster General
"And all conveyancers of letters" for their warm humanity,
And the gardeners for their private benevolence
And intricate knowledge of the language of flowers,   *20*
And the milkmen for their universal human kindness.

This morning I understood that he loved to hear—
As I have heard the soft clink of milk bottles
On the rickety stairs in the early morning,

And how terrible it must have seemed
When even this small pleasure was denied him.   *25*
But it wasn't until tonight when I knelt down
And slipped my hand into Zooey's waggling mouth
That I remembered how he'd called Jeoffry "the servant
Of the Living God duly and daily serving Him,"
And for the first time understood what it meant.   *30*
Because it wasn't until I saw my own cat

Whine and roll over on her fluffy back
That I realized how gratefully he had watched
Jeoffry fetch and carry his wooden cork
Across the grass in the wet garden, patiently   *35*
Jumping over a high stick, calmly sharpening
His claws on the woodpile, rubbing his nose
Against the nose of another cat, stretching, or
Slowly stalking his traditional enemy, the mouse,
A rodent, "a creature of great personal valour,"   *40*
And then dallying so much that his enemy escaped.

And only then did I understand
It is Jeoffry—and every creature like him—
Who can teach us how to praise—purring
In their own language,   *45*
Wreathing themselves in the living fire.

PHILIP LEVINE   (1928–   )

Animals Are Passing from Our Lives

It's wonderful how I jog
on four honed-down ivory toes
my massive buttocks slipping
like oiled parts with each light step.

I'm to market, I can smell   *5*
the sour, grooved block, I can smell
the blade that opens the hole
and the pudgy white fingers

that shake out the intestines
like a hankie. In my dreams   *10*
the snouts drool on the marble,
suffering children, suffering flies,

suffering the consumers
who won't meet their steady eyes
for fear they could see. The boy   *15*
who drives me along believes

that any moment I'll fall
on my side and drum my toes
like a typewriter or squeal
and shit like a new housewife   *20*

discovering television,
or that I'll turn like a beast
cleverly to hook his teeth
with my teeth. No. Not this pig.

SEAMUS HEANEY   (1939–   )

The Skunk

Up, black, striped and damasked like the chasuble
At a funeral mass, the skunk's tail
Paraded the skunk. Night after night
I expected her like a visitor.

The refrigerator whinnied into silence.   *5*
My desk light softened beyond the verandah.
Small oranges loomed in the orange tree.
I began to tense as a voyeur.

After eleven years I was composing
Love-letters again, broaching the word "wife"   *10*
Like a stored cask, as if its slender vowel
Had mutated into the night earth and air

Of California. The beautiful, useless
Tang of eucalyptus spelt your absence.
The aftermath of a mouthful of wine   *15*
Was like inhaling you off a cold pillow.
And there she was, the intent and glamorous,
Ordinary, mysterious skunk;
Mythologized, demythologized;
Snuffing the boards five feet beyond me.   *20*

It all came back to me last night, stirred
By the sootfall of your things at bedtime,
Your head-down, tail-up hunt in a bottom drawer
For the black plunge-line nightdress.

ROBERT LOWELL   (1917–1977)

Skunk Hour

(For Elizabeth Bishop)

Nautilus Island's hermit
heiress still lives through winter in her Spartan° cottage;   *austere*
her sheep still graze above the sea.
Her son's a bishop. Her farmer
is first selectman in our village;   *5*
she's in her dotage.

Thirsting for
the hierarchic privacy
of Queen Victoria's century,
she buys up all   *10*
the eyesores facing her shore,
and lets them fall.

The season's ill—
we've lost our summer millionaire,
who seemed to leap from an L. L. Bean   *15*
catalogue. His nine-knot yawl
was auctioned off to lobstermen.
A red fox stain covers Blue Hill.

And now our fairy
decorator brightens his shop for fall;   *20*
his fishnet's filled with orange cork,
orange, his cobbler's bench and awl;
there is no money in his work,
he'd rather marry.

One dark night,   *25*
my Tudor Ford climbed the hill's skull;
I watched for love-cars. Lights turned down,
they lay together, hull to hull
where the graveyard shelves on the town. . . .
My mind's not right.   *30*

A car radio bleats,
"Love, O careless Love. . . ." I hear
my ill-spirit sob in each blood cell,
as if my hand were at its throat. . . .
I myself am hell;   *35*
nobody's here—

only skunks, that search
in the moonlight for a bite to eat.

They march on their soles up Main Street:
white stripes, moonstruck eyes' red fire   *40*
under the chalk-dry and spar spire
of the Trinitarian Church.

I stand on top
of our back steps and breathe the rich air—
        a mother skunk with her column of kittens swills the garbage pail.   *45*
She jabs her wedge-head in a cup
of sour cream, drops her ostrich tail,
and will not scare.

APPENDIX A
Writing About Poetry

Making an Approach

Throughout this book we have seen that you can approach a poem from many different angles. This may seem overwhelming. Just remember, though, that the place to begin is always *with the poem itself*. Before you even think of writing a paper on a poem, sit down with the poem and read it over several times, slowly, taking notes as you go. Look up any words that confuse you or don't seem quite right in the context of the poem. The poet may well have taken a common word and used it in a strange way, so it will help to have in mind different levels of meaning. Examine the poem carefully for the kinds of things we have identified in *An Invitation to Poetry:* the poet's use of metaphor and symbol, irony, or whatever seems appropriate. Always ask yourself who is speaking and in what context, because there is no other way to identify tone and point of view. The most difficult area of approach to a poem was discussed in Chapter 14, in the section about *reading from the outside in.* It isn't easy to determine what hidden factors may have gone into the determination of a poem, what prejudices, beliefs, quirks, and so on, led the poet to a particular view of things. Tread carefully, and make sure that you can back up whatever assertions you make by some direct quotations from the poem itself. There's simply no point in spinning off notions that don't relate directly to what the poet actually put on the page.

Common Mistakes

The most common mistakes students make are the result of not looking closely enough at a poem. Some students think that a critic simply has to talk about the poet's life and times—that criticism, in other words, is really a form of biographical writing. It isn't. Biography is probably the *last* thing you should consider when writing a paper on a poem. As we've said, begin with the words on the page, and ask yourself how these words work together to produce the effects of language associated with poetry. Look first at the poem's **diction**—the vocabulary, the types of words used—for clues to the poet's meaning and style. A student of mine once thought that Robert Frost's poem, "The Oven Bird," was about a Thanksgiving turkey because he had not heard of the oven bird, and did not bother to look up the term. Read the poem carefully for evidence of rhymes or regularity of meter. Students frequently don't even notice that a poem is, for instance, a sonnet, or that it is written in blank verse (unrhymed iambic pentameter). The physical shape of a poem is also significant. If you half close your eyes and squint at the page, the poem should take on an abstract shape. Think about this shape. How does it relate to the poem's meaning? Why did the poet, consciously or unconsciously, give the poem that shape? The presence of mostly short or mostly long lines is also evidence you might be able to use in your critical evaluations.

From Explication to Argument

The word **explication** derives from *explicare,* to unfold. A student writing a paper on a poem should move carefully through that poem, line by line or section by section, "unfolding" it as one might unfold a wallet to display its contents. In most ways, an explication is a careful explanation of a poem, a meticulous inspection of all that it holds. You will probably not be asked to write a paper on a poem that's extremely long, such as Milton's *Paradise Lost,* but if you are, be sure to isolate small passages that stand on their own. Explication assumes a relatively brief text that can be discussed in close detail.

Straight explications are fairly easy to write because you don't have to think about making much of an argument. You simply run through the poem in a chronological way, perhaps even beginning with the title, commenting and elucidating as you go. You try to *notice* as much as possible, explaining how the poet achieves various effects that enhance or produce the poem's meaning.

Analysis and argument assume greater mental dexterity and intellectual power. You must *think hard* to make a real argument. The main point is that you must actually *have* an argument in the first place. But what does an argument about a poem consist of? You might, for example, wish to prove that one poem written on a given topic succeeds better than another poem on the same topic. Comparisons make good arguments. You might also want to explore a point that strikes you as possibly being true. The scientific method applies to the arts as well: Work with a hunch, a "thesis." Look for evidence to support that thesis, taking note that "evidence" in a literary paper consists of quotations from the text or the poem under discussion. In a final paragraph, you should form a conclusion based on the evidence. Ideally, in the course of the paper you will have proven the truth you already guessed at the paper's outset.

A Sample Paper

A well-written student paper follows. The student, a sophomore at Middlebury College, writes about Robert Frost's poem "Out, Out—" (the first poem in the Anthology section of this textbook).

The Boy's World and a King's World:

A Reading of Frost's "Out, Out—"

On the surface, Robert Frost's "Out, Out—" reads like a poem about a farm boy who dies in a hideous accident. It seems like a very pessimistic poem about a very small subject: the death of an insignificant member of a rural world that has long since been out of step with modern industrial society. But Frost is asking us to look beyond this boy's world to the larger world. The boy's death, in fact, is highly symbolic, the poem's images themselves taking us far beyond the specific scene described to layer after layer of meaning, to a significance not unlike the five mountain ranges "one behind the other / Under the sunset far into Vermont" that Frost speaks of at the poem's beginning.

Ostensibly, the poem is about the inexplicable cruelty of a situation wherein a boy accidentally cuts his hand off while sawing wood. The boy is called in to supper by his sister, who witnesses the horrible scene:

> At the word, the saw,
> As if to prove saws knew what supper meant,
> Leaped out at the boy's hand, or seemed to leap—
> He must have given the hand. However it was,
> Neither refused the meeting. But the hand!
> The boy's first outcry was a rueful laugh,
> As he swung toward them holding up the hand
> Half in appeal, but half as if to keep

> The life from spilling. Then the boy saw all—
> Since he was old enough to know . . .

The boy, of course, "saw all spoiled."

In the modern world, it's unlikely that such an accident would lead to death, would spoil "all." Even in "Out, Out—" the doctor comes to the boy pretty quickly, but he can do nothing but put him in "the dark of ether." It's as if modern science is suddenly up against something older and stranger and more powerful in the boy's "accident." To suggest this mysterious aspect of things, Frost makes the saw come alive. The saw "seemed to leap" at the hand as if animated by a weird force. The boy has been picked out for death, for whatever reasons, and it will do no good simply to mend the boy by technological means. The boy, a wise boy, has already "seen all spoiled."

He has seen that in his rural world there is no place for a boy who can't pull his oar. Frost's rural world is integrated. Man and nature work together. Nature acts, in fact, like a partner in holy matrimony. Any severance (a hand, a heart) leads to disaster, and man and nature can no longer move together. More practically, the boy can no longer be of service to his family. He would have to become a dependent, in a world where this spells misery for all. The hand stands for power and the ability to survive. Its loss means more than just the loss of a limb. The boy, like his family, understands this implicitly; the family "turned to their affairs" because they understood the proper place of the boy's accident and death in their world. Tragedy, for them, is sad but endurable.

That Frost wants us to look beyond this simple scene comes out in the title, "Out, Out,—" an allusion to the lines in Shakespeare's *Macbeth* where Macbeth has just learned of his wife's death by her own hand. He sees life as a tale "Told by an idiot, full of sound and fury, / Signifying nothing." Unlike the boy, Macbeth is responsible for the loss of meaning in his world. He is guilty, and his guilt has indirectly caused his wife's death and will, soon, cause his own. But, unlike the boy in Frost's poem, he struggles against his own fate. He doesn't understand his place in the context of the universe, even though he has had a powerful say in making of this context—which the boy has not. We have, finally, to admire the boy more than Macbeth, since he "sees all" and Macbeth does not.

This comparison between a boy's rural world and a king's larger one forces us to conclude that Frost wants us to look beyond the farmyard fence. He invites us to think about our own life, to ask whether or not we have understood the conditions of our life and have accepted them. Frost also makes us appreciate the quality of life lived by the farm boy, who has the opportunity to smell the "Sweet-scented stuff" every day, to look out at the Vermont hills, and to have significant—though dangerous—work. Macbeth's life, though "larger," seems paltry by comparison. And Macbeth's inability to accept his own fate is a sign of the poverty in his life, a poverty not found in the life of the conventionally rural "poor" of Frost's poem.

The Physical Format of a Paper

Write on plain, white typing paper, 8 1/2 by 11 inches. *Don't use onion skin,* though erasable paper is all right, as long as it doesn't smudge. Leave margins at least 1 1/4 inches wide all the way around. (In other words, you should leave room for your instructor's comments.) Put your name, your instructor's name, your course and section number, and the date in the upper right-hand corner. Center the title below this information. (You may wish to make a separate title page that includes all of this information.) Number every page, and include your name on every page before the number (For instance, a student named Jones would write *Jones—2*). You can put the numbers at the bottom, centered, or in the upper right-hand corner of the page (though not the first page if you're numbering in the upper right-hand corner, because it might get confused with the other information you've put there). Be sure to staple the paper (in the upper left-hand corner) and *keep a carbon or a photocopy.* Many papers get lost because the students failed to keep a copy.

How to Quote Poetry

Titles of poems should be enclosed in quotation marks—for example, "The Road Not Taken." Book-length poems or poems of extraordinary length should be underlined—thus, <u>The Iliad</u>. (Note that underlining a manuscript word means that, if the page were printed, the word would be in *italics.*)

Put quotation marks around any poetry you quote within a sentence or paragraph of your own:

When Robert Frost says "Two roads diverged in a yellow wood," he refers to an autumnal forest. The speaker says: "long I stood / And looked down one as far as I could / To where it bent in the undergrowth."

Notice two things about the preceding paragraph. First, the individual lines of poetry are separated by a slash (/); it is crucial in poetry that you always do this, to indicate where the line breaks occur. Second, quotations can begin and end anywhere; you can even change the final punctuation from, say, a period to a comma to make it fit smoothly into the grammar of your sentence. *Always make sure that the sense of your quotations runs in with the sense of your own statements.*

If you are quoting more than three lines of poetry, it is best to set the poetry off with a line of space, type it single-spaced, and indent ten spaces from the rest (a five-space indent makes a proper paragraph indention). Setting the quotation off like this means you *don't* need quotation marks. Here is an example:

The speaker in Frost's "The Road Not Taken" is meditating on what to do when he reaches a fork in the path:

> Two roads diverged in a yellow wood,
> And sorry I could not travel both
> And be one traveler, long I stood
> And looked down one as far as I could
> To where it bent in the undergrowth.

But he does not take this road. Rather, he takes "the other, as just as fair."

Notice that a period has been put after "undergrowth" instead of the semicolon that appears in the original poem. This was done for reasons of grammatical consistency.

Sometimes you'll want to leave out something from a passage you are quoting. In that case, use three dots, called **ellipses** (. . .), to indicate where something has been omitted. For example:

Robert Frost's speaker in "The Road Not Taken" looked down one path as far as he could "to where it bent . . . Then took the other."

If you want to quote a lengthy part of a poem but leave out some lines or stanzas, use ellipses centered on a blank line, as in the following example:

Frost's speaker in "The Road Not Taken" looked down one path as far as he could:

> To where it bent in the undergrowth;
> Then took the other, as just as fair
> And having perhaps the better claim
>
> . . .
>
> Oh, I kept the first for another day!
> Yet knowing how way leads on to way,
> I doubted if I should ever come back.

The main thing to remember is that you have to respect the text. Quote it accurately and, when making ellipses, try not to distort the poem's meaning.

Avoiding Footnotes

In most cases, footnotes are unnecessary. They are occasionally used to amplify or explain something in the body of the paper, but you should avoid using them in this way. Say what you have to say in the paper's main body. If something is genuinely a digression or side-track, put it in parentheses (like this, for instance). When you quote from a secondary source, such as a book or magazine article, identify the source sufficiently in your discussion so footnotes aren't needed. For example, if you are writing about a poem and want to quote a critic of that poem, do it as follows:

Writing about Frost's "Design," Robert Harris says that "Frost's focus is on the possibility of an evil God acting behind the scenes" (Harris 37).

In this case, the student has cited the name of the author and the page of the book where the direct quotation is found, putting this information in parentheses. The full publication details on each source mentioned are provided in the bibliography or list of "Works Cited" at the end of the paper.

Compiling a "Works Cited" List

When working with source materials, be sure to record the information you will need for a "Works Cited" list *while you are taking notes.* This will make life easier when you write the paper. It's a good idea to use small notecards and to put one bibliographical citation on one card. Write down the page numbers involved, all publication data, such as where the book or article was published, when, and by whom. If you are citing a translated book or an anthology, be sure to include the translator's name or the editor's. If you are quoting from an article in a periodical (such as a magazine), be sure to get the inclusive page numbers of the article. It is a good idea to write the library call numbers of any book cited on the card, too; that way, you can relocate the book in a hurry if you have to.

Remember: the purpose of a "Works Cited" list is to help the reader identify the quotation and look it up if he or she wants to. So include all pertinent details. Get this information down correctly on your notecards the first time, and you will find it quite simple to type up the final list.

Before typing the list, put the cards in alphabetical order by the author's last name. If there is no author directly cited, as in an encyclopedia entry, use the first significant word in the title for alphabetizing. For instance, put the following entry on the list of works cited under I: "The Inventiveness of Wordsworth."

Use the common forms of abbreviation for bibliographical terms, such as "trans." for translator or "ed." for editor. You will often see "n.d." for no date, UP for University Press, OUP for Oxford University Press, and so on. The names of publishing houses may be shortened—e.g., Harcourt instead of Harcourt Brace Jovanovich. For documents published by the Government Printing Office, use GPO in your citation. If you are not sure of the correct abbreviation or think your abbreviation may not be clear to the reader, avoid using it.

When typing up your list, center the title—Works Cited—at the top of a new page, about an inch down. Double-space all lines. Begin your citation flush to the lefthand margin. When an entry is longer than one line, indent continuation lines of the citation five spaces.

Formats for Entries in "Works Cited"

The following formats are used for citing specific kinds of entries.

1. For a book with one author:

   Frye, Northrop. The Great Code: The Bible and Literature. New
   York: Harcourt, 1982.

2. For a book with two authors:

   Bryan, Margaret B., and Boyd H. Davis. Writing About Literature and
   Film. New York: Harcourt, 1975.

3. For a book with more than two authors:

   Smith, John R., et al. Poetry and Science. New York: Holt, 1975.

4. For a book in an edition other than the first, be sure to record what edition you cited:

   Samuels, Harold. Reading Modern Poems. 2nd ed. New York: Atheneum,
   1981.

5. For a book in a series of books:

   Ryf, Robert S. Henry Green. Columbia Essays on Modern Writers, No.
   29. Ed. William York Tindall. New York: Columbia UP, 1967.

6. For a translated book:

   Eco, Umberto. The Name of the Rose. Trans. William Weaver. New
   York: Harcourt, 1983.

7. For an edited book:

> Schorer, Mark, ed. <u>Modern British Fiction.</u> New York: OUP, 1961.

8. For an anonymous book:

> <u>Irish Folk Tales.</u> Trans. P. W. Findley. New York: Freeman, 1981.

9. For a signed article from a periodical:

> Smithson, Henry. "Poetry and Music." <u>Poetry Studies</u> 22 (Oct.
> 1981): 27–35.

10. For signed encyclopedia articles:

> Goodwin, George C. "Mammals." <u>Collier's Encyclopedia.</u> 1976 ed.

11. For an anonymous encyclopedia article:

> "Universities." <u>Encyclopaedia Britannica: Macropaedia.</u> 1974 ed.

In general, when quoting material from a periodical publication of any kind, cite the author, the name of the article, the journal, its volume number, the date of publication (in parentheses) and the page numbers of the entire article. When the author is not given, begin with the title of the article. There are endless varieties of publications, and you might not find the particular format you need mentioned above. Consult the 1984 *MLA Handbook* for exact information about how to cite sources.

Integrating and Citing Sources in Your Paper

It is important that quotations—from poems or from critics—be carefully integrated into the body of your paper so there is no disruption of the normal sequence of thought and grammar. Make sure the quotation "fits in" nicely, as in the following example:

Wordsworth's solitary reaper stands alone in a field, "a symbol of contemplation,"
as John Barber says in <u>Wordsworth's Imagery</u> (Barber 149).

As with poems that you quote, you may shorten a quotation by using ellipses (. . .) to indicate words left out. Be careful not to distort an author's meaning, however, by careless deletion.

Note, again, that the proper way to cite a reference source is to name the author and the page number on which your quotation appears.

If you want to cite two or more works by the same author, use shortened versions of the titles in your in-text citations, as in the following passage (the books referred to are Joan Didion's <u>The White Album</u> and <u>Slouching Toward Bethlehem</u>):

With her cool eye for the telling detail, Didion records the absurdities of a Las Vegas marriage ceremony (<u>Slouching</u> 79–83). In a later collection, she lays bare the absurdities of California's Governor's Residence, which has remained "unlandscaped, unfurnished, and unoccupied since the day construction stopped in 1975" (<u>Album</u> 67).

When it is not possible to include the author's name in your statement, you must include it in the parenthetical reference along with the shortened title. In compiling your list of "Works Cited," alphabetize multiple works by a single author according to title, using the *first word* as your key letter.

APPENDIX B
Writing Your Own Poems

Having read a lot of poems written by others, you may want to try your hand at writing your own poems. It doesn't matter whether or not you'll ever become another Milton or Shakespeare; the point is that writing poems of your own can only increase your appreciation and understanding of the art of poetry. Writing a sonnet, for instance, will make you aware of the difficulties involved in trying to get fourteen lines of verse to rhyme in a specific way and still make sense! It isn't easy.

You shouldn't be intimidated by the great poems of the past. Shakespeare, Milton, and Keats are not your competition. You are trying to do the best *you* can do. No one else's poetry matters, at least not at this stage in learning to write poems. Many people never become poets or even try to compose their own poems because they immediately see how trivial or incompetent their work looks by comparison with that of the great poets. That's foolish. Begin where you are, with whom you are. Everyone can write a poem that has value and meaning for oneself and, probably, for some friends.

Most poems begin with abstract ideas that are, somehow, converted into concrete language. You should keep a daily journal in which you write down odd phrases that interest you, words that you like, and images that come into your mind. You can never tell what might set a poem in motion—a point made nicely in a poem by Alastair Reid:

An Instance

Perhaps the accident of a bird
crossing the green window, a simultaneous phrase
of far singing, and a steeplejack

poised on the church spire, changing the gold clock,
set the moment alight. At any rate, a word
in that instant of realizing catches fire,
ignites another, and soon, the page is ablaze
with a wildfire of writing. The clock chimes in the square.

All afternoon, in a scrawl of time,
the mood still smoulders. Rhyme remembers rhyme
and words summon the moment when amazement
ran through the senses like a flame.
Later, the song forgotten, the sudden bird
flown who-knows-where, the incendiary word
long since crossed out, the steeplejack gone home,
their moment burns again, restored
to its spontaneity. The poem stays.

Note that the "incendiary word," the word that started the poet thinking
and writing the poem, got crossed out. That's quite common. You may
not find out what poem you want to write until you've written a long
way into it. Suddenly, the "real" poem will dawn on you.

We've talked a lot about concreteness in *An Invitation to Poetry*. A
general rule to follow is this: *Show, don't tell*. What this means is that you
shouldn't write *about* ideas. You should try to embody ideas in specific
images. Don't write a poem in which you say you are depressed, for
instance. Write a poem about a rain-drenched day: find objects in the
real world, images, to convey a sense of depression. Avoid abstract words
like *happiness, solitude,* or *beauty*. Show your readers an image that makes
them feel happy or conveys an impression of solitude or confronts them
with beautiful language.

It often helps to think of a poem as having one central image. Try
to avoid crowding contradictory images into the same poem. Keep to
one thing, and develop it. Look back at William Blake's poem, "The Sick
Rose" (p. 39). See how he follows through one idea, transforming that
idea into a little myth. He sticks to the subject, and he never gets "talky."
He is willing to present the image and let the readers draw their own
conclusions.

One word of warning: Never end a poem with a moral. If a poem
has a "moral," a point of some kind that you want to convey, the poem
should carry this meaning in itself. You should not have to repeat it at
the end in different, probably less concrete, language. Allowing readers
to discover a moral for themselves makes for a more meaningful poem.

You should not be afraid of rhyme and meter. Writing a poem in
a specific form, such as the sonnet, is probably too difficult for a first
attempt, but you can at least begin with a simple meter and rhyme. Try

writing in a four-beat line with four-line stanzas, rhyming ABAB CDCD
EFEF:

> Perhaps the place for you to start
> is with a simple, rhyming poem;
> it doesn't matter if your art
> has tendencies to wander, roam
>
> away from this quite simple rhyme
> and meter. You should find this fun
> (if you, in school, can find the time)
> and maybe even learn that one
>
> can be a poet without strain.
> The fact is, anyone can write
> a mediocre poem and gain
> a little something from it. Right?

Remember that no poet ever wrote a good poem in one or two
drafts. You've got to revise and revise and revise. That's part of the joy
of writing. Vision comes from revision. As you work, changing words
and phrases, playing with rhymes and meters, you'll gradually create
the poem you want to write. A character in a novel by E. M. Forster
remarks, "How do I know what I think till I see what I say." Writing
forces us to see what we think. Our rough drafts are imperfect versions
of what we think. Revision is a way of working *toward* our real sentences,
the words that will become us.

Every person has a unique voice, a way of talking that is like nobody
else's. You've got to find that unique voice in your writing. Revise your
work in such a way that you move closer and closer to saying things in
a natural way, a familiar way. Rhyme and meter should not distort your
natural voice. If they do, you're not using them well. Remember: Rhyme
is a kind of echo, and meter is nothing but repetition. If you find it
easier to begin with **free verse,** do so. But pay attention to line breaks.
Don't just break up a prose sentence arbitrarily and call it poetry. It's
not. Make a decision every time. And be able to back up your line breaks
with some kind of reasoning.

Finally, you should also make sure your poem creates a unified
impression in the reader's mind. *Don't include too many ideas.* When you
begin a poem, you build up certain expectations. Don't leave the reader
hanging. Build on what you've written, and make sure that you follow
through from start to finish. For instance, if you begin with an image
of autumn leaves falling on the ground, don't end the poem in summer—
unless that's the point of the poem, and you have worked your way

through the seasons. A poem should gather momentum, moving from the first word to the last in a single arc of music and meaning. This is not easy to accomplish, but—when it happens—you will understand why John Keats once told a friend "how great a thing it is" to be a poet, and what "great things are to be gained by it." There is nothing quite like writing a good poem, seeing your own sense of the world translated into firm, clear, perhaps even beautiful, language.

Acknowledgments

A. R. AMMONS. "So I Said I Am Ezra" from *Collected Poems, 1951–1971,* copyright © 1971. Reprinted by permission of W. W. Norton and Co., Inc.

W. H. AUDEN. "Fleet Visit," copyright 1955 by W. H. Auden; "O What Is That Sound," copyright © 1937, renewed 1965 by W. H. Auden; "Miss Gee," "Musée des Beaux Arts," "Lay Your Sleeping Head," copyright © 1940, renewed 1968 by W. H. Auden. From *Collected Poems* by W. H. Auden, edited by Edward Mendelson. Reprinted by permission of Random House, Inc. and Faber and Faber Ltd.

WENDELL BERRY. "The Old Elm Tree by the River" and "The Country of Marriage" from *Collected Poems* by Wendell Berry, copyright © 1984 by Wendell Berry. Reprinted by permission of North Point Press.

ELIZABETH BISHOP. "The Fish" and "Seascape" from *The Complete Poems: 1927–1979,* by Elizabeth Bishop, copyright © 1940, 1941 by Elizabeth Bishop, renewed 1968, 1969. Reprinted by permission of Farrar, Straus and Giroux, Inc. and Faber and Faber Ltd.

GWENDOLYN BROOKS. "We Real Cool" from *The World of Gwendolyn Brooks,* copyright © 1959 by Gwendolyn Brooks. Reprinted by permission of Gwendolyn Brooks.

GEOFFREY CHAUCER. From *The Canterbury Tales,* trans. Neville Coghill, copyright © 1951 by Neville Coghill. Reprinted by permission of Penguin Books, Ltd.

LUCILLE CLIFTON. "Homage to My Hips" from *The Two-Headed Woman,* © 1980 by the University of Massachusetts Press. Reprinted by permission of Curtis Brown, Ltd.

ALFRED CORN. "Grass" from *The Various Light,* copyright © 1979 by Alfred Corn. Originally published in *The New Yorker.* Reprinted by permission of Viking Penguin Inc.

GREGORY CORSO. "The Mad Yak" from *The Vestal Lady on Brattle* by Gregory Corso. Reprinted by permission of City Lights Books.

E. E. CUMMINGS. "anyone lived in a pretty how town," copyright 1940 by E. E. Cummings; renewed 1968 by Marion Morehouse Cummings. Reprinted from *Complete Poems, 1913–1962,* by E. E. Cummings by permission of Harcourt Brace Jovanovich and Grafton Books.

J. V. CUNNINGHAM. "For a College Yearbook" from *The Collected Poems and Epigrams of J. V. Cunningham,* copyright © 1971 by Swallow Press. Reprinted by permission of Ohio University Press.

PETER DAVISON. "Cross Cut" from *A Voice in the Mountain* by Peter Davison. (First published in *The Atlantic.*) "The Ram Beneath the Barn" from *Praying Wrong: New and Selected Poems, 1957–1984* by Peter Davison. Copyright © 1984 by Peter Davison. Reprinted by permission of Atheneum Publishers, Inc.

JAMES DICKEY. "Cherrylog Road" and "The Dusk of Horses" from *Helmets,* copyright © 1962, 1963 by James Dickey. Reprinted by permission of Wesleyan University Press. These poems first appeared in *The New Yorker.*

HILDA DOOLITTLE. "Evening" from *Collected Poems,* by H. D. copyright © 1982 by the Estate of Hilda Doolittle. Reprinted by permission of New Directions Publishing Corporation.

KEITH DOUGLAS. "How to Kill" from *The Complete Poems of Keith Douglas,* edited by Desmond Graham, copyright © 1978 by Oxford University Press. Reprinted by permission of Oxford University Press.

RICHARD EBERHART. "The Fury of Aerial Bombardment" and "The Groundhog" from *Collected Poems, 1930–1985* by Richard Eberhart, copyright © 1986 by Richard Eberhart. Reprinted by permission of Oxford University Press and Chatto and Windus, Ltd.

T. S. ELIOT. "The Love Song of J. Alfred Prufrock" from *Collected Poems, 1909–1962* by T. S. Eliot, copyright 1936 by Harcourt Brace Jovanovich © 1963, 1964 by T. S. Eliot. Reprinted by permission of Harcourt Brace Jovanovich and Faber and Faber Ltd.

ROBERT FROST. "For Once, Then, Something," "Design," "Stopping by Woods on a Snowy Evening," "The Road Not Taken," "Home Burial," "The Silken Tent," and "Out, Out—' from *The Poetry of Robert Frost,* edited by Edward Connery Lathem. Copyright 1923, 1930, 1939, © 1969 by Holt, Rinehart and Winston. Copyright 1936, 1942, 1944, 1951, © 1958 by Robert Frost. Copyright © 1964, 1967, 1970 by Lesley Frost Ballantine. Reprinted by permission of Henry Holt and Company.

NIKKI GIOVANNI. "Kidnap Poem" from *Re-Creation,* copyright © 1970. Reprinted by permission of Broadside Press.

LOUISE GLUCK. "Happiness" from *Descending Figure* by Louise Gluck, copyright © 1976, 1977, 1978, 1979, 1980 by Louise Gluck. Reprinted by permission of The Ecco Press.

ROBERT GRAVES. "Ulysses," "Rocky Acres" and "She Tells Her Love While Half Asleep" from *The Selected Poems of Robert Graves* by Robert Graves. Reprinted by permission of A. P. Watt, Ltd.

PAMELA WHITE HADAS. "The Ballad of Baseball Annie" from *From Pocahontas to Patty Hearst* by Pamela White Hadas, copyright © 1983. Reprinted by permission of Alfred A. Knopf, Inc.

MICHAEL S. HARPER. "New Season" from *Dear John, Dear Coltrane,* by Michael S. Harper, copyright © 1970 by Michael S. Harper. Reprinted by permission of the University of Illinois Press.

ROBERT HASS. "Meditation at Lagunitas" from *Praise* by Robert Hass, copyright © 1979. Reprinted by permission of The Ecco Press.

ROBERT HAYDEN. "Those Winter Sundays" is reprinted from *Angle of Ascent,* New and Selected Poems by Robert Hayden, with the permission of Liveright Publishing Corporation. Copyright © 1975, 1972, 1970, 1966 by Robert Hayden.

SEAMUS HEANEY. "Personal Helicon," "Digging," "The Forge," "Sunlight," and "A Constable Calls" from *Poems: 1965–1976* by Seamus Heaney, © 1980 by Seamus Heaney. "The Skunk" from *Field Work* by Seamus Heaney, copyright © 1979 by Seamus Heaney. Reprinted by permission of Farrar, Straus and Giroux, Inc. and Faber and Faber Ltd.

ANTHONY HECHT. "The Dover Bitch" from *The Hard Hours* by Anthony Hecht, copyright © 1967 by Anthony Hecht. Reprinted by permission of Atheneum Publishers, Inc. and Oxford University Press.

EDWARD HIRSCH. "Wild Gratitude" from *Wild Gratitude* by Edward Hirsch, copyright © 1985 by Edward Hirsch. Reprinted by permission of Alfred A. Knopf, Inc.

A. E. HOUSMAN. "Into My Heart an Air that Kills," "With Rue My Heart Is Laden," and "To an Athlete Dying Young." From *The Collected Poems* by A. E. Housman, copyright 1939, 1940, © 1965 by Holt, Rinehart, and Winston. Copyright © 1967, 1968 by Robert E. Symons. Reprinted by permission of Holt, Rinehart and Winston; The Society of Authors as the literary representatives of the Estate of A. E. Housman; and Jonathan Cape, Ltd.

LANGSTON HUGHES. "The Weary Blues" from *The Selected Poems of Langston Hughes.* Copyright © 1926 by Alfred A. Knopf, Inc. Reprinted by permission of Alfred A. Knopf, Inc.

TED HUGHES. "The Horses" and "The Thought-Fox" from *New Selected Poems,* copyright © 1957 by Ted Hughes. Reprinted by permission of Harper and Row and Faber and Faber Ltd.

RANDALL JARRELL. "The Death of the Ball Turret Gunner" from *The Complete Poems of Randall Jarrell,* copyright © 1945, renewed 1972 by Mrs. Randall Jarrell. Reprinted by permission of Farrar, Straus and Giroux, Inc. and Faber and Faber Ltd.

ROBINSON JEFFERS. "Hurt Hawks" from *The Selected Poetry of Robinson Jeffers,* copyright © 1928, 1956 by Robinson Jeffers. Reprinted by permission of Random House, Inc.

ERICA JONG. "In Praise of Clothes" from *Loveroot* by Erica Jong, copyright © 1975 by Erica Jong. "Jubilate Canis" from *At the Edge of the Body,* copyright © 1979 by Erica Mann Jong. Reprinted by permission of Henry Holt and Company.

RICHARD KENNEY. "Witness" from *The Evolution of the Flightless Bird,* copyright © 1984 by Richard Kenney. Reprinted by permission of Yale University Press. "Harvest" from *Orrery* by Richard Kenney, copyright © 1985 by Richard Kenney. (First published in *The Atlantic.*) Reprinted by permission of Atheneum Publishers, Inc.

GALWAY KINNELL. "The Bear" from *Body Rags* by Galway Kinnell, copyright © 1967 by Galway Kinnell. Reprinted by permission of Houghton Mifflin Company.

D. H. LAWRENCE. "Gloire de Dijon," "Piano," and "Humming-Bird" from *The Complete Poems of D. H. Lawrence,* edited by Vivian de Sola Pinto and F. Warren Roberts, copyright © 1964, 1971 by Angelo Ravagli and C. M. Weekley, Executors of the Estate of Frieda Lawrence Ravagli. Reprinted by permission of Viking Penguin Inc.

SYDNEY LEA. "Young Man Leaving Home" from *Searching the Drowned Man* by Sydney Lea, copyright © 1979 by Sydney Lea. Reprinted by permission of the University of Illinois Press.

DON L. LEE. "Man Thinking About Woman" from *Directionscore: New and Selected Poems*, copyright © 1971. Reprinted by permission of Broadside Press.

DENISE LEVERTOV. "The Ache of Marriage" from *Poems: 1960–1967*. Copyright © 1964 by Denise Levertov Goodman. Reprinted by permission of New Directions Publishing Corporation.

PHILIP LEVINE. "My Son and I," "On the Murder of Lieutenant José del Castillo by the Falangist Bravo Martinez, July 12, 1936," "Animals Are Passing from Our Lives," and "Belle Isle, 1949" from *Selected Poems* by Philip Levine, copyright © 1984 by Philip Levine. Reprinted by permission of Atheneum Publishers, Inc.

ALUN LEWIS. "All Day It has Rained" from *Raiders Dawn* by Alun Lewis. Reprinted by permission of Allen & Unwin, Ltd.

ROBERT LOWELL. "History" from *History* by Robert Lowell, copyright © 1973 by Robert Lowell. "Man and Wife" and "Skunk Hour" from *Life Studies* by Robert Lowell, copyright © 1959 by Robert Lowell. Reprinted by permission of Farrar, Straus and Giroux, Inc. and Faber and Faber Ltd.

J. D. MACCLATCHY. "Hummingbird" from *Stars Principal* by J. D. MacClatchy, copyright © 1986 by J. D. MacClatchy. Reprinted by permission of Macmillan Publishing Company. First appeared in *The New Yorker*.

ARCHIBALD MACLEISH. "Ars Poetica" from *New and Collected Poems, 1917–1976* by Archibald MacLeish, copyright © 1976 by Archibald MacLeish. Reprinted by permission of Houghton Mifflin Company.

PAUL MARIANI. "North/South" from *Prime Mover* by Paul Mariani, copyright © 1985 by Paul Mariani. Reprinted by permission of the author and Grove Press.

EDNA ST. VINCENT MILLAY. "The Strawberry Shrub" from *Collected Poems* by Edna St. Vincent Millay, copyright © 1958, 1962, 1967 by Edna St. Vincent Millay and Norma Millay Ellis. Reprinted by permission of the Literary Executor for Norma Millay Ellis.

ROBIN MORGAN. "The Mermaid" from *Lady of the Beasts* by Robin Morgan, copyright © 1976 by Robin Morgan. Reprinted by permission of Random House, Inc.

MARIANNE MOORE. "Poetry" from *Collected Poems* by Marianne Moore, copyright © 1951, renewed 1969 by Marianne Moore. Reprinted by permission of The Macmillan Company and Faber and Faber Ltd.

EDWIN MUIR. "Horses" from *Collected Poems*, copyright © 1960 by Willa Muir. Reprinted by permission of Oxford University Press and Faber and Faber Ltd.

MARY OLIVER. "The Truro Bear" from *Twelve Moons: Poems* by Mary Oliver, copyright © 1978 by Mary Oliver. Reprinted by permission of Little, Brown and Company.

GREGORY ORR. "We Must Make a Kingdom of It" from *We Must Make a Kingdom of It* by Gregory Orr, copyright © 1986 by Gregory Orr. Reprinted by permission of Wesleyan University Press.

ROBERT PACK. "The Thrasher in the Willow by the Lake" from *Waking to My Name* by Robert Pack, copyright © Robert Pack. "Prayer for Prayer" from *Faces in a Single Tree* by Robert Pack, copyright © 1984 by Robert Pack. Reprinted by permission of David R. Godine, Publisher, Boston.

JAY PARINI. "To His Dear Friend, Bones" and "Skater in Blue" from *Anthracite Country*, copyright © 1982 by Random House. Reprinted by permission of the Elaine Markson Agency.

MARGE PIERCY. "A Work of Artifice" from *Circles on the Water* by Marge Piercy, copyright 1969, 1971, 1973 by Marge Piercy. Reprinted by permission of Alfred A. Knopf.

ROBERT PINSKY. "First Early Mornings Together" from *Sadness and Happiness* by Robert Pinsky. Copyright © 1975 by Princeton University Press. "Serpent Knowledge" from *An Explanation of America* by Robert Pinsky. Copyright © 1979 by Princeton University Press. Reprinted by permission of Princeton University Press.

SYLVIA PLATH. "Death & Co." from *The Collected Poems of Sylvia Plath*, edited by Ted Hughes. Copyright © 1963 by Ted Hughes. Reprinted by permission of Harper and Row and Faber and Faber Ltd.

EZRA POUND. "The Return" and "Hugh Selwyn Mauberly" from *Personae* by Ezra Pound, copyright 1926 by Ezra Pound. Reprinted by permission of New Directions Publishing Corp. and Faber and Faber Ltd.

JOHN CROWE RANSOM. "Janet Waking," "Blue Girls," and "Bells for John Whiteside's Daughter" from *Selected Poems, Third Edition, Revised and Enlarged* by John Crowe Ransom, copyright © 1927, 1952, 1955 by John Crowe Ransom. Reprinted by permission of Alfred A. Knopf and Laurence Pollinger, Ltd.

HENRY REED. "The Naming of Parts" from *A Map of Verona* by Henry Reed. Reprinted by permission of Jonathan Cape Ltd.

ALASTAIR REID. "Curiosity," "Oddments, Inklings, Omens, Moments," "A Lesson in Music," "An Instance," and "Horses" from *Weathering*, copyright © 1979 by Alastair Reid and published by E. P. Dutton and Cannongate, Ltd. Reprinted by permission of Alastair Reid.

THEODORE ROETHKE. "Orchids," "My Papa's Waltz," "Child on Top of a Greenhouse," "Elegy for Jane," "Wish for a Young Wife," and "I Knew a Woman" from *Collected Poems* by Theodore Roethke,

Index of Literary Terms

Index of Poets, Poems, and First Lines